WORLDS APART

Worlds Apart

GENRE AND THE ETHICS OF
REPRESENTING CAMPS, GHETTOS,
AND BESIEGED CITIES

Benjamin Paloff

Columbia University Press
New York

Columbia University Press
Publishers Since 1893
New York   Chichester, West Sussex

Copyright © 2025 Columbia University Press
All rights reserved

Library of Congress Cataloging-in-Publication Data
Names: Paloff, Benjamin, author.
Title: Worlds apart : genre and the ethics of representing camps, ghettos, and besieged cities / Benjamin Paloff.
Description: New York : Columbia University Press, 2025. | Includes bibliographical references and index.
Identifiers: LCCN 2024042607 (print) | LCCN 2024042608 (ebook) | ISBN 9780231215107 (hardback) | ISBN 9780231215114 (trade paperback) | ISBN 9780231560627 (ebook)
Subjects: LCSH: Internment camps in literature. | Survival in literature. | Internment camp inmates' writings—History and criticism. | Holocaust survivors' writings—History and criticism. | Autobiographical memory in literature. | Truth in literature. | Literature and history. | LCGFT: Literary criticism.
Classification: LCC PN56.C663 P35 2025 (print) | LCC PN56.C663 (ebook) | DDC 809/.93358—dc23/eng/20241223

Cover design: Milenda Nan Ok Lee
Cover photo: Benjamin Paloff

GPSR Authorized Representative: Easy Access System Europe, Mustamäe tee 50, 10621 Tallinn, Estonia, gpsr.requests@easproject.com

The greater the anxiety to be inside death and to avoid it at the same time, the more the critical immortality of reason turns into a sense of death and mourning, in the exhausting search for infinite representations of death.
—ACHILLE BONITO OLIVA, *THE IDEOLOGY OF THE TRAITOR: ART, MANNER AND MANNERISM* (TRANS. MARK EATON AND PAUL METCALFE)

Text is always testament—not only in the sense of witnessing—but as last word, the utterance of a dead person. Writing—dying.
—EMMANUEL LEVINAS, *CARNETS DE CAPTIVITÉ, SUIVI DE ECRITS SUR LA CAPTIVITÉ ET NOTES PHILOSOPHIQUES DIVERSES*

Let us make a film in which the representation of Fascism would engage with the fascism of representation.
—GILLIAN ROSE, *MOURNING BECOMES THE LAW: PHILOSOPHY AND REPRESENTATION*

Contents

Acknowledgments ix
A Note on Translation and Transliteration xiii

HAVE WE BEEN MISREADING THE CAMPS?
(AN INTRODUCTION) 1
   1 Fraud 18
   2 Parabiography 48
   3 Real-Life Fiction 76
   4 Comedy 133
   5 Horror 157
WHY READ CAMP LITERATURE?
(A CONCLUSION) 179

Notes 195
Bibliography 233
Index 245

Acknowledgments

No book is written by only one author, and when you work on something obsessively over many years, just about anyone foolish enough to express an interest in your obsession becomes an unwitting contributor. My interlocutors in confronting the issues raised in the following pages are simply too numerous and far-flung to name. Still, I feel compelled at the beginning of these acknowledgments to offer a kind of thanks more traditionally held until the end: to Megan and our children, Elliot and Zeke, for living with me as I was all too willingly living with this darkness—thank you. I dedicate this work to them.

I began researching this book during a three-year postdoctoral fellowship with the Michigan Society of Fellows, a richly interdisciplinary environment that helped me find my own priorities in navigating the frighteningly expansive corpus of concentration camp and siege literature. I am especially grateful to Hussein Fancy for having my back (feedback, pushback) in those early days and ever since. I also continue to benefit daily from the curiosities and insights of my colleagues at the University of Michigan's Departments of Slavic Languages and Literatures, Comparative Literature, and English; the Center for Russian, East European, and Eurasian Studies; the Copernicus Center for Polish Studies; and the Frankel Center for Judaic Studies. For this project, particular thanks go to Tatjana Aleksić, Julia Hell, Daniel Herwitz, Mikhail Krutikov, Ewa

Małachowska-Pasek, Christi Merrill, Brendan Nieubuurt, Yopie Prins, Jindřich Toman, Silke-Maria Weineck, and Geneviève Zubrzycki.

Once I confronted the bottomlessness of the relevant material and my own sometimes contradictory responses to it, I would never have been able to shape my reflections into a book without the exceedingly encouraging and stimulating intellectual home provided by a yearlong External Faculty Fellowship at the Stanford Humanities Center. I am grateful to all the fellows who shared their limited time and boundless intelligence, especially Lilla Balint, Vincent Barletta, Regina Kunzel, Nariman Skakov, Edith Sheffer, and Bronwen Tate. Other friends and colleagues in North America and around the world have gifted me helpful insights, probing questions, and vital inspiration: Polina Barskova, Jonathan Bolton, Edyta Bojanowska, Clare Cavanagh, Frances Foley, Jan Tomasz Gross, Irena Grudzińska-Gross, Adam Hradilek, Bożena Keff, Sabine Koller, Michał Paweł Markowski, Bill Martin, Joanna Niżyńska, Harsha Ram, Gabriella Safran, Thomas Seifrid, Leona Toker, Karen Underhill, Alissa Valles, Emily Van Buskirk, Caroline Winterer, and, in memoriam, Leon Neuger, Svetlana Boym, and Vladimir Gitin. I am in debt to them all.

My research on this book has received additional financial and institutional support from the University of Michigan's Office of the Vice President for Research, the Associate Professor Support Fund, and the LSA Michigan Humanities Award. Even with these resources, however, the book would not be possible without the often invisible labor of dedicated staff and volunteers at the memorial sites, museums, and libraries where I conducted much of my research: the camp museums of Auschwitz-Birkenau, Buchenwald, Dachau, Flossenbürg, Majdanek, Ravensbrück, Sachsenhausen, Terezín (Theresienstadt), and Treblinka; the Galician Jewish Museum (Kraków), Mémorial de la Shoah (Paris), Mémorial des Martyrs de la Déportation (Paris), Militärhistorisches Museum der Bundeswehr (Dresden), the POLIN Museum of the History of Polish Jews (Warsaw), Pawiak Prison (Warsaw), Topography of Terror (Berlin), and the United States Holocaust Memorial and Museum (Washington, DC); and the collections of Beinecke Library (Yale University), the Hoover Institution (Stanford University), the Jewish Historical Institute (Warsaw), and Památník Národního Písemnictví (Prague). I thank them here for their invaluable assistance, a welcoming working environment, and, on occasion, hot tea.

Exceptional editorial advice from Emily-Jane Cohen during the early compositional stages deeply influenced the book's development. Its final form, meanwhile, owes just as much to Christine Dunbar, my editor at Columbia University Press, who provided unwavering enthusiasm, direction, and above all patience with her sometimes recalcitrant ward.

Drafts of material from this book were first presented as papers at the national conferences of the American Association of Teachers of Slavic and East European Languages; the American Comparative Literature Association; the Association for Slavic, East European, and Eurasian Studies; and the Modern Language Association; or else as invited talks at Harvard University; the University of California, Berkeley; the University of Illinois, Chicago; the University of Michigan; the University of Southern California; and Yale University. I thank the organizers of these events, as well as their participants.

A portion of chapter 5 was originally drafted in Polish and published as "O Robinsonie warszawskim, czyli poeta chodzi do kina (i wraca do domu rozczarowany)" in *Warszawa Miłosza*, edited by Marek Zaleski (Warsaw: IBL PAN, 2013).

A Note on Translation and Transliteration

The texts discussed in the following pages were originally composed in Czech, French, German, Polish, Russian, or Yiddish, among other languages, and often had tangled publication histories, with some having been written in one language but first published in another, so that an early translation might become the de facto "original" from which subsequent translations are entered into international circulation. Some sources are available in multiple English versions. Others have never been translated at all.

While I strive to keep the reader properly oriented to the cultural and linguistic origins of these materials, everything here is presented in English. The translations are my own unless otherwise indicated in the citations. To facilitate access to the original language of each text for those interested in considering it, I also provide untranslated quotations from primary sources in the notes. Slavic languages, including Russian, appear there in their standard orthography. Yiddish has been transliterated. In most instances, I have standardized spellings.

WORLDS APART

Have We Been Misreading the Camps?

(An Introduction)

> The disaster, unexperienced. It is what escapes the very possibility of experience—it is the limit of writing. This must be repeated: the disaster de-scribes.
>
> —MAURICE BLANCHOT, *THE WRITING OF THE DISASTER* (TRANS. ANN SMOCK)

This book is about literary accounts of survival in concentration camps, ghettos, and besieged cities in Europe in the middle of the last century. Specifically, it is devoted to texts produced by authors who experienced these spaces firsthand, but who then chose to represent their experiences using the devices of literary fiction. But the questions that haunt this study, and that pertain most readily to the theory of genre and the ethics of representation, apply more broadly to life writing and the literary narration of personal and collective trauma in general. They ask a series of questions: What is the relationship between personal art and public, historical truth? Are there circumstances under which a fictional narrative more accurately reflects a historical reality than a collation of factual data can? And, ultimately, is there a way for us to read literary representations of life in extremis that simultaneously acknowledges the power of invention and avoids the trap of sentimental self-delusion?

Early in the twenty-first century, American television audiences and cultural observers were treated to an unusual piece of public theater that illustrated these age-old epistemological questions to a degree rarely seen on a daytime talk show. James Frey, author of an acclaimed memoir of drug addiction and recovery, was sitting on a couch between Nan Talese, his editor and a doyenne of the New York publishing world, and Oprah Winfrey, the iconic talk show host whose relatability and trustworthiness were such that by 2017 there was a groundswell of interest in having her run for president of the United States.¹

This occasion, however, was not the usual induction into Oprah's Book Club, coveted by authors and editors alike as a virtual guarantee of massive sales and multiple printings. That had already happened some months earlier, in October 2005, when Winfrey listened with demonstrative compassion as Frey shared his harrowing struggle with substance abuse and all the violence, suffering, and humiliation that had gone with it.² Now things were different. Winfrey was glaring at Frey like a disappointed parent. Several weeks earlier, the Smoking Gun, a website devoted to debunking dubious claims in the media, had published a damning dissection of Frey's book.³ It revealed that the time he had spent in a jail cell for one incident of booze-addled misconduct amounted to a few hours, not the eighty-seven days he had claimed. Some of the injuries he purported to have sustained in run-ins with drug dealers and other addicts had been heavily exaggerated. An especially memorable passage in which Frey recounts a root canal without anesthetic, told in agonizingly minute, present-tense detail, turned out never to have occurred.

Frey's second appearance on *The Oprah Winfrey Show*, in January 2006, had the flavor of an interrogation, with Talese serving as counsel for the accused. The author, an outraged Winfrey now suggested, was a fraud. And just as her viewers had been deeply moved by Frey's initial discussion of *A Million Little Pieces*, they shared Winfrey's opprobrium as he fumbled through the excuses and equivocations of someone who has been caught in a lie. "I don't feel like I conned everyone," Frey tried to explain to his host. "Because the book is about drug addiction and alcoholism and nobody's disputing that I was a drug addict and an alcoholic." Winfrey was visibly unconvinced. So, too, was her audience: in the wake of the broadcast, a number of readers filed a class action lawsuit against both the author and the publisher for having "wasted their time"; the case was later settled. Frey's publisher recalled and pulped the remaining unsold copies.⁴

Between Frey's initial success and his unmasking, there seemed to have been no diminishment in his audience's emotional investment in his story. There was, rather, a reassignment of that investment from one purpose to another. As much as audiences had connected with Frey's narrative when they believed it to be wholly factual, they rejected it with equal zeal when they learned it was not.

The vital matter that arises from this episode offers a twist on the question that Blakey Vermeule poses in her 2009 book *Why Do We Care About Literary Characters?*[5] Why, we might just as well ask, do we care about *real* ones? The very notion of a "real" character confronts us with some epistemological challenges that the controversy surrounding Frey's book can help us untangle. Why does it matter that Frey strayed from the facts if his telling does, in the aggregate, faithfully represent his experience? Or to approach the same question in such a way as might apply equally to texts that make no claims to facticity whatsoever: If I read a text and find myself deeply moved by the world represented therein, what difference should it make to me whether the events described actually happened, or whether the person speaking in that text ever shared the same world where I am now writing this sentence? I don't know him or her, I wasn't there, so why should facticity—that there is no "him" or "her," there is no "there"— have any effect on my experience as a reader at all?[6]

What Is, in Fact, True?

The argument that unfolds in the following pages is contentious, though not prescriptive. In the years I have devoted to reading the literature that has emerged from the experience of survival in concentration camps, ghettos, and besieged cities, and that I will sometimes refer to by the reductive shorthand of "camp literature," I have indeed come to be convinced that both the interpretive frameworks by which I was introduced to these texts, as well as the moral assertions underpinning those frameworks, are fatally flawed, and that they are apt to lead later generations of readers to troubling misreadings of literary representations and the very phenomena they represent. What I offer in this book is therefore a corrective, certainly, albeit not one that claims to be the only "right" way to read a novel about the Shoah or a short story drawn from the experience of Soviet labor camps. Instead, I lay out a critique of the hermeneutic paradigm that has accrued to camp literature over the decades since the Second World War, a critique grounded in the incongruity between Anglo-American notions of genre and the ethics of representation as it pertains to lived historical trauma. I then elaborate that critique in its confrontation with texts whose generic peculiarity deliberately disrupts received wisdom about what constitutes the truthful representation of history in literature. I conclude in a more polemical vein, arguing for the moral urgency of camp literature in the new millennium, an urgency that I posit is quite different from what has dominated public discussion of this literature until now.

My argument in this book can be summarized as follows: The literature of survival in concentration camps, ghettos, and besieged cities cannot be read using a conventional approach that equates facticity with truthful representation, since the very fact of the author's having survived the experience obscures the paradoxes that are fundamental to the experience that he or she strives to represent. Foremost among these paradoxes is that life in a concentration camp, ghetto, or besieged city is marked by a persistent sense of precarity and an equally persistent boredom with that same precarity. That is, such existence is characterized by an awareness of the mortal danger one finds oneself in, on the one hand, and the nullification of that awareness through the monotony of its persistence, on the other. Daily life, Primo Levi tells us, was "made up of boredom and interwoven with horror."[7]

This interplay between danger and boredom is illustrated powerfully by Viktor Shklovsky's definition of artistic representation as a device for shocking readers out of the "automatization" of repeated experience. In one of the twentieth century's most frequently cited definitions of literary art, Shklovsky remarks, "Automatization eats away at things, at clothes, at furniture, at our wives, and at our fear of war."[8] Shklovsky's formulation has often been brought into service as a diagnosis of a general human condition, one that art is poised to remedy, and not as a forceful characterization of its author's contemporaneous experience, though that is very much what it reflects. When Shklovsky first published these words, in 1917, his own "fear of war" during the Siege of Petrograd was actual. He understood that it could not be conveyed to someone who has not lived through a comparable experience unless the author of a new telling were to employ techniques that effectively force readers to "see" experience in new ways.[9]

Even before the reader encounters camp literature, the automatization that Shklovsky describes is working against the author's effort at truthful representation. This is most readily evident in the text's peritextual data. With the author's name under the title and a copyright date chronologically later than the events described in the text, it is clear that the writer has survived the dangers he or she describes. The precarity represented in the text is diminished by the text's very existence. We know that the author will survive, since we are literally holding the evidence of that survival.

For this reason, literary authors who represent their own camp experiences have at times done so not through fact-based testimonials, evidentiary dossiers, or memoirs, as the vast majority of nonliterary witnesses have done, but by drawing on the techniques of literary fiction. In the process, however, they violate the terms of what Philip Lejeune has famously described as the "autobiographical pact."[10] The contract's standard terms are uncomplicated. The author promises the reader that what is presented in the text as experiential did in fact occur more or less as depicted. Despite whatever distortions may be inherent in the translation of experience into verbal representation, such a text purports to be an honest and trustworthy account of a historical reality, one that will remain congruent with adjacent sources pertinent to the events the author describes. The reader, in turn, agrees to trust that the author's account is truthful, that the events depicted in the text really did occur, and this despite the extraordinary quality that makes those events worthy of textual representation and memorialization in the first place.

Yet one ought not to suppose, as too many critics of life writing continue to do, that the terms of Lejeune's autobiographical pact are enforced equally across all jurisdictions. On the contrary, Lejeune undertook his research into the nature of autobiography in a postwar European context in which the autobiographical pact he describes was, and indeed remains, significantly looser than in the Anglo-American literary marketplace. The intellectual trajectory of continental European thought in the twentieth century differs markedly from that of the United States and United Kingdom in regard to the nature of meaning, to *how* texts mark truthful signification, insofar as in Europe we witness an evolving understanding of how truth is constituted in, and emerges from, discourse itself, its internal and at times contradictory dynamics, and eventually its interaction with interpretive communities.[11] The Anglo-American environment is remarkably different. Conditioned in the first half of the twentieth century by the dominance of philosophical pragmatism, especially as elaborated by William James and John Dewey, that tradition would rely upon a generic distinction between fiction and nonfiction to signal to readers whether the content of a given text should be understood as factual and therefore truthful.

Retail Genres: The Spatial Divisions of Represented Space

The neat generic divide between fiction and nonfiction is immediately evident in the institutions that promote and distribute literature in much of the English-speaking world, where we are taught this division early and explicitly, through our teachers' instruction and the physical arrangement of our school and municipal libraries, and even of our bookstores. Fiction and nonfiction are often cataloged under completely different systems.[12] While a retail outlet of any size most likely subdivides its nonfiction into different areas of interest, or even into different literary subgenres, such as essay or biography, we maintain a strict sequestration between fiction and nonfiction on the same subject. One would no more expect to find Czesław Miłosz's essayistic *The Captive Mind* (*Zniewolony umysł*, 1953) next to his novel *The Issa Valley* than to see *The Last of the Mohicans* beside a history of the American frontier.

Such distinctions are just as clearly evinced in our paratextual and peritextual conventions—for example, in how books are characterized in cover copy, blurbs, advertising, and critical reviews.[13] The genre designation printed on the cover of a book or in the U.S. Library of Congress data within its pages, in fact, tells booksellers and librarians where to put it, which in turn tells the reader how to read it. In the following pages I will often draw attention to these external genre markers, and especially to how they evolve as a given text is translated and reprinted over time, very often ending up presenting simply as "nonfiction" a text that had begun its life as a novel.

Though odd to us, grouping Miłosz's poems, essays, critical writings, and fiction together would be utterly unremarkable in a Polish bookstore, where the fundamental division is not a separation of fiction from nonfiction, but of domestic texts from foreign ones. So long as their treatment is "literary," broadly defined, books originally written in Polish will be collected as *literatura polska* (Polish literature), regardless of genre, while those written in a language other than Polish will be similarly grouped as *literatura obca* (foreign literature). This organizing principle is replicated throughout Central and Eastern Europe and, with slight variations, in much of the world. In the same way that our Anglo-American institutional separation between fiction and nonfiction both reflects and reifies our approach to facticity in the literary text, the more fluid distinction favored elsewhere accommodates and fosters literature that complicates or altogether explodes that boundary. In the traditions that produced most of the texts I discuss in this book, "fact-checking," even for an (auto)biographical or testimonial text, seems a peculiarly American institution.[14]

In some sense, it is. Though the term "fact-checking" gained currency in American journalism immediately after the Cold War—there is no equivalent term in Russian, Polish, or Czech, nor a standard set of practices to warrant one—it was early in that conflict, and in reference to it, that Dwight Macdonald observed the American "triumph of the fact," which in Macdonald's understanding means that "a boldly asserted lie or half-truth has the same effect on our minds as if it were true, since few of us have the knowledge, the critical faculties or even the mere time to discriminate between fact and fantasy."[15] Macdonald's point was not that Americans were scrupulous in their attention to the facticity and accuracy of the information they received from a rapidly developing mass media; on the contrary, he believed that most consumers of information were disturbingly passive in accepting as true even flimsy innuendo.[16] But they nevertheless demanded that such innuendo be presented to them *as fact*, that the lie or misdirection bear the imprint of what the American political satirist Stephen Colbert would term "truthiness."[17] Colbert's durable neologism became a keyword in the commentaries surrounding the James Frey scandal.[18] But already half a century earlier, according to Macdonald, American media audiences desperately wanted to believe that what they were hearing was *true* and were altogether prepared to accept it as such, so long as that's how it was presented.[19] Not coincidentally, this is when the phrase "based on a true story" first sees regular use in the marketing of English-language literature and film.[20]

The long decades of the Cold War and the concurrent proliferation of autobiographical accounts of survival in the concentration camps, ghettos, and besieged cities of Nazi- and Soviet-occupied Europe brought these accounts into increasing competition with each other, and consequently the insistence on facticity, or at least on its appearance, has become an insufficient guarantee of reaching a distracted audience. No longer is a story's claim to "truth" enough to warrant the reader's attention. Now the "true" story must also be "extraordinary," "amazing," and eventually "unbelievable," which necessarily promises two things that, taken together, would seem paradoxical: the story will be entirely true to life, but the life it encapsulates will be so unusual, even unrelatable, as to *seem* fictional. Such a text will thereby satisfy the reader's desire for the remarkable while also assuring them that the fantastic—here, the superhuman strength and good fortune required for one to survive a death trap—is possible, within reach, "true," or, at the very least, potentially true. And because the historicity of the survivor's circumstances has been thoroughly documented and studied—that is, only those more committed to ideology than to historical evidence can deny that context, regardless of how the author represents his or her survival in it—the text's principal burden is not to reestablish the facts but to demonstrate the exceptional quality of the hero's navigation of those facts.

This arrangement creates conditions for profound interpretive error. On the one hand, it conditions the reader to assume that a text that purports to present verifiable facts is therefore a fundamentally truthful representation of reality—and, *mutatis mutandis*, that a text that is shown to contain authorial inventions or manipulations *cannot* be an honest account of a lived experience. On the other hand, it encourages the reader to assume that a powerful representation, one that affects the reader with its appeals to imagination or sentiment, is truthful and therefore factual. Ironically, the very same "extraordinary," "amazing," and "unbelievable" details that might draw our skepticism in a narrative of everyday life become the grounds for our faith in the telling of life in extremis. The reader does not feel affected by the narrative because it is true; rather, by a strange seizure of authorial control, the reader assumes that the narrative must be true because he or she has been affected by it.

Here we begin to see that the danger posed by misreading camp literature extends well beyond the potential for mistaking a fictional text for historical record. In its most pernicious form, using one's own sentimental attachment to a text as a barometer of that text's authenticity lends itself to an insidious moral relativism, since the reader enjoys the affirmation that comes whenever what is true (or just, or good) is measured by what he or she wishes to believe. Plato's warning against self-deception as the root of evil action assumes new urgency when we consider that the persistence of the concentration camp as a modern institution can be ascribed at least in part to the inconvenience of recognizing it as an institution of the present, rather than as an artifact of a finalized past whose lessons we have already fully digested.

The Reality of Representation Versus the Representation of Reality

What concerns us here—namely, representation's claims on truth, or how text corresponds to experiential reality, if it does so at all—reaches far beyond camp literature and its reception. It is arguably the most fundamental dilemma in Western epistemology. Which species of text can make the stronger claim on our sense of reality, whether an authorial invention or a textual record supplied by someone who once breathed the same air I am now breathing, presents an inflection of the problem of "closure," the knot whose Gordian solution we are demanded to perform virtually every moment of our conscious lives, or at least whenever we are called upon to assume as true that which we cannot know to be true. If not for such leaps of faith, we would be incapable of recognizing other persons as subjectivities equal to ourselves, let alone of believing that events represented in text refer to real-life circumstances that *did* occur at some point in the same past that has led to *our* present. Assuming another's subjectivity or the past's reality demands that we ignore the objections of the skeptical epistemologist.

In applying the same violent solution to text, if only to slice through its artifice and establish its referential posture toward the reality behind it, our convention is to assert that there is an infinitude of factual data not in evidence, yet eternally available to the seeker. In other words, the possibility of filling in *factual* details, those that would be immutable with respect to the author or reader, forms the basis for the text's historicity. One can always imagine otherwise unarticulated features of an imaginary world; this is what the practice of writing fan fiction is all about. But the immutability of the historical fact, distinct from a given author's interpretation or stylization, locks the historical text within a spatiotemporal specificity that is both recoverable and universal, or so the assumption requires.

It is easy to see how everyday life would become unlivable without taking so much of the world for granted. One simply cannot buy groceries, succeed in one's work, and care for a family while actively questioning the existence of the supermarket, the office, and kinship. Necessary though these assumptions may be to our daily lives, however, they do not always stand up against serious scrutiny, which quickly reveals how much more of the imagined past is imagined than actually past. In a Platonist jab against the human tendency to fantasize the past, Suetonius tells us that the Emperor

Tiberius would torture the "grammarians" of his court by asking them to produce the referential trivia absent from mythic narratives: "Who was Hecuba's mother? What name did Achilles assume when he was among the girls? What song did the Sirens sing?"[21] These questions are, of course, rhetorical. For Tiberius, the surfeit of potential responses demonstrates that there is no one recoverable and universal history here, which is how we know that we aren't dealing with history at all.

But one could just as easily take the opposite tack. Referring to the same Suetonius passage in the seventeenth century, Thomas Browne made so bold as to suggest that, "though puzzling," the questions posed by Tiberius "are not beyond all conjecture"—one could certainly venture some guesses—whereas the histories that might attach to ancient bones anonymously buried "were a question above Antiquarism."[22] Browne's challenge is not to be taken lightly. It suggests that the choice to define reality as encompassing a surplus of available and articulatable data—in contrast to fantasy, which is always coterminous with the data of which the narrative itself consists—can itself be turned on its head. Reality, Browne seems to suggest, is *too* specific, *too* contingent, so that lost details may simply be beyond the future historian's reach. Invention, on the other hand, can always be augmented by more invention. Supposing that Browne did not himself believe that Odysseus *actually* heard the singing of aquatic half-women, we can conclude only that the emperor's jeering interrogation *could* be satisfied, at least potentially, through the very practices of humanistic inquiry, by interpolating potential responses that fit those parts of the narrative that have already been furnished. However, when facing the material remains of lived reality—literally, the bones of the dead—there is only guesswork. The plenitude of historical data becomes overwhelming, an ever-present white noise akin to silence. Browne admonishes us that the conventional distinction between historical reality and invention is, when it comes to narrative, unconducive to *responsible* reading. It does not tell us how better to know the bones of the dead. Perhaps more to the point, it does not tell us why we might want to.

Three centuries after Browne, camp literature places this problem into special relief *through the extremity of the representation*. Here I am not referring to the extreme nature of how these spaces were experienced, the convention shaped by a long line of readers, from Theodore Adorno to Terrence Des Pres and Tzvetan Todorov.[23] Indeed, it is beyond my task, and surely beyond my power, to describe a calculus for ranking human experiences according to intensity, rarity, or awfulness. Rather, I am suggesting that the "terminal paradoxes" (Milan Kundera's term) that these spaces expose within representation itself outline the extremes of reading and interpretation.[24] In considering the fragmentary traces left over from concentration camps, ghettos, and besieged cities, much as for Browne in his examination of burial urns, our confrontation with the material remnants of the anonymous dead evokes perplexity. We know there are stories here, we're holding the evidence in our hands, we are seeing it with our eyes, but these stories defy our efforts at unequivocal, objective, factual—that is, historical—articulation.

The Camp: A Paradoxical Object of Representation

The principal paradox of camp representation, I have already suggested, is that the survivor's account belies the precarity that is central to the experience that the survivor wishes to represent. Here paradox is already inscribed within the object of representation.

Of the paradoxes we could name in regard to concentration camps, ghettos, and besieged cities, the most significant is that these are institutions, with all the infrastructural norms and organizational rules that the term implies, that are every bit as constitutive of modernity as the school, the clinic, the church, and the prison, but they are invisible. Unlike the school, the clinic, the church, or the prison, we cannot pay a visit to the concentration camp or besieged city as such. The modern world is so unimaginable without these spaces that denying their historicity has itself become synonymous with fantastical revisionism, and yet it is the experience of these spaces that we reflexively describe as "unimaginable," "incredible," and "extraordinary." Despite efforts from some corners to conflate these invisible institutions—for example, by generalizing carceral sites to include prisons *and* forced labor camps—such a maneuver ignores a fundamental fact: one can visit a prison, or one might drive by a prison twice a day on the way to and from work, whereas the forced labor camp, which no conception of the modern world can do without, remains beyond general experience, a space in mind but beyond knowledge. Another way we know that a concentration camp is not a prison is that the camps to which I am referring *contained* prisons, as well as idiosyncratic versions of the other basic institutions I have mentioned. As Imre Kertész notes in his sharp rebuttal to Hannah Arendt's thesis on the "banality of evil," the concentration camp was rather an uncanny institution, though not because people were enslaved and murdered there. What made a place like Buchenwald uncanny, according to Kertész, is that "in the middle of the camp was a hospital where they tended to the ailing."[25]

There was also a small zoo installed for the benefit of SS members and their families in 1938, just as Jews were being added to Buchenwald's population of political prisoners. Unlike most of the facilities erected for German soldiers and their families, the zoo could be seen unobstructed from the main camp, with only a path separating the electrified barbed wire from the wrought iron ringing the bear pit (figure int.1). Just a few feet away from where prisoners were being starved to death en masse, they could easily glimpse animals being generously fed and looked after. When such paradoxes are inscribed physically in the landscape, they naturally invite ironic reflection on the theatricality of one's own experience. It is not an invitation that many are willing or able to accept, especially under conditions of duress. Yet for those inclined toward artistic representation, and particularly for those who were already practicing writers and artists

Figure Int.1 The bear pit in Buchenwald with the main camp fence. Also visible nearby are the crematorium (with chimney) and a guard tower. *Source*: photograph by the author

before entering this "world apart," the question of how to represent the experience without eliding its paradoxes often becomes an integral feature of the experience itself, as the authors themselves frequently attest.

Other paradoxes constitutive of these spaces further underscore their challenges to representation. They are deeply hierarchal human institutions whose defining feature is the reduction of the human to "bare life," a condition well beyond the experiential horizon of most readers. They exist in space and time, yet they are a sequestration of space and time, their borders often blurry or mutable, their temporality meaningless, since no one could say for sure when the confinement or siege would end and, as its conditions became engrained into the endlessly repetitive routines and performances of this alternative everyday, one might just as easily forget when they had begun. A space like Auschwitz, the survivor and author Ka-Tzetnik 135663 (born Yehiel Dinoor) testified at the trial of Adolf Eichmann in Jerusalem, had a temporality "different from what it is here on earth," since "every split second ran on a different cycle of time."[26] For those inducted into the Soviet Gulag system, and, in certain instances, the Nazi concentration camps as well, confinement came with a fixed sentence to be served, but the number of years assigned had, as Alexander Etkind has put it, "no predictive value."[27] A commonplace of survivor narratives is the confession that, decades after release, one nevertheless continues to live in the camp, not simply because of the recurrence of trauma (the Freudian paradigm), but because survival required a complete assimilation into the suspension of norms that these spaces embody. Thus the spaces came to be characterized as their own self-referential reality—the "world apart" (Gustaw Herling-Grudziński), the "world of stone" (Tadeusz Borowski), the "planet of Auschwitz" (Yehiel Dinoor/Ka-Tzetnik), the "concentration universe" (David Rousset) or "Gulag archipelago" (Alexander Solzhenitsyn), "the world of concentration camps" (Jorge Semprún). In this connection, it is worth mentioning another commonplace that will appear frequently in the chapters to follow: the predictable death of the fool who *fails* to assimilate, who attempts to live according to the norms not of the "world apart," but of the world *before*. Anyone who succumbs to the illusion that he is about to be released because he has served his sentence is almost guaranteed never to reach the outside.

How can one represent such paradox without eliding it, without taming one side of the contradiction in favor of the other? Viktor Shklovsky had this kind of paradox in mind when he formulated his notion of *ostranenie* (estrangement, defamiliarization), impressing upon us the necessity of a sophisticated representation that makes the quotidian new and frightening, not by brushing its mundanity aside, but by showing it to us in all its uncanny splendor. Experiential reality, Shklovsky argues, is irreducible to fact. The "world apart" of the concentration camp or besieged city provides the extreme of that irreducibility.

The Parallax View: Reading Responsibly

The paradoxes communicated in camp literature require *parallactic* strategies in reading them. Parallactic reading scrupulously preserves both sides of the paradox, taking into account the factual detail together with the embellishment, the data alongside its stylization, allowing the experiential reality to speak *through* its self-conscious fictionalization. Reading this literature responsibly, *responsively*, means not only accepting that a text fictionalizes its author's lived experience, but also recognizing how that fictionalization communicates essential, and essentially factual, information. It means fully valuing transhistorical social formations within the historical contingency of their manifestation.

I do not propose this parallax merely as a means of avoiding the need to elide paradox, for example, by removing the book from the shop's window display and shelving it conveniently as either nonfiction or fiction. After all, the parallax view, as Slavoj Žižek demonstrates, is not a *strategy* of the viewer, or not only that, but rather (or also) a property of the object, which demands such a strategy by changing in response to our attention, which it anticipates and conditions, by shifting position in response to our response.[28] In contrast to the spaces these texts represent, which are distinguished by their invisibility even as many of them are hidden in plain sight, *literary camp representations always know they are being watched*. They beg our attention with their dramatic and often shocking images. They anticipate and rely upon scripted emotional responses. And they are constructed self-consciously through received genre conventions that long predate the modern institution of the concentration camp.

Our discussion approaches these deliberate genre manipulations by touring the spectrum across which genre itself positions the text relative to historical experience, beginning with chapter 1, "Fraud." Fraudulent accounts of camp experience, as well as of similar instances of what might be termed "open confinement," exploit the generic norms of earlier, now canonical texts. They allow us to see most readily how a parallactic reading can nevertheless extract valuable historical insights from distorted facts and outright fabrication.

Read parallactically, with an eye to the truths that emerge from behind a lie, hoaxes and misrepresentations help us establish a generic baseline for what more truthful representations might look like. I hasten to stress that we are not pursuing an ideal of a text that is *absolutely* true to life. Indeed, an underlying assumption in my own reading of this material, and one shared by the vast majority of those authors and thinkers to whom I refer, is that the truthfulness of any representation cannot be discussed in absolute terms, and that this—the text's ultimate indeterminacy—is precisely why reading these texts responsibly means reading them parallactically. The next two chapters after "Fraud" therefore address two different modes of combining actual, lived experience and fictional representation. Chapter 2, "Parabiography," considers texts by authors who project their own survival into fictionalized versions of themselves, using allegory, composite characters, and novelistic techniques to communicate aspects of their experience that echo biographical facts without repeating them. Often, though not always, told in the third person, such texts lend themselves to controversy and public confusion, since readers are immediately confronted with the task of reconciling whatever they know about the writer's life with obvious and less obvious fabrications. That task becomes more difficult still when the author and his or her textual avatar share a name and experiences corroborated by facts and documents external to the text, which otherwise relies on the devices of literary fiction. These texts, the most troublesome instances of what I call "real-life fiction," are the focus of chapter 3.

The distress that this body of literature can cause in the reader is not limited, however, to those instances where the text's genre boundaries are blurred, since it is entirely possible for the audience to have an untroubled grasp of a text's genre while still finding that genre unsuitable or inappropriate for its subject. We see this most readily with comedic representations set in concentration camps and siege conditions. Since the immediate postwar period, films and novels representing the survival of such conditions through comedy have consistently provoked shock, distress, and public opprobrium, regardless of whether the authors of those texts can attest to the historical accuracy of their own accounts or, for that matter, whether they can use their experience to claim license to joke about it. In these instances, which are the subject of chapter 4, the experiences portrayed by the person who knew them firsthand are misaligned with the audience's expectations of what those same experiences are *supposed to mean* for the author. For the uncomfortable reader or viewer, it is as though the survivor-author, failing to understand his or her own experience of survival, has chosen the "wrong" genre for its representation. But as we will see, by casting an ironic eye on events whose paradoxes can be flattened by the tragic or sentimental, comedy proves especially adept at exposing those paradoxes and placing them at the center of the representation. In this sense, comedy performs its own parallactic reading in front of and alongside the audience, making the paradoxes of camp representation an object of representation in itself. It can come as no surprise, then, that the first feature film to represent the filmmakers' own experience as Jews in Nazi concentration camps—*Our Children* (*Undzere kinder*, 1948), the last Yiddish-language feature made in Poland—also foregrounds the question of how best to represent the Shoah to those who did not experience it for themselves.

Without discounting the demand that we historicize our reading of these spaces, I contend that the norms governing their representation are basically the same whether we are talking about Theresienstadt, Auschwitz, Sachsenhausen, Kolyma, Leningrad during the blockade, Warsaw during the Warsaw Uprising (or the Warsaw Ghetto during the Warsaw Ghetto Uprising a year earlier), or Prague for a Jew in hiding. The historicizing imperative confuses the industrial scale of confinement, enslavement, and murder, prompting the coinage of a new term, "genocide," with the advent of the phenomenon itself, as though prosecutorial necessity might shape reality after the fact. But, to articulate yet another paradox, the subjective experience of such spaces is itself transhistorical, and the texts that I treat insert themselves, often explicitly and self-consciously, into a literary tradition that goes back centuries and extends, I argue in the book's penultimate chapter, to the present day, in the form of postapocalyptic science fiction.[29]

At its heart, then, this book is a meditation on the *ethics of representation*. I argue that the literary representation of concentration camps, ghettos, and besieged cities, those spaces that I refer to collectively as "worlds apart," exposes the ethical limit of literary representation as such, demanding that the reader constantly interrogate the text's claims on historical experience while also remaining fully immersed in the author's narrative construct. This is, of course, an impossible demand, one that the reader can only approach asymptotically—thus my characterization of it as the ethical limit. In practice, what these texts demand is a double resistance on the part of the reader. First, they call on us to resist equating historical data with historical experience, since these texts show us time and again that the raw facts of an individual's life in a concentration camp or besieged city most often fail to convey the most essential paradoxes of that experience, such as the monotony of terror and the uncanniness of the everyday. The reflexive attachment to the incontrovertible, the objective, the factual, the dispassionate, trivializes the survival experience—quite literally, by reframing its narrative details as trivia. But these texts also call on us to resist the temptation to reclassify those stories to which we form a sentimental attachment as historical data, to believe that fiction is fact merely because it confirms what we wish were true about human perseverance, endurance, self-sacrifice, or similar staples of survival literature. Surrender to either tendency is, this book argues, the enemy of *responsible* reading.

When it comes to literary representations of these worlds apart, the responsible reader will recognize the truth value behind artistic inventions without ever losing sight of how what triggered that recognition was a fabrication, not a historical fact. The same reader will also command the informational traces of real historical events in such a way as to see what those details ignore, obscure, or distort in actual human experience. All of which is to say that the literature of concentration camps, ghettos, and besieged cities, by using artistic devices not only to connect readers with the actual world around us, but also to impart inconvenient knowledge about our often failed ethical relation to each other, makes demands on us that are at once unreasonable and wholly necessary.

CHAPTER I

Fraud

> So misery becomes fiction, fiction pornography,
> pornography becomes real tears.
> —DUBRAVKA UGREŠIĆ, *THE CULTURE OF LIES:
> ANTIPOLITICAL ESSAYS* (TRANS. CELIA HAWKESWORTH)

The September 11, 2001, terrorist attack on New York City produced many individuals later lauded as heroes for their bravery, perseverance, and self-sacrifice. Among the least likely of these was Tania Head, who had ostensibly been working on the seventy-eighth floor of the World Trade Center's South Tower, squarely within the impact zone when hijackers crashed United Flight 175 into the building. Severely burned in the ensuing blaze, she would not have survived, by her own account, if not for the help of Welles Crowther, a twenty-four-year-old equities trader who rescued at least a dozen people that day before he was himself killed in the building's collapse. In the darkest moments of her ordeal, Head was propelled forward by the thought of the dress she was going to wear at her upcoming wedding. She managed to survive, but her fiancé, who worked in the North Tower, never made it out. Swiftly recovering from her injuries, Head became active as a public advocate for the interests of September 11 survivors, sharing their stories and eventually becoming president of the World Trade Center Survivors' Network. Newspapers covered her leading major political figures, including Mayors Rudy Giuliani and Michael Bloomberg and New York governor George Pataki, on tours of the World Trade Center site.

Those same newspapers also eventually caught her in her lie.

Alicia Esteve, who presented herself to the world as Tania Head, had never actually worked at the World Trade Center. She had never even visited the building. A native of Barcelona, she first came to the United States in 2003.[1]

That our mass media was complicit in Esteve/Head's years-long fraud is beyond question. After all, in both advertising and journalism, mass media exists to mirror our own public appetites back at us—in a sense, to feed us what we have already said we wish to consume. At the same time, such a fraud benefits from two factors that, at least in the short term, seem to inoculate the perpetrator from the rigorous scrutiny that would expose the inconsistencies between our shared reality and the fraudster's misrepresentation. First, accounts of serious personal loss and trauma, especially those that resonate with the current concerns and sensitivities of popular discourse, may be treated more delicately than stories less likely to arouse outrage when openly challenged. Second, the Tania Head case reflects a broad and reliable market interest in tales of survival, effectively guaranteeing persistent attempts to erode the boundary between cathartic entertainment and historical record.

My principal contention in this chapter is that our desire for stories like Tania Head's—sometimes outlasting, as we will see, the exposure of the fraud—stems less from an enduring interest in accessing historical fact than from an appetite for the shape of the stories themselves. As a number of scholars have pointed out, particularly with regard to the Shoah, the tragic tale told within a historical context lends a narrative design to variegated, amorphous historical events, thereby allowing the audience to see the confirmation of a certain view of history, the confirmation of their own worldview, in the confirmation of narrative expectations that the text itself projects.[2] In other words, we assume the tragic tale of survival to be true not only because we have been trained not to question the authenticity of traumatic narratives, but because the tale's conformity to narrative expectation raises no red flags.[3] To be sure, there is some added value bound to the principal character's survival, the reassurance we feel in watching someone endure overwhelming, even otherworldly, tribulations and come out intact on the other side. But there are plenty of similar stories that end with the principal characters' damage or death, whether in the ordeal itself or in its epilogue. The important thing for the audience is that the text dutifully present the key story elements of a survival narrative and that it order those elements appropriately to orchestrate an emotional response that is predicted within, and required by, the conventions of the genre.

The Tania Head story does just that. It begins with a heroine who is unremarkable, and therefore maximally relatable. Her survival needs to be a demonstration of fate's capriciousness and her own will to go on, not a function of abilities, resources, or privileges that, in real life, may well improve one's chances when society no longer affords its protections. Though she herself serves as an everywoman, her circumstances are anything but common, which both allows us to envision ourselves enduring situations we are unlikely ever to know and, at the same time, prevents us from challenging Head's account by testing it against our own experience. Her story must be, and will often be described as, at once "unbelievable," even "impossible," yet nonetheless "true."

The epistemic disconnect of the same object being simultaneously "impossible" and "true" can be overcome only in a world of either fiction or miracles. The fervent wish for the latter often occludes the insight that we are dealing with the former. This gives rise to yet another paradox, one inherent not to the survival experience itself, but to its representation: the more the narrative satisfies the demand for rising action, the more it should stretch the audience's trust. After all, the skeptical reader might ask, How is it that the survivor is able to escape narrowly so many times, yet their situation always seems to go from bad to worse? More importantly, how is it that the evolution of their circumstances seems to have been preordered from bad to worse?

As Head's story progresses, she is subject to increasingly dire trials along a downward path. Such a descent, or *katabasis*, into the underworld counts among the fundamental structures in human narrative, with broadly similar versions in Vedic and Greek myth and epic literature, its Roman epigones, the New Testament, and elsewhere. In *Inferno*, Dante tells us that he and his guide must reach the lowermost pit of the "city of woes" before finally catching a distant glimpse "of the beautiful things that Heaven bears, / Where we came forth, and once more saw the stars."[4] Just as the popular addiction narrative must feature increasingly harrowing episodes of suffering and depravity before the hero hits "rock bottom" and begins the ascent toward salvation, Head must reach a point where she no longer feels that she can go on. At this crucial moment, typically when she is near total despair, the hero receives an emblem of hope, or a helping hand—in Head's narrative, the wedding dress and the self-sacrificing equities trader, respectively—that restores her on the path toward survival.

With this help, she triumphs. Yet she is not unscathed. What she has lost in the ordeal is gone forever, her scars visible and invisible.[5]

"If that were from a novel," Terrence Des Pres comments on an account of the Warsaw Ghetto Uprising, "how easily we might speak of rites of passage; of descent into hell; of journey through death's underworld.... For despite the horror, it all seems familiar, very much recalling archetypes we know from art and dreams."[6] In Tania Head's story of surviving the September 11 attacks we find a classical hero quest, a genre piece, as easily reducible to essential plot elements as a folktale or a children's book.[7] In their telling, the historical details become mere backdrops to stories that are functionally ahistorical, essentially the same. When a fraud like the one perpetrated by Head/Esteve is then exposed, commentators will typically ask how anyone could have been taken in by it in the first place. After all, the contours of her account are so generic, while the details are extraordinary, straining credulity. "Extremity makes bad art"—Des Pres, again—"because events are too obviously 'symbolic.' The structure of experience is so clear and complete that it appears to be deliberately contrived."[8] Shouldn't the combination of the vague and the outlandish in Tania Head's story have triggered our skepticism?

But this is the wrong question. We don't buy into this kind of story *in spite of* its conformity to basic narrative norms; we buy into it *because* it observes those norms. As I have already suggested, it is often the text's dutiful obeisance to norms and expectations that we are responding to.

Once we move beyond this question, a more challenging one arises: Can the very falsehoods that shape this fraud provide us with vital insights into the actual experience it falsifies? Can they show us, through a kind of *via negativa*, how to access human circumstances that are otherwise sealed beyond our own horizon of expectations?

I have to state firmly: My purpose here is not to redeem acts of misrepresentation, exploitation, and duplicity, quite often perpetrated cynically or desperately, whether for material gain or public attention.[9] Nor am I proposing that the reader's positive response to a false representation should somehow mitigate the deception or supersede the historical record. It is, rather, my argument here and throughout this book that the only way one can read these representations responsibly is to cultivate a vigilance over how fact, representation, and response condition each other. And that imperative is just as necessary, if not more so, in cases of fraud.

Sympathy for the Fraud, Ridicule for the Survivor:
Wilkomirski, Defonseca, Rosenblat

Three relatively recent cases of fraudulent Holocaust memoir, and especially the divergent afterlives these cases have generated in public discourse, help illustrate precisely what value such texts can have for the critical reading of history. The first is Binjamin Wilkomirski's *Fragments* (*Bruchstücke*, 1995), a memoir of surviving Nazi concentration camps and subsequent orphanhood as a child. The second is Misha Defonseca's 1997 memoir, also of being orphaned by Nazis, including (as a seven-year-old) a two-thousand-mile winter trek in search of her parents and, at a critical moment, being cared for by a pack of wolves. Finally, there is Herman Rosenblat's 2008 memoir of surviving Schlieben, a subcamp of Buchenwald, with the help of a little girl who passed him apples across a barbed wire fence, only to meet the same girl on a blind date in New York thirteen years later, marry her, and live happily ever after. Both Wilkomirski's and Defonseca's books were internationally acclaimed before they were exposed as frauds. The wide publicity for Rosenblat's story drew enough scrutiny that, the memory of the earlier scandals still fresh, the book was never actually released.

Just as with James Frey's *A Million Little Pieces*, Oprah Winfrey played a central if inadvertent role in all three frauds. That is not a coincidence: the kinds of misrepresentations purveyed by these authors speak to the popular imagination of a broad, nonspecialist audience that tunes in specifically for personal narratives of overcoming. Several years before the Frey controversy, Winfrey used her considerable cultural influence to promote both Wilkomirski's book and Defonseca's. She also featured a recorded interview with Herman Rosenblat and his wife on her show before their story was called into question. In each instance, it was the "incredible" or "amazing" aspect of the survival narrative that seemed to warrant the special attention paid to it. "That whole, the whole book," a visibly upset Winfrey told Frey in their confrontational second segment on *A Million Little Pieces*, "one of the reasons why we're all so taken with the book is because it feels and reads so sensationally that you can't believe that all of this happened to one person."[10]

But it is the aftermath of the frauds' exposure that needs our attention. Rosenblat, who actually did survive the concentration camps as a Jewish child in Nazi-occupied Europe, was prevented from releasing his book, *Angel at the Fence*. Though the story was sufficiently compelling that a children's book "based on" Rosenblat's tale, *Angel Girl*, was published in 2008, Rosenblat himself was criticized in the popular press, notably by other camp survivors, for distorting reality for personal financial gain.[11] Monique de Wael, the Belgian woman who, as the Jewish survivor Misha Defonseca, had written an account of wandering Europe with a pack of wolves, was also a victim of Nazi atrocities, though she is not Jewish: her parents were arrested and executed as members of the antifascist resistance in Belgium, leaving her to fend for herself.[12] Once her fraud was revealed—the detail of having been rescued by wolves drew particular ridicule—de Wael dropped any pretense of the account's veracity, though one can still easily find her book in Holocaust collections, and even in the bookstores of concentration camp and Holocaust memorial museums. Wilkomirski, meanwhile, is not only not a Jew, but he never had any personal experience of Nazi brutality. Born Bruno Grosjean (later adopted as Bruno Dösseker), he has spent his entire life, including the war, in Switzerland, which as a neutral state was never invaded by Germany. And yet, of these three cases, Wilkomirski's has arguably been treated with the greatest sympathy by journalists and scholars.

How is it that Rosenblat, the Jewish survivor of Schlieben, comes to be regarded as a sentimental phony for fantasizing the circumstances of his actual survival, whereas Wilkomirski, whose life story has no factual basis in the experiences he claims, remains a topic of serious discussion for a memoir known to be fake? The answer lies in how Wilkomirski's book has been reshaped and quite literally repackaged as a demonstration of responsible reading.

Schocken, the American publisher of Wilkomirski's *Fragments*, at first resisted questions about the book's veracity. When the evidence against the book became undeniable, the editors recalled the title from bookstores and hired Stefan Maechler, a Swiss historian, to investigate the author and to reconstruct how and why the fraud had been perpetrated. Schocken then published Maechler's complete account under the title *The Wilkomirski Affair: A Study in Biographical Truth*, in 2001, bound together with the original text of *Fragments*.[13] The publisher makes *Fragments* available only as an appendix to Maechler's report, which dwarfs it in size and scope.

Beyond merely fact-checking *Fragments*, which is almost completely fabricated, Maechler's text effectively reconstructs the process by which Bruno Dösseker came to identify with, and as, Binjamin Wilkomirski, ultimately assuming the memories and Jewish identity of a character he had created. As a child, Dösseker had survived orphanhood, abuse, and neglect so severe that he eventually came to regard his own life as a Holocaust narrative. Maechler is careful not to justify, excuse, or even to offer a psychological explanation for Wilkomirski's behavior, but his research does reveal such striking correlation between what Dösseker lived through and those experiences he assigns to Wilkomirski that, read alongside Maechler's investigation as a parallel text, *Fragments* appears as an allegorical representation of profound childhood misery and deprivation. Once the falsehood is revealed as such, Maechler's book appears to suggest, it becomes possible to discern the authentic experience behind it.

The Correspondences of Truth and Fiction

This kind of parallelism between the fictional representation and its factual basis is deeply rooted in Western literature. Literary realism, in particular, cannot dispense with it, though the epistemological origins of such an allegorical telling are much older than nineteenth-century fiction. Plato uses allegorical parallelism as the basis of his loophole for poets wishing not to be expelled from the Republic: misrepresentation, the crime of poets who fill our heads with all manner of things that have no manifestation in the real world, is excusable only insofar as the inventions may prove useful in teaching real-world virtues.[14] Somewhat closer to our own time, in one of the numerous metanarrative turns of his own fictionalized autobiography (or autobiographical fiction), Marcel Proust describes how his younger self-projection learned not to mind too much when his beloved Albertine lied to him, since, in having learned to recognize her lies and to expect them, he could immediately hear within them the truth they were intended to conceal.[15] This "correspondence" theory of truth allows the young Marcel access to both the factual reality he seeks and its inflections and implications, exposing not only what Albertine is *actually* doing, but also how she wants him to see it.

Although the notion of truth-in-correspondence complicates any crude tracing of the border between fiction and nonfiction, it does not necessarily require us to revise our genre distinctions. It calls on us to reconsider the *uses* of genre. Genre is, in Michael Riffaterre's seemingly intuitive formulation, what allows us to determine whether the information conveyed by a text should be accepted as reflecting or representing reality outside of that text: "The only reason that the phrase 'fictional truth' is not an oxymoron, as 'fictitious truth' would be, is that fiction is a genre, whereas lies are not."[16] As useful as this formula can be in helping us think through the distinction between imaginative literature and deception, however, it cannot hold up for long against the very human tendency to categorize, to place encountered artifacts into determinative generic groups. Such is the case with the lie, the very thing that Riffaterre uses to illustrate his point about fiction. In communicative praxis, a lie is indeed defined by its *lack* of generic markers that would tell an audience how to read it correctly: the audience must understand the falsehood as truth if the deception is to be effective. But once the lie is exposed as a lie, it quickly acquires all the generic markers that would allow the audience to understand it parallactically, both for its referential content (it means something other than what it says) and its intentional context (it was originally offered as a deception). As Derrida describes the lie, nesting it within ironizing layers that reveal the lie as inextricable from its discursive function ("a definition of the traditional definition of the lie, as I believe I must formulate it here"), "the lie is not a fact or a state; it is an *intentional* act, a lying. There is not *the* lie, but rather this saying or this meaning-to-say that is called lying."[17] Once "a lying" is affixed with the generic marker *a lie*, the lie is no longer capable of lying.

Riffaterre's definition of the lie, by contrast, is too schematic to accommodate the diversity of ways we measure any representation's truth claims. That range suggests so many complicating factors that in 2012, in the wake of several high-profile journalism scandals, *Slate* published an infographic, only slightly tongue-in-cheek, ranking fourteen genre-based professions (from "Fantasy Writer" and "Science Fiction Writer" to "Journalist" and "Memoirist," the latter represented pictorially by James Frey) along a scale of "Can I Make Stuff Up?"[18] In considering this same question in regard to the textual traces of concentration camps, ghettos, and besieged cities, we must resist the temptation to predetermine who has the authority to speak. In dealing with fraud, the central concern is instead whether the representation we are encountering already supplies the reader or audience with the basic parameters for proper use. We need to consider not whether the text "tells the truth" before its future interpreter has encountered it, but whether it directs that interpreter sufficiently in how to arrive at a true image of what the text represents.

The uncontentious historical fact, the "raw data," claims a *symmetry* with reality. By removing the agent of perception from view, it is representation that advertises its proximity to the thing it represents. Like perceptions, facts do not claim to *be* reality, but at the same time they are not art, which Bertold Brecht admonishes us shortly after the war is not life but rather a reflection of life made "with special mirrors."[19] Art often announces its manufactured, manipulated nature to us; when its artfulness consists in deception, as in the *trompe l'oeil*, it is through its own self-disclosure that we come to appreciate its artfulness. In this way, art casts the reality to which it refers in a new light, as Viktor Shklovsky promises it will. "Art, it is said, is not a mirror, but a hammer," Leon Trotsky notes, in a formulation frequently misattributed to Brecht: "it does not reflect, it shapes."[20]

Understanding how artistic representation shapes the reality it represents first requires a critical appreciation of the distance between the historical data and the artistic text. The precise nature of that distance varies from one text to another. Some texts may claim a congruence with reality: they do not contradict anything that is, but they fill in missing details. This is the most overtly "novelistic" of the techniques of historical and autobiographical fiction, which routinely supplies third parties with thoughts and speech that the author could not *not* have invented.

Other texts, or sometimes passages within a text, rely less on congruence with historical facts than on correspondence, as we have seen in the example of Proust. For Proust, "a fact is never a simple fact"; his writing is "much more an account of his own thoughts awakened by a collision with a fact, rather than just the facts themselves."[21] This is how the Polish artist and author Józef Czapski frames Proust in lectures delivered to other prisoners in 1940 and 1941 at the Soviet labor camp in Griazovets. The fullness of the truth—the reality, along with how it is perceived—is accessed through correspondence. Such a text makes no claim to factual accuracy. On the contrary, it tells us where and how its fabrications occur. But it also claims that its narrative corresponds to factual realities available to the reader holographically, as it were, through active, parallactic reading, or through what Lejeune calls "*the phantasmatic pact*," an "indirect form of the autobiographical pact" whereby the reader encounters novels "not only as *fictions* referring to a truth of 'human nature,' but also as revealing *phantasms* of the individual."[22]

Any or all of these modes of representation—the cold recitation of facts, congruence, or correspondence—can be operative in a telling that claims to be autobiographical. Even a lie can be brought into the service of truthful representation, so long as its generic status as a "lie" is fully available to the reader and applied appropriately to the reading. The very fact that practical recontextualization allows us to parse what is factual, what is exaggeration, and what is invention or supposition, as we do whenever we compare, say, the literary text to the historical or biographical realities represented therein, distinguishes the fraudulent accounts of Wilkomirski, Defonseca, and Rosenblat from what Harry Frankfurt designates simply as *bullshit*—that is, a representation manufactured without regard for what is true and what is not.²³ A fraud that successfully dupes its audience, even for a short time, does so through its assiduous attention to the formal *generic* markers of authenticity.

Once the responsive reader is aware of the incongruities between authentic history or biography and what is represented in the fraud, however, it becomes possible for that fraud to be recovered as a truthful representation of lived experience, as a text whose falsifications become the "special mirrors" that Brecht ascribes to art. These mirrors, corrected by a parallactic reading of the representation and the undistorted reality behind it, accurately convey a paradoxical experience that a "straight" telling could only falsify as lacking paradox. It is on this basis that Wilkomirski's *Fragments*, now subsumed into Maechler's *The Wilkomirski Affair*, is reborn as an ethically useful reflection on both the crimes that the Nazi regime perpetrated against Jewish children and the deprivations and abuses inflicted on children by an indifferent and neglectful society, fusing these themes in a single fictionalized account.²⁴

The Passion of Binjamin Wilkomirski: Recovering the Fraud for Ethical Use

With the correspondence theory of narrative truth in mind, we may now return to the paradox of how the public, critical, and scholarly afterlives of the pseudo-memoirs of Binjamin Wilkomirski, Misha Defonseca, and Herman Rosenblat diverged once their frauds were exposed. How is it that the book contract for Rosenblat, an actual concentration camp survivor, was canceled before the book could be released; Misha Defonseca, who as child had in fact been orphaned when her parents were arrested by the Nazis, lost a multimillion-dollar lawsuit brought by her own publisher; yet the work of Bruno Dösseker, who never lived under either Nazi or Soviet occupation and experienced neither regime's system of open confinement, remains readily available as an appendix to Stefan Maechler's careful and well-received study?

A question that initially appears as a paradox of reception—the actual concentration camp survivor is dismissed for his mendacity, whereas the Swiss musician is read more sympathetically as a victim of childhood trauma—resolves itself: Binjamin Wilkomirski's *Fragments* can be recovered for ethical use *because* it is now fully recontextualized by the discourse on memory and trauma that has surrounded it, most notably in Maechler's book. Maechler reframes Dösekker's fraud for the reader, assiduously reconstructing the author's real tribulations and leaving no doubt regarding the authenticity of his suffering. This is not to say that what Rosenblat and Defonseca endured as children was any less traumatic, or even that their respective tellings could not be similarly reframed to shed light on their real lived experiences, thereby redeeming their falsehoods to some degree. But that is not how their narratives are presented to audiences now.[25] Maechler's book, on the other hand, constitutes a record of the historian's parallactic reading, one that moves back and forth between those biographical facts of Dösekker's life that Maechler has reconstructed and their fictionalized echo in Wilkomirski's text. Seen through Maechler's parallax vision, we, too, can find the same truth-in-correspondence, as Maechler states directly:

> Because even the most personal memories are always prestructured by society, Wilkomirski fell back on collective memory in order to articulate his own memories, and chose images that had no direct connection with what had happened to him but that seemed to express the quality of his experience. He made use of the Shoah as the source of his metaphors. Wilkomirski, an outsider to his own society, became a Jew, the prototypical outsider in the modern world. Wilkomirski, who carried with him a past as tormenting as it was incomprehensible, became the victim of unutterable horror. A fabricated narrative about a concentration camp victim has the advantage of being understood and accepted everywhere, because the remembrance of the Shoah has established itself as collective knowledge beyond its German-Jewish context, and in the last decades, memoir literature has grown even more extensive. The chances for unconditional

acceptance of such a narrative are far greater than they would be for the story of an unhappy, illegitimate, adopted working-class child.[26]

Maechler's phrasing in this passage, which comes near the end of his book (in a chapter pointedly titled "The Truth of the Fiction"), sounds almost as though Dösekker has made a conscious calculation to represent his personal trauma through a readily accessible and popular literary genre, that of the memoir of surviving the Nazi genocide of European Jewry. The portrait of Dösekker that emerges from Maechler's book, however, is much more ambiguous: Dösekker appears to have real difficulty parsing where his real life ends and his invention begins, so that he often seems to identify wholly with—in fact, *as*—the fictional Binjamin Wilkomirski. Whether we regard Dösekker's elaborate performance as Wilkomirski as evidence of cynical calculation or of a personality disorder brought about by extensive childhood trauma, the passage's closing sentence does offer a damning critique—not of Dösekker/Wilkomirski, but of a contemporary public that is as ravenous for tales of extraordinary historical survival as it is indifferent to the unremarkable, ubiquitous, present-day sufferings of neglected and abused children. In this way, the question of whether the fraud can be recovered for ethical use becomes obsolete. Maechler has already done it.[27]

Such an effort to pull the text back from readerly dismissal has required an extraordinary *re*contextualization, most obviously by the inversion of the text-apparatus relationship in Maechler's book, where Wilkomirski's *Fragments*, formerly the primary text through which readers came to know the imagined life of one Benjamin Wilkomirski, is now an appendix to *The Wilkomirski Affair*, through which readers come to know the life of the real Bruno Dösseker.[28] In *The Wilkomirski Affair*, we see a child severely traumatized by real childhood deprivation and abuse, and we follow the process by which Dösekker comes to identify so powerfully with his own allegorical narrative that he accepts it as biographical fact. Neither Rosenblat nor Defonseca have been the beneficiaries of such an effort. For the former, the narrative of the attempted fraud superseded the narrative of survival, and the book was never published. For Defonseca, the fraud's exposure became its own story of the author's cynical manipulation of others, so that those details of survival that had earlier been most exceptional, and therefore most worthy of our attention—not just the little girl's living among wolves, but her Zelig-like appearance in far-flung settings featured prominently in the literature of open confinement, such as the Warsaw Ghetto—became the targets of hostility and ridicule. A Belgian feature film based on Defonseca's book had the unfortunate fate of having been completed just as the fraud was exposed. It was never widely distributed.

Reading parallactically is, in essence, reading ironically, with an eye to engaging, as Roland Barthes says of irony, "the question that language puts to language."[29] Recovering Dösekker's pseudo-memoir for ethical use requires a willingness to engage it through the layers of its deception, by reading its representations against the backdrop of what we know to be fact. The distinction that Barthes draws between "the poverty of Voltairean irony" and "another irony which, for lack of a better word, we shall call *baroque*, because it makes play with forms and not with beings," may be especially useful here.[30] For we cannot read a text like *Fragments* in its original presentation as a specimen of "Voltairean irony" at all—that is, as an instance of cutting doublespeak in which both speaker and audience are aware of the tension between what is said and what is meant. It is only when we assume an appropriate ironic distance toward the text—a distance that is enacted by Maechler's study and physically embodied in the repackaging of *Fragments* as the appendix to *Maechler's* book—that we can revisit it as a "play with forms," which we can then read as a meaningful and useful commentary on the treatment of children, both in situations of collective confinement and in the isolation of the solitary, abused orphan. Reading *Fragments* parallactically means first to perform the ironizing operation of divorcing the text from its decidedly unironic intentions and reading it instead through how it manipulates the received form of the Holocaust survival memoir.

Naturally, for some the facts of Dösekker's deception do not compel the deliberate, parallactic reading that could activate truth-in-correspondence, even if his tragic *self*-deception evidences an originary trauma.[31] Avishai Margalit, for example, advances an unwavering ethical critique of Dösekker's intention to perpetrate a fraud. "I use *experience, authentic,* and *fake* as objective categories," Margalit writes. "A mere act of identification with children in the Holocaust does not establish identity as one of them."[32] Margalit is obviously correct—we do not invent reality through our will alone—and in this respect Dösekker's book is indeed an irretrievable fake. At the moment of the text's first arrival, its deception does not tell us how to read it. Such an intentionalist critique, however, refuses to account for what Linda Hutcheon has pointed to as the "'performative' happening" of irony as an "interaction of interpreter, ironist and text."[33] The ironist need not even recognize himself as such. We regularly read situations, statements, and facts ironically, regardless of whether they were intended as such or, for that matter, had an "intentional" origin at all. *Fragments* does not provide instructions for an adequate—truthful—interpretation *at the moment of the text's first arrival*, but we are no longer in that moment. As the heirs to a history that has deepened and evolved on its way to us, we are invited to read the book parallactically, observing the echoes among the actual history of Nazis hunting Jewish children, Dösekker's survival of childhood abuse and neglect, and the fraudulent reframing of the latter as an instance of the former

Fraud Contra Post-Truth

When it comes to engendering the ironic distance that allows irony to happen, nothing is more effective than the mere passage of time. In time, new meanings and contexts accrue to the text, and in time new circumstantial data and intertextual references fall within the audience's expanding horizon of expectations. These two processes are, in fact, mutually conditioning, which is how "aesthetic experience can enter into a communicative relation with the everyday world or any other reality and annul the polar opposition of fiction and reality," as Hans Robert Jauss observes.[34] While the fraud is still being perpetrated, before it is exposed as such, there can be no "communicative relation with the everyday world," since the fictional text, as pseudo-historical data, lays claim to a symmetry with the world it represents. There is simply not enough distance between the historical reality and its representation for the reader to generate meaning between them. This is very much the point of the fraud: not, as with bullshit (à la Frankfurt), to frustrate the distinction between reality and invention, but to have the invention substitute for the reality. Yet at the moment the fraud becomes known *as* fraud, the distance that allows for a "communicative relation" between reality and representation opens up, ready to be filled with interpretation. We no longer accept the fiction as fact. We ask instead what the fact of the fiction says or means—not for itself, not within the text's fictional framework, but here, in *our* world.

In this respect, Kevin Young's assessment of the Wilkomirski affair, while tracking closely with the intentionalist ethical critique articulated by Margalit, collapses against cultural history. "The hoax is the very absence of truth," Young writes, "which usually means that art is absent too—hoaxes regularly substitute claims of reality for imagination, facts for form, acting as if artifice is the antithesis of art."[35] The impulse to expel the hoax from the Republic of Art is as understandable as Plato's insistence on exiling imaginative arts from the ideal republic, both rejections motivated by a sincere concern for the damage falsehood does to our shared polity. It is also no less outlandish. The fraud cannot mark "the very absence of truth," since it is only in the presence of the truth that the fraud can be understood as fraud. And rather than signal that "art is absent too," the fraud's unveiling reveals how artful it had been, how effectively its apparent lack of artifice had constituted a studied illusion of authenticity.

Again, contra Riffaterre, a lie *is* a genre—once it is exposed as a lie. Take James Frey's *A Million Little Pieces*, whose exposure sparked a media frenzy and a lasting public discussion about truthful representation. It was reissued by its publisher, its paratextual markers changed. Originally bearing the designation "Memoir/Literature" on its back cover, the book is now marked as "Fiction/Literature," and a telling disclaimer has been added in bold print to the copyright page: "This book is a combination of facts about James Frey's life and certain embellishments. Names, dates, places, and events have been changed, invented, and altered for literary effect. The reader should not consider this book anything other than a work of literature."[36] (It is a curious formulation: Is a rigorously factual history or memoir not also "a work of literature"?) Later editions contain further notes from the author and publisher. The rich conversation surrounding Frey's book has also replaced the fraud-inflected epitext, which had praised the raw brutality of the memoir, with a conversation rooted in the fraud's exposure and offering detailed instructions on how to navigate the text's weaving of fact and fiction. This epitext even encompasses Oprah Winfrey, who was instrumental in the fraud's initial success and subsequent exposure. In 2011, she invited Frey back to her show for a reconciliation that likely helped revive his career.

For those who take the absolute position articulated by Margalit and Young, it may be irrelevant that recontextualization allows us to parse which features of a fraudulent narrative reflect actual experience. Such an audience regards misrepresentation as pollution—not as a threat to the author who has perpetrated the fraud, and who might suffer reputational and financial damages as a result of being exposed, but as a threat to the very experience that the text represents. This threat is especially acute when the representation pertains to world-altering traumas like those inflicted by the Nazi and Soviet regimes, whose last witnesses are quickly passing from this world, and for which there is no shortage of vocal denialists, apologists, and equivocators. To those combating historical revisionism and obfuscation, doesn't another false memoir provide ammunition for the enemies of truth?

The fear that the fraudulent representation pollutes our understanding of authentic history can be assuaged simply by referring to the distinction between lived experience and invention. The fraud is defined as such *because* there is an authentic history to which we can refer parallactically. Rather than negate reality, the fraud refers us back to reality. It does this first by inserting itself into an informational matrix to which it must convincingly conform—in order to succeed as fraud. It does this again as it is being unmasked as a fraud, through its failure to cohere with the facts on hand. And finally, once the fraud has been fully recontextualized, as Wilkomirski's *Fragments* is in Maechler's book and elsewhere, it is presented anew in a preformed parallactic frame, which guides audiences in reading it *against* agreed-upon facts. If there had been no Nazi or Soviet camps in Europe and Central Asia, if there had been no ghettos or besieged cities, if thousands had not been forced to live a shadow existence in urban ruins and forests and secret cellars—in effect, if the fraudulent representations did not necessarily point us toward the authentic lived experiences of others, though not of the authors themselves—then the frauds would be meaningless. What makes a tale like Wilkomirski's fraudulent is not that there were never Jewish orphans surviving or perishing in Nazi-occupied Europe. *Fragments* is a fraudulent text because these children *did* exist, though Bruno Dösseker, for all his real suffering, was not one of them.

This is why it is a critical error to conflate these frauds with the rise of "fake news" and "post-truth," ideas that have once again come to prominence with the resurgence of populism and nationalism in the 2010s. "Post-truth" and "fake news" align more properly with Frankfurt's definition of bullshit: they cynically degrade the distinction between fact and fiction so that publics are left without the capacity to distinguish one from the other and, eventually, without the basic conviction that the distinction matters.

Fraud, on the other hand, inadvertently points the responsive reader to everything she would need to debunk the fraud.

The way we know that fraudulent camp narratives do not necessarily damage the history of lived experience is that they have been with us from the beginning of camp representation.

The Kolitz Case: "Yosl Rakover Talks to God"

In 1946, a short story appeared in a Yiddish-language newspaper published in Buenos Aires. Entitled "Yosl Rakover Talks to God" ("Yosl Rakover redt tsu got"), it presents itself as a first-person testament from the last days of the Warsaw Ghetto, where the eponymous speaker addresses God directly about the fate of his community. In its original context, there is no doubt that the text is fictional, authored by Zvi Kolitz, a Lithuanian-born Jew who had spent most of the war in British Mandate Palestine and later settled in New York. Following its initial publication, however, an admiring reader sent a transcript of the story, now absent its author's name or any indication that it was fictional, to Israel, where it was published by Avram Sutzkever in the Yiddish-language journal *Di goldene keyt* (The golden chain) in 1954. From there it would circulate in German, French, Hebrew, and English translations, almost always with an explicit indication that it is an authentic document whose anonymous author had perished in the Warsaw Ghetto, or at least without any indication that the actual author was still alive and had never experienced what the text relates.[37]

That subterfuge is engineered directly into Kolitz's composition, which opens with a statement regarding its own provenance that the credulous reader could easily mistake—that countless readers *have mistaken*—for fact: "In one of the ruins of the Warsaw Ghetto, preserved in a little bottle and concealed amongst heaps of charred stone and human bones, the following testament was found, written in the last hours of the ghetto by a Jew named Yosl Rakover."[38] This makes Kolitz's story a ready-made example of the power of peritext to determine the parameters for the text's interpretation. After its history was reestablished in the late 1980s and 1990s, in successive textological efforts by Frans Jozef van Beeck, Jeffry V. Mallow, and Paul Badde, Kolitz's story is now most readily accessible in much the same form as Wilkomirski's *Fragments*: it appears as a small portion of a larger volume, where it is framed by an extensive peritextual apparatus.[39] In the Vintage International edition, clearly labeled "Fiction/Literature" on the back cover, that apparatus includes Badde's detailed reconstruction of the text's history (a compact analogue to Maechler's recontextualization of the Wilkomirski text); Emmanuel Levinas's theological essay "Loving the Torah More than God," written in 1955 as a commentary to "Yosl Rakover Talks to God"; and Leon Wieseltier's afterword reflecting on the ethical challenges inherent in addressing historical trauma through fiction.

Even so substantial an effort to contextualize Kolitz's fiction, however, is bound to fail against our collective desire that a moving story about historical trauma prove to be true to life, as was indeed the case when a colleague introduced Kolitz's text to me as a historical document. It just so happens that this instance of recommending the fiction as fact occurred in the context of a conversation about Frey's *A Million Little Pieces*, which the same scholar also believed to be a factual memoir; he had encountered both texts initially as nonfiction and had had no reason to reevaluate that first impression. He remained particularly moved by an unsettling passage in Frey's book, referenced frequently in the book's initial critical response, in which Frey describes how a dentist repaired four of his teeth, including performing a double root canal, without administering anesthetic—one of many episodes from the book that were later revealed to have never taken place.[40]

Such confusion is to be expected. When the audience has a strong response to the act of reading, the very power of the response seems to call on us to reconcile the sometimes contradictory data that produced it.[41] If we believe that the external historical information in which the text is nested is authentic, and the feelings that the text triggers certainly feel real to us, then we are inclined to accept the representation in toto, especially because unmasking the representation's inauthenticity presents an equally forceful challenge to the authenticity of feelings we know we are experiencing, to say nothing of the doubts such a challenge would pose to our confidence in historical understanding. Thus K. K. Ruthven notes how the same power of the literary memoir to "supplement" our understanding of historical realities also opens the (mis)interpretive space where "bogus but well-written 'memoirs'—which may result from copycat behavior induced by the heroization of disaster—circulate more widely than the cruder texts of nonwriters who actually experienced the events they narrate. In that respect, they are substitutional supplements masquerading as supplementary supplements."[42] What is at stake in our encounter with the "unbelievable" or "amazing true story," then, is not merely our satisfaction in having invested our time and energy well, but our very sense of the real. No one wants to be gaslighted by a book.

In attempting to reconcile these potential contradictions, to reassert the distinction between historical fact and authorial invention, even the attentive reader might end up replacing one fiction with another. Van Beeck's commentary on Kolitz provides an excellent example. Sandor Goodhart points out how, in his eagerness to find an echo of Christian redemption in both Kolitz's story and Levinas's interpretation of it, van Beeck misinterprets both, believing the story's Yiddish original to have been "pirated" from its later English translation and using that alternative textology to support his idiosyncratic reading of Levinas:

> Not unlike Zvi Kolitz himself, in other words, van Beeck's well-intentioned efforts achieve a contrary effect. Where Kolitz wants to write fiction (as a way of dealing with the realities he experienced) but finds that that fiction takes on a life of its own and is mistaken for reality, so van Beeck wants to construct a document (as a way of dealing with his own interests and the realities he has experienced) that would move fiction back to reality but finds that documentation in turn constructs a new fictional character—a Jewish "pirate" who has expanded Kolitz's English text to Yiddish, a text by Levinas making the claims van Beeck says he makes—and that such fictional translations likewise assume their own role in the life of scholarship surrounding this particular story. The issues at stake in other words would appear to be the same both within the story and without.[43]

As the textological history of "Yosl Rakover Speaks to God" makes clear, Kolitz never sought to obfuscate his own authorship or the story's generic status as fiction. On the contrary, over the course of decades he repeatedly attempted to correct the error of readers, editors, and journalists who insisted on treating his invention as an authentic trace of the Warsaw Ghetto, with which Kolitz was not personally familiar. Yet among those readers were skilled literary professionals like Sutzkever, who *had* experienced the ghetto firsthand, and who nevertheless found Kolitz's story convincing as an authentic document.[44] With "Yosl Rakover Talks to God," we find ourselves in the presence of a fraud without a perpetrator, a fiction whose audience has repeatedly refused to accept it as fiction. Given the choice between believing the story's own dramatic statement of origin—that it had been "preserved in a little bottle and concealed amongst heaps of charred stone and human bones"—and trusting the author's competing claim that this is just one of many short stories he wrote over a long career, the reader has very often chosen to take the story's word over the author's.

Why?

Responses to this question are almost unanimous in locating the authenticity of Kolitz's story not in its putative origin in the ghetto, but in its representation of how Jewish thought might approach the challenge that atrocity and cataclysm pose to religious faith. This is very much in line with the reading that Levinas applies in his now famous essay, where he characterizes the text as "literary fiction, to be sure; but fiction in which all of us who survive recognize ourselves with a sense of vertigo."[45] Does this mean that Levinas recognized Kolitz's story as a story, rather than as the testament of a man who had actually died in the ghetto? Not necessarily. Levinas betrays no interest in the text's historical origins.[46] Rather, what Levinas seems to identify as "fiction" is the very construct of the text, which offers itself as Rakover's final prayer. A private prayer spontaneously delivered under duress is not a literary composition, and what Levinas seems to suggest in calling the text "literary fiction" is not that there never was a Yosl Rakover who perished in the Warsaw Ghetto, but that the text, even if it were authentic, constitutes a public, artistic representation of a survivor's private lament rather than that lament as such, and that it performs its task so effectively—so *authentically*—that "all of us who survive recognize ourselves."

Levinas's private notes from the Nazi POW camp where he spent most of the war—years marked by his attempts, ultimately aborted, to reformulate his experience in draft novels written within the camp itself—repeatedly revisit the question of how fictional representation relates to historical reality, a relation that Levinas describes as the reassertion of human time. "The historical novel recreates the time of history," he writes to himself. "It is above all a question of temporal perspective. In history, history unfurls to the rhythm of the age—of history. In the novel, to the rhythm of a human life. The present can be given only by the historical novel and not by 'history.'"[47] Once again, history as such occupies its own temporality beyond the scale of the human encounter, so that to speak about history means to speak in the absence of human subjectivity, which necessarily negates the human experience of that same history.

There were undoubtedly countless prayers (accusations, remonstrations, questions, curses) addressed to God from within the spaces of open confinement that characterize the Second World War, addresses that, never formalized as text, will forever remain beyond the scope of documentary history, which is why we can reasonably conclude that Kolitz's story encompasses a historical reality inadequately represented in that documentary history. "If Kolitz presumes to think and to feel like the final survivor in a room of corpses in the final hours of the Warsaw Ghetto," Leon Wieseltier remarks, "it is because such is the founding presumption of fiction. To seek the true it leaves the real."[48] "Yosl Rakover Talks to God" therefore becomes legible as a true representation of historical experience, not in the sense that there was an actual author of these thoughts named "Yosl Rakover," but because there were far too many real Yosl Rakovers to name.[49]

This is why Levinas, who is elsewhere highly critical of art that aestheticizes lived experience, characterizes the text as "both beautiful and true, true as only fiction can be."[50] It also points the way to how Kolitz's fiction, a generic status repeatedly erased and reasserted throughout the text's history, can serve the kind of ethical function that a reader like Levinas insists upon. For even when the reader does not have access to the text's tangled history, the prosthesis that most readily enables a parallactic reading, the text itself demands that it be read as representative of anonymous individual experiences. Thus, when Rabbi David Weiss commemorated the Warsaw Ghetto Uprising in 1967 by declaring the community's intention to honor "the countless thousands and millions of our people like Yossel [sic] Rakover," the fact that there was no Yosl Rakover—a fact then unknown to Weiss, as it has been to a great many others who have used Kolitz's text in religious commentaries—becomes irrelevant.[51] The history against which Rakover is revealed to be fiction is also the history in which "millions of our people like . . . Rakover" were undeniably real.

How does an artifact like Kolitz's story, written deliberately as fiction to reflect on an actuality to which only fiction provides access, relate to one like *Fragments*, which offers itself fraudulently as testimony? Is "Yosl Rakover," as Stephan Feuchtwang has suggested, "the reverse of *Fragments*," because "when Zvi Kolitz claimed he was its author and that it was fiction, he, not it, was denounced as a fraud"?[52] This is unconvincing. For one thing, while some readers bristled at the notion that the real author of

"Yosl Rakover" was living and had no firsthand experience of the Warsaw Ghetto, it is far from the case that Bruno Dösseker/Binjamin Wilkomirski escaped accusations not only of having authored a fraudulent text, but of being a fraud personally. For another, some readers who are inclined to treat Holocaust testimonials as a corpus of sacred literature wholly reject Kolitz as an imposter, a position argued forcefully by David Roskies, who claims that "Mr. Kolitz's story, by being untrue to the facts, falsifies the Holocaust in larger ways."[53] But this position appears to flip the ratio between representation and a reality that always far exceeds it. It is not Rakover's fictionalized cri de coeur that "falsifies the Holocaust," but the material facts of the Holocaust that reveal the Rakover text to be a fabrication.

Blake Eskin offers a more productive comparison, one that accounts for actual reader response rather than condemning it, when he notes that *Fragments* and "Yosl Rakover Talks to God," rendered in English by the same translator and released by different imprints of the same American publisher, "can be seen as companion volumes": "Both . . . are brief, didactic fables. In each, there is something simplistic and fundamentally false that allows uninformed readers to make an emotional investment that requires a reader's complicity in making a story come true."[54] All texts, of course, fictional or otherwise, demand "a reader's complicity in making a story come true." What distinguishes a fictional narrative of open confinement from authentic survival testimony is that the former is composed with the express intention of harnessing that complicity, of garnering that "emotional investment" by performing tragedy for an audience, whereas the latter inserts itself into an evidentiary corpus, without which that testimony might otherwise appear confusing or disjointed. In effect, fiction initiates the audience into the worlds it simulates within the text, while testimony presumes a broad familiarity with a single, historically contingent world that is forever inaccessible to all but the unlucky few.

The Kolitz case powerfully illustrates how, once its machinations have been exposed, "fraud" is not simply a misrepresentation perpetrated deliberately by an unscrupulous author. It is more accurately a kind of textual encounter in which the text's features are misaligned with the text's use, such as when the prayer of the fictional Rakover is used as evidence of the actual death of an actual Rakover. In a 1972 letter, Kolitz himself took the persistence of this error as evidence of his having communicated an essential *truth* about life and death in the Warsaw Ghetto:

> The refusal of this particular error to die, and the fact that many persons, and capable ones to boot, like Mr. Sutzkever, who were in the ghetto (which is not the case with me), saw "Yosl Rakover" as something that gives authentic expression to the spiritual turmoil of a believing Jew in the last hours of the Warsaw ghetto—all of this is certainly a source of satisfaction to me. But there is a further testimony here. It is the testimony of my own spiritual turmoil, which did not subside with my giving it a fictional (and, I hope, artistic) expression; it went to the depth of the pain of a people that has the awesome right to take God to court.[55]

Rather than charge himself with inauthenticity, Kolitz does the opposite: he reasserts—as he did repeatedly, over decades, against "the refusal of this particular error to die"—the dynamic interdependence of authenticity and invention whenever historical reality is given a "fictional... expression." What is authentic, according to Kolitz, is not that Rakover was ever a living, breathing individual, but the "expression" itself, since it corresponds accurately to the experience of "many persons... who were in the ghetto." To the extent that we might insist on reading the text as testimony, it is testimony not from the Warsaw Ghetto, but of the author's "own spiritual turmoil," which no one is in a position to deny. As with the frauds of Dösseker, Defonseca, Rosenblat, and any number of other historical obfuscators, the epistemological chain of truth-in-correspondence becomes clear once the reader is granted access to all the relevant data. The impersonal, historical tragedy is real; the authors' personal tragedies are also real. Reading the fraud *as fraud*, we readily see how the fiction mediates between them.

Such an explanation does not necessarily mitigate the outrage of those who have been lured into the textual encounter under false pretenses—whether the author is a willing partner in public misprision, as with *Fragments*, or a reluctant one, as with "Yosl Rakover." An audience that feels duped is hardly likely to feel less so for having had the subterfuge explained to them. What an example like the Kolitz case demonstrates is how such outrage is rooted not in our mental image of authorial intent, or not only in that image, but in the sense of the text being out of place, mislabeled, misshelved, calling into question neat definitions of the historical past and those who purport to be speaking on its behalf. We are outraged at imposture, Susan Stewart remarks, because it signals "the manufactured and collaborative, as well as contradictory, nature of all identity, and, just as we can see obscenity as an utterance out of place, [we can] see imposture as an identity out of place."[56] Falsely claiming to have endured a concentration camp or besieged city is certainly an obscenity, but recontextualizing the claim as fraud restores it to its proper place, where the text's mediation between the personal reality of the author's experience and the impersonal reality of the historical past becomes a new, layered text of its own.

The Performance of Falsehood: From Fraud to Parabiography

Two essential features distinguish fraudulent narratives of open confinement from the "real-life fiction" that remains my principal concern in this book. Most obviously, in fraud the biographical facts of the author's life simply contradict the narrative information conveyed by the text. What the author claims to have endured, or else to know from firsthand experience, never occurred as related. As we have seen in the different reception histories of Wilkomirski, Defonseca, and Rosenblat, especially after their respective frauds were exposed, even in instances of outright deception, it is often unhelpful to equate the facts with truth and invention with falsehood, since the correspondence between the actual facts of the author's life and the narrative details provided in the text can be both real and powerful. Read allegorically, with an eye toward specific congruencies between the life and its textual trace, the narratives can be read as simulations of lived historical experience rather than as evidence, which is precisely why these narratives initially attract so strong a readerly response. "The factual details that realist discourse seems to amass in acts of documentation," Michael Rothberg observes in reference to Barthes's description of the "reality effect" that such discourse aims for, "are mere ruses that simulate and do not refer to reality."[57] Or, rather, they refer to reality not by documenting it, but by simulating it. By exploiting the generic conventions of survival narratives, these texts succeed in providing the reader with the faintest visceral experience of the camp, of the life in hiding, of the familiar yet extraordinary twentieth-century Robinsonade, without ever openly acknowledging that the experience has been a simulation from the beginning.

The second difference between fraud and real-life fiction is in the ironic distance that would be required to read the respective texts responsively. In real-life fiction, as we shall see, that irony is woven directly into the narrative fabric. The author needs the audience to interpolate actively between the narrative data provided by the text and the external realities to which they refer in modified, abbreviated, or altogether distorted form. Often, this is achieved by underscoring those instances where the narrative effect depends upon a *congruence* with fact, rather than a strict conformity or adherence to it. The author herself highlights, whether structurally or explicitly or both, the *literariness* of the telling. She might announce at the outset that a major character is a composite of actual persons or a deliberately inverse self-portrait. She might incorporate editorial commentary, including asides on the mimetic process, into the representation, foregrounding the representation of these spaces *within* the spaces' representation. The result is a text that, acknowledging the complexity and potentially confusing claims it is making on truth, furnishes its audience with the tools to untangle them and, very often, clear instructions for their use.

But it is rare for the fraudster to expose the fraud—at least, not intentionally, not immediately—and for as long as the lie remains unexposed it continues to function as a deception. Just as Riffaterre suggests, it does not yet constitute a genre, since it does not share any of the rules of engagement that genre implies. Identifying the fraud as fraud, however, activates its rich genre characteristics, exposing interpretive expectations whose satisfaction allows the fraud to be perpetrated successfully in the first place.

This is how a book like *Fragments* can be recovered for ethical use: as a *lie*. Once a statement is duly labeled a "lie," the label provides a highly functional set of genre norms that allow us to interpret the text. With an increasingly clear elaboration of the author's actual biography, textual self-representation, and historical data, the parallax reading becomes possible, even rewarding in its own right. Exposing the fraud opens an ironic distance between the false representation and the actual history it misrepresents. Arguably, it is this distance, rather than the truth of any particular supporting detail, that the fraud seeks to conceal, since audiences readily allow storytellers a measure of "license" in amplifying or tailoring illustrative details, so long as those details are not "major"—that is, so long as they do not significantly alter the representation as a whole by opening an ironic distance between the representation and the reality behind it. Yet once that ironic distance announces itself, the fraudulent text passes from lie-as-deception to lie-as-genre. It becomes possible to read the truth of the experience through the lies of its telling.

Fraud as such places the burden of supplying its parallel text—the paratextual discussions, verifiable facts, consensus history, etc., that allow us to separate fact from invention and to make sense of how they align or diverge—squarely on the audience, leaving open the possibility that the deception that has already been exposed could resurface when a new reader encounters the text outside of its real context. The unsuspecting patron of a used bookstore who chances upon a first edition of Wilkomirski's *Fragments* or Defonseca's *Surviving with Wolves* or else Laurie Friedman's *Angel Girl*, "Based on a True Story"—that is, on Herman Rosenblat's untrue story—might have no way of knowing that these texts are fraudulent. Visual texts complicate this situation further, since they carry a heightened aura of authenticity, the assumption that "seeing is believing." Someone who stumbles upon a copy of *The Ghetto* (*Das Ghetto*, 1942), an unfinished Nazi propaganda film shot inside the Warsaw Ghetto in the months before mass deportations to Treblinka began, could regard the soundless footage as evidence of Jews' indifference toward their own suffering (figure 1.1), which is precisely what the propagandists had intended in staging their scenes and framing their shots.[58] Noting the arrival of the film crew in her diary in May 1942, Rachela Auerbach had no illusions about their intentions, which she characterizes as "anti-Semitism seasoned with pornography."[59] Alternatively, the viewer could access much of the same material through *A Film Unfinished*, Yael Hersonski's 2010 documentary about *The Ghetto* that also *contains* that earlier film. Hersonski's presentation of the Nazi propaganda film includes footage of survivors of the Warsaw Ghetto watching and commenting on what they see, comparing their lived experience to its deliberate misrepresentation in the propaganda text. Dramatic reenactments of how *The Ghetto* was created and rediscovered augment the ironic distance necessary for a responsive, responsible reading of a film originally intended to deceive. Voiceover commentaries provide additional information, contrasting sharply with the silence of the original silent film, while footage from the making of *The Ghetto* helps reconstitute the filmmakers' distortions of reality (figure 1.2). "Forty-five years passed," Hersonski announces, "from the moment the unfinished propaganda film was discovered until chance revealed another film reel containing outtakes, frames from the raw footage left on the cutting-room floor. Images that were never meant to be seen now revealed

Figure 1.1 The unfinished Nazi propaganda film *The Ghetto* (1942) repeatedly stages scenes of Jews' indifference toward the suffering of other Jews (00:44:18). *Source:* public domain

repeated attempts to stage moments over and over again until a take seemed credible enough."[60] Encountering *The Ghetto* through *A Film Unfinished* is, in this sense, analogous to reading Wilkomirski's *Fragments* through Maechler's *The Wilkomirski Affair*, an exhaustive biographical study of how the text and the persona of its author came into being. In both instances, a responsive, parallactic reading is only possible when the audience has sufficient information to recognize deviations from historical or biographical fact and the interpretive tools for understanding what those deviations signify.

When one insists on performing this kind of laborious reading, even fake testimonials can become interpretable objects. It is worth noting in this regard that, as of 2024 (i.e., decades after their narratives were exposed as frauds), we can still find video testimonies by Wilkomirski, Defonseca, and Rosenblat among the more than fifty thousand survivor testimonies that make up the USC Shoah Foundation's Visual History Archive, among our foremost repositories of survivor accounts. In Wilkomirski's archived

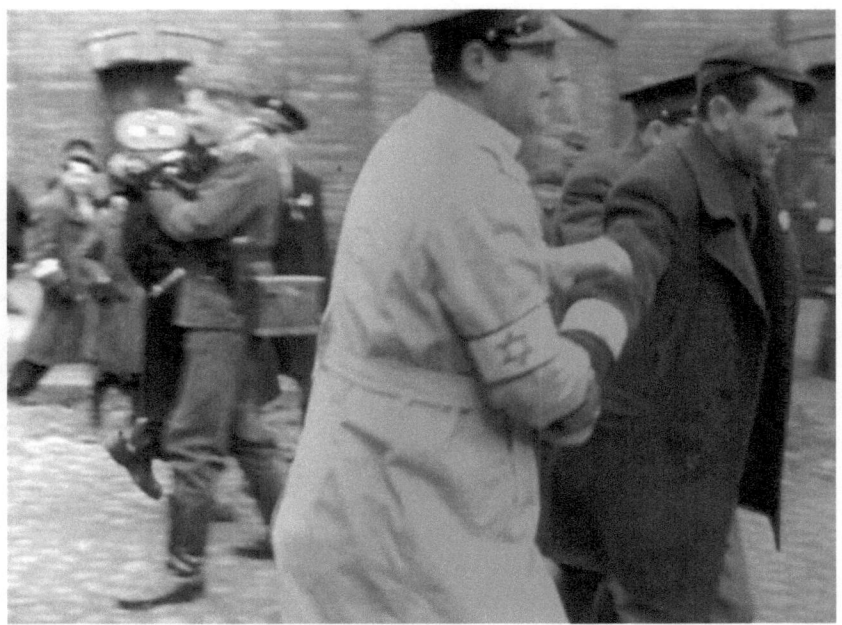

Figure 1.2 *A Film Unfinished* (2010) highlights evidence of how the propaganda film *The Ghetto* was staged (00:50:02). *Source*: *A Film Unfinished*, dir. Yael Hersonski (New York: Oscilloscope Laboratories, 2011)

Figure 1.3 Binjamin Wilkomirski video testimony (00:23:40). *Source*: Visual History Archive of the USC Shoah Foundation

Figure 1.4 Misha Defonseca video testimony (00:22:30). *Source*: Visual History Archive of the USC Shoah Foundation

testimony (figure 1.3), a large Star of David pendant is clearly visible in his open collar. In her video (figure 1.4), Misha Defonseca wears an exceedingly large *chai* ("life") medallion.[61] Both are symbolic necklaces identifying their bearers as Jews, though neither Wilkomirski nor Defonseca is ethnically Jewish. Their alter egos, however, are, and we might therefore consider these worn emblems as costumery that helps complete the roles each has adopted as personal biography. Herman Rosenblat, the only one of the three who actually was a Jew and actually did survive a concentration camp, wears no such emblem in his taped testimony (figure 1.5), but he also makes no mention in the video of the extraordinary love story that he recounts in *Angel at the Fence*. This is because Rosenblat's testimony was recorded in January 1995, almost a year before he began telling the fabrication publicly.

A standard feature of real-life fiction of open confinement is its insistence on that ironic distance, which is prerequisite to parallactic, responsive reading, but which is simultaneously the primary cause of the genre confusion that suffuses these texts' reception. Audiences frequently do not know whether the text they are encountering is fiction or nonfiction, not because the text claims to be one while actually being the other—that is, fraud—but because the text insists on being both fiction and nonfiction at the same time.

Figure 1.5 Herman Rosenblat video testimony (00:13:24). *Source*: Visual History Archive of the USC Shoah Foundation

This fuzzy boundary between genres conventionally defined by their mutual exclusion is not so much a destabilization as an adept exploitation of the fact that life writing is not, nor has it ever been, generically stable. Philippe Lejeune points out that critical definitions of autobiography, as generic definitions more generally, are inherently normative: rather than attempt to describe the available corpus in its entirety, they formulate 'what is the essence, or the model of the genre" first, only then to include those texts that most readily confirm the definition: "In order to define, the critic is going to be led not only to say what the genre is, but what it *must* be in order to be what it is. . . . The operation is circular: it corresponds to a rationalization of the horizon of expectation."[62]

Concerned that the positivist critic's normative definition of life writing overdetermines genre and does so to the exclusion of actual lived experience, several important mid-century writers chose to represent their survival of uncanny spaces by making the interplay of invention and historical fact an explicit compositional feature of their work—in essence, to foreground irony not only as a rhetorical device, but as the rhetorical symptom of the situational paradoxes they had experienced firsthand. These texts, explicitly *parabiographical*, challenge positivist normativity by asking, *Is it still a lie when the speaker always tells you how, when, and why she is lying?*

CHAPTER II

Parabiography

> The subject of testimony is the one who bears witness to a desubjectification.
> —GIORGIO AGAMBEN, *REMNANTS OF AUSCHWITZ: THE WITNESS AND THE ARCHIVE* (TRANS. DANIEL HELLER-ROAZEN)

"In the war years people eagerly read *War and Peace*—to check themselves (and not Tolstoy, in whose truth-to-life no one doubted). And the reader said to himself: yes, this means that I have the right sense of things. It means this is what it's like. Whoever was strong enough to read eagerly read *War and Peace* in besieged Leningrad."[1]

This is how Lidiia Ginzburg opens *Notes of a Blockade Person* (*Zapiski blokadnogo cheloveka*, 1984–1989), a literary representation of her own experience and that of her immediate social circle during the nearly three-year Siege of Leningrad, from September 1941 to January 1944. Though it has generally been known in English by the title of Alan Myers's translation, *Blockade Diary*, it is not a diary.[2] It was, first of all, penned four decades after the events it describes, the first portions appearing in the Leningrad literary journal *Neva* in 1984. And then there's the oddity of that opening paragraph, dramatically *un*-diaristic in its signaling to the reader that what follows is not simply a recitation of dates and events. Here, in the very first sentences of what has become one of the most important texts bearing witness to a demographic catastrophe, one in which nearly a million civilians lost their lives and countless others were reduced to cannibalism to survive, Ginzburg offers an unambiguous articulation of the function of the literary text in extremis. It is not to provide entertainment, distraction, purpose, or hope in the face of precarity, or at least not primarily so.[3] The reason Ginzburg's "reader" absolutely had to find a copy of *War and Peace* was to confirm through fiction that reality is real.[4]

But how? How does a literary text tell us essential things about our world that other sources—including, in Ginzburg's formulation, our own firsthand experience of that world—cannot? The most immediate answer is that even our own experiences consist of meaningless data points, discrete impressions that lack sense until they are bound together in some narrative sequence. It is the sequential ordering structure of the narrative, its "emplotment," and not its constituent points, that generates meaning. It is the form of the narrative, rather than its infinitely reproducible (and often predictable) content, that forces an impression on audiences left unaffected by historical data accessible elsewhere. We know this already from our own lives, from the impossibility of "making sense" of our experiences in the moment of their occurrence, and perhaps from our own quixotic efforts to "figure out what it all"—any *it*, any *all*—"means." This is why the reading of *War and Peace* in besieged Leningrad is initially not about verifying reality as such (which requires an additional epistemological step), but about testing whether "I have the right sense of things": *eto ia chuvstvuiu pravil'no*—literally, that "I am feeling this correctly." For Ginzburg, whether I am living under bombardment or reading about someone living under bombardment, I am taking in the data of experience. Reading about my own experience becomes a way of calibrating the very senses through which the world arrives to me.

Ginzburg's formulation assumes that there is a Kantian gulf between the world as it is and the world as we think we know it. Even the phrasing she applies to verisimilitude in Tolstoy's representations of wartime trauma strongly suggests that we are dealing not with life itself, but with information that demands interpretation: what I have translated as "truth-to-life," *adekvatnost' zhizni*, is more literally "correspondence to life." And as we have already seen in fraudulent representations of surviving open confinement, with any "correspondence" theory of truth it is essential that the interpreter have a command of the genre, of the rules governing this particular representation, in order to arrive at an appropriate understanding of the object represented.

The need to command these interpretive rules arises not only as a by-product of literary tradition, which offers extensive instruction in how to dupe the uninformed reader with a well-crafted tale of woe, or from the rapid development of information technologies that spread and digitally canonize misinformation. Rather, it is symptomatic of the change in representation that Erich Auerbach identifies first with Stendhal and more powerfully with Balzac, for whom "history" was not a "scientific investigation of transactions which have already occurred, but of comparatively free invention" oriented toward an accurate portrayal of the *present*, that which "is in the process of resulting from history," so that the author "regards his creative and artistic activity as equivalent to an activity of a historical-interpretive and even historical-philosophical nature."[5] And this change in representation was not merely a shift in fashion or style for its own sake, but, as Hayden White has forcefully argued, representation adapting itself to aspects of reality that had never before been objects of representation, and that, in the "'holocaustal' events" of the twentieth century, were themselves new to historical consciousness.[6] For White, the new need to represent experiences that occur simultaneously on an individual and a mass scale—that is, from perspectives that are invisible to each other—creates a condition where "it seems as difficult to conceive of a treatment of historical reality that would not use fictional techniques in the representation of events as it is to conceive of a serious fiction that did not in some way or at some level make claims about the nature and meaning of history."[7]

Ginzburg's view of this shift, revisited many times over a career-long inquiry into the textual representation of experience, aligns cleanly with White and specifically with Auerbach, whose observation about the generalized, composite personality of the hero in the classical tradition serves as the point of departure for Ginzburg's investigation of how personality is represented in text, whether as a unique interiority or a collective type, "as if his life flowed in abstracted and general outlines."[8] Like White and Auerbach before him, Ginzburg regards the evolution of novelistic representation as a response to concurrent changes in how society conceives of interiority. As we see in Ginzburg's striking reference to *War and Peace* at the beginning of *Notes of a Blockade Person*, the "holocaustal events" of the twentieth century call on us to place fact and fiction into dynamic conversation, lest the private be excised falsely from the public, the individual from the collective, the momentary from the historical.

From Composite to Self: Lidiia Ginzburg's Parallax View

Of special interest in Ginzburg's approach in *Notes of a Blockade Person* is her decision not to write primarily from her own first-person perspective, but instead to invent a third-person hero through whom she could mediate between individual and collective experiences: "I needed to show not only the general life [*obshchuiu zhizn'*], but the blockade existence [*blokadnoe bytie*] of a single person. This is a composite and conventional [*summarnyi i uslovnyi*] person (which is why he is called 'N.'), an intellectual in peculiar [*osobykh*] circumstances."[9] Ginzburg's formulation carefully outlines the paradoxes of the kind of representation she is undertaking. She intends to show "the general life" of a person living in mid-century Leningrad, since that is the baseline, the backdrop against which "blockade existence" plays out. The phrasing *blokadnoe bytie* is markedly philosophical: *bytie* is everyday life, a mode of existence, or being as such, which, under siege, has been dramatically altered. By inventing N., Ginzburg takes the most basic paradigm of life writing—a representation of what makes the individual unique and extraordinary in circumstances where most others are neither—and inverts it. In *Notes of a Blockade Person*, it is the circumstances that are "peculiar"—*osobye*, from *osoba*, "individual person"—whereas the person generically named "N.," Russian literature's preferred monogram for otherwise anonymous provincial towns and tertiary characters, is "composite and conventional." In describing this character as "conventional," Ginzburg uses a polysemous term, *uslovnyi*, whose potential meanings encompass not only the conventionality of this fictional creation, but also his being "contingent" (he is invented for a specific purpose), "referential" (he is used as the measure of a typified intellectual's experience of *blokadnoe bytie*), and especially "pretend," a "stand-in," the kind one might use in a model, game, or, in this case, a reenactment staged on the page.

But it is Ginzburg's characterization of N. as *summarnyi*, "composite," that demands special attention. For this is the same word that Ginzburg uses when she echoes Erich Auerbach's analysis of the hero in ancient literature, who is far less individuated than the circumstances around him: "In ancient literature, the specificity of the material world and the specificity of psychic life are not correlated. The material world may be detailed, while the hero remains composite [*summarnyi*], because the empirical world has not yet penetrated into the mechanisms for the determination [*obuslovlennosti*] of his behavior."[10] Here, in a critical-theoretical text, Ginzburg offers the same tension between the generalized human type (the "composite," *summarnyi*) and the representation whose uniqueness is "determined" by convention (*obuslovlennost'*, from *uslovie*, "convention," "contingency," etc.). In this vision, it is only as the nineteenth century flows into the twentieth that we see literature catching up with the need to represent the human being not as a composite type, but as a unique interiority.[11] What Ginzburg proposes in telling her own story through N. is a reversion toward the classical paradigm, where the storyworld is specific, consisting of "peculiar circumstances," whereas the hero is an abstraction, a type composited from among the Leningrad intelligentsia that included Ginzburg herself.

As a contrastive example, one might look to Olga Bergholz, Leningrad's most celebrated poet of the siege, who spoke to Leningrad's inhabitants in popular radio broadcasts during their catastrophe and then shaped public memory of the experience in later writings. Bergholz is notable for having produced both a conventional "blockade diary," which records her more or less unvarnished impressions of life in a besieged city, and *Daytime Stars* (*Dnevnye zvezdy*, 1955), which relies on novelistic techniques and a self-conscious turn toward propaganda, with the author telling the reader directly that "the Essential Book"—that is, the book that captures the essence of its author's truth—"shuns neither collective heroes, nor speculation, nor fiction; it does not refuse any of the wonders of art, and above all—not for a moment does it refuse the great task of communist propaganda."[12] It is only by regarding Bergholz's two texts simultaneously and parallactically, tracing the overlaps and incongruencies of their representations of the same events, that the reader can glean both the facts of her experience and the shape that experience assumed in memory.

Ginzburg's approach in *Notes of a Blockade Person*, on the other hand, accomplishes its two essential goals in a single work. The first goal, which she has already announced explicitly, is to create an accurate, true-to-life portrait of a person who is individuated not by personal idiosyncrasies, but rather by the special circumstances of "blockade existence." N.'s movement through Leningrad casts light on these circumstances, not the other way around. "Blockade existence," and not the intellectual called "N.," is Ginzburg's most urgent subject. In the book's second typescript, Ginzburg expounds briefly on how she views this composite figure, suggesting that N. is not a person, but "rather, a point for entering the circumstances, from which other circumstances and other people are revealed. This character and everything here related have arisen from various accounts, from concentrating my own and others' experiences."[13] While there is noticeable ambivalence in Ginzburg's conceptualization of N.—he is an individual, but also a collective; a subjective personality, but also the reflection of a generalized reality; an avatar of Ginzburg, though encompassing her friends' experiences as well—he is above all a focalization point, a *tochka prilozheniia obstoiatel'stv*, that allows her to shift from sociological observation and first-person recollection to narrating action in the third person. And unlike the language of the retrospective sociologist describing what appear as interminably repetitive circumstances (i.e., during the blockade, we would do this, we would do that), N.'s actions are more frequently perfective: he completes an act not knowing what will come next.

The second purpose in telling her story through a composite character is more subtle, though no less essential: he embodies the author's own sense of personality in tension with itself, an internal otherness that the unity of the first-person "I" occludes. "In Ginzburg's case," Emily Van Buskirk argues, "the way to 'deal' with otherness is to distance this other from the 'I' through the creation of an episodic character, while creating a near-identity of distanced voices and perspectives on these experiences": "Not only does the third person highlight otherness, but it also works particularly well when one wants to tell a story of failure (whereas most first-person autobiographies are in some manner success stories). In Ginzburg's quasi-autobiographical texts, the 'he' is a traumatized self, who is trying to understand his moral failures through a division into actor/sufferer and critic/judge."[14]

The composite N. is at once Ginzburg and not Ginzburg, the expression of both her inner experience and her quasi-objectivized judgments of herself, with the internal and external perspectives bundled together within the convention of the third-person fictional hero. He is a public performance of a personality divided against itself, struggling against internal contradictions and situational paradoxes that the autobiographical "I," in its equally conventional unity, could only falsify. That Ginzburg, a homosexual woman in a relentlessly homophobic society, presents her textual stand-in as a man makes that struggle against the self all the more resonant and poignant.

The sense of struggle against oneself, in fact, resonates powerfully with the fraudulent works we have already considered. Texts like Wilkomirski's *Fragments* and Defonseca's *Surviving with Wolves*, as we have seen, express authentic trauma, but they do not express that trauma authentically, insofar as the traumas that the actual authors had endured in childhood are not those represented in their written accounts. The authors of fraudulent accounts have followed Brecht's injunction that we "Erase the traces!," thereby creating what Walter Benjamin imagines as pure artifice or simulacrum.[15] Benjamin's concept of authenticity relies upon the traceability of the transmissible (reproducible) object to its origin: "The here and now of the original underlies the concept of its authenticity."[16] That link is especially elusive when the original object is not an identifiable image or thing, but rather the experience of a particular here and now, where both the experience and the place are inaccessible to virtually all those who encounter their textual representation. It is precisely this lacuna that instances of fraud exploit: they can convince readers that they are authentic because most readers cannot access the original experience and place that we might otherwise refer to in testing the representation's authenticity.

In *Notes of a Blockade Person*, however, Ginzburg *does not* "erase the traces." On the contrary, she repeatedly instructs the reader in how, when, and why her depiction of life in besieged Leningrad deviates from documentary history. Then why, we might ask, does she take any liberties at all? When the perpetrator of fraud fabricates his or her own story, the motivation for doing so, whether one is seeking fame or fortune or a complex and misguided reckoning with one's actual past, is usually easy enough to trace once the falsehood has been exposed. One way or another, people usually lie because they want to get away with something. As long as there are atrocities there will be victims, and as long as there are victims there will be those who are willing to victimize the victims further by appropriating whatever pathetic shadow of restitution their status as victims might afford. What would be the point of announcing one's deviations from fact at the very outset?

The answer, again, is that Ginzburg is depicting not herself, but a "blockade person," who is simultaneously Lidiia Ginzburg and not Lidiia Ginzburg. The Siege of Leningrad is a special, "peculiar circumstance" that forces an intellectual such as herself into a paradoxical existence, one that demands an equally paradoxical representation, allowing us to see the "blockade person" from within and from without at the same time. *Notes from a Blockade Person* is neither memoir nor diary nor autobiography, genres whose conventions the text explicitly repudiates. It is, more accurately, a *parabiography*, a text that deliberately provides false information about the author in order to access a more truthful portrait of that author's paradoxical existence.

Parabiography as Genre: Artur Sandauer's
Notes from the City of the Dead

Ginzburg's representation is less a description of wartime Leningrad than a reenactment of how, under such conditions, a member of the Soviet intelligentsia experienced life as a split self. Autobiography, Ginzburg self-consciously determined, was inadequate to the task of truthful representation, since the first-person speaker of the autobiographical text can, at best, write *about* internal psychological fissures from within the text's unified voice. Just as the survivor-memoirist is challenged to convey the possibility of his or her own demise, a possibility already foreclosed before the book is opened, the autobiographer will have a hard time reenacting the state in which the "I" does not know to which of several competing or contradictory selves the pronoun "I" refers.

The solution to this paradox, according to Artur Sandauer, is not autobiography, but *parabiography*. Sandauer, a major Jewish literary critic, coined the term as he approached the task of writing about his coming-of-age in interwar Poland; his survival in Nazi-occupied Sambor (now Sambir, in western Ukraine), from which he escaped before the local ghetto was liquidated and most of its inhabitants murdered; and his professional flourishing in the postwar Polish academic and literary establishments, which he could accomplish only by working against what he perceived to be the markedly Jewish inflections of his worldview and language.[17] It was 1948, Sandauer tells us directly in one of the passages of reflective commentary interspersed throughout his *Notes from the City of the Dead* (*Zapiski z martwego miasta*, 1963), and he had been planning to write about his life before the war.[18] But in revisiting his earliest literary efforts, Sandauer was "chilled by their unflawed Polish, their impeccable rhymes and metaphors," the linguistic scars of having been born "on the boundary of two nationalities and classes," requiring him to turn against himself, against his own Jewishness: "Through the gutter smell, through the wheezing of peddlers, through the moaning of beggars, I was running for the stairs, where I would stand momentarily at the top in order to shake off everything that had stuck along the way, to become fixed and civilized."[19] Sandauer imagines a sharp divide between his small Jewish neighborhood of Blich—"a settlement of Jewish poverty and darkness," called "Bleich" in German, a generic term for undeveloped land suitable for sun-bleaching linen—and the town's elevated main square just a short walk away, "a district of culture and Polish language" to which he "quite literally had to climb."[20] Among the assimilated Jewish intelligentsia of prewar Eastern and Central Europe, it was not uncommon for the sense of sociocultural insecurity, or even inferiority, to express itself as a rebellion against what Osip Mandel'shtam dismissed as the "tongue-tied and language-less language" (*kosnoiazichie i bez"iazichie*) of his father's generation.[21] That language, inflected with Yiddish phrasing and intonation, is for such writers strongly associated with poverty, backwardness, and exclusion from modernity, an association that Sandauer amplifies when he refers to the "peddlers" as *handełes*, a term often used with anti-Semitic derision to denote the poor rag-and-bone men who would pass from courtyard to courtyard buying and selling old clothes. As a Jewish writer working in Polish, Sandauer had felt a need to excise any traces of his ethnic heritage from his language—in effect, to be more Polish than a Polish writer, who need not hesitate from deploying a Yiddishism for stylistic effect—and in the process found his personality divided against itself in a way that traditional autobiography, totalizing its subject ex post facto, could only obscure.

In Paris shortly after the war, Sandauer found himself grappling with Jean-Paul Sartre's arguments in "Reflections on the Jewish Question" ("Réflexions sur la question juive," 1945–1946), in which Sartre insists that Jews need to resist the kinds of assimilation that Sandauer and others had struggled to achieve:

> Jews, [Sartre] asserted, dwelling among strangers, should guard against assimilation, preserving their fidelity to themselves and their nation. Lovely! But for the Jew who is already assimilated and sits on the border between two nationalities: to which of them is he to be faithful? And doesn't that fidelity—especially during a period of raging anti-Semitism, when dual nationality is like having a pack of enraged dogs within you—have to signify fidelity to one's own fissure, to one's own . . . inauthenticity? And so, polemicizing mentally with Sartre, I began to create Mieczysław Rosenzweig, a character—as his very name already suggests—split in two, on the one hand deeply inauthentic, because he hates himself, and on the other endowed with a sort of higher-order authenticity, since it gives voice to this situation clearly and without mincing words.[22]

For Sandauer, an "authentic" self-representation would necessarily encompass those ways in which his circumstances had forced him into "inauthenticity." The unity of the autobiographical "I," in this view, becomes fiction and deception, while authorial gestures underscoring "one's own fissure," illustrated most colorfully by the invention of an avatar with an unmistakably Polish given name and an equally obvious Jewish surname, reflect a truthful accounting of, and reckoning with, the paradoxes of the author's circumstances and how he has accommodated himself to them. Saddling the parabiographical version of himself with repugnant prejudices and ideological orthodoxies, Sandauer is able to portray his real ambivalence and inner conflict more accurately.

Sandauer concludes his explanation for the invention of Mieczysław Rosenzweig by relaying a story that he claims to have been told by one of the Jewish gendarmes tasked with escorting Jews who had been rounded up in "actions" to the train platforms, from which they would be loaded onto cattle cars and transported to camps. For the Jews of Sambor, such roundups meant almost certain death: the trains were bound for Bełżec, purpose-built as a death camp, and fewer than two hundred of Sambor's roughly eight thousand Jews survived the war. Those awaiting the transport knew what lay ahead of them. The gendarme, according to Sandauer, recounted how, facing death, the Hasidim from Blich encountered the gentrified Polonized Jews who lived around the town square, an encounter between two inimical ways of life that would normally occur only on major holidays, when the assimilated Jews might descend to Blich to worship at the Great Synagogue. Spontaneously, the gathered Hasidim lift their voices in chorus to sing the Shema, Judaism's core confession of faith in the unity of God, an act reified when the otherwise secular Jews from the town square join them in prayer. Only one man stands off to the side, refusing to be subsumed into the collective—and not just the social collective, but the sublimation of the individual into a common, textually predetermined narrative:

> I realize that in this story, which otherwise corresponds to all the canons of occupation poetics (in nearly all novels from these times, Jews recite the Shema on their way to their deaths, thereby giving expression to their tribal bond and to their optimistic faith in the survival of their nation)[23]—that in this story the refusal to take part in a collective dying prayer creates a particularly sharp dissonance. And yet

I have reason to believe that that gesture of double refusal with which my father, a socialist and non-believer, throughout his life at odds with both the darkness of Blich and the snobbery of the Town Square, had rejected the proposition of reconciling with his native community, that the contrarian and willful smile with which he went to his death—that these were no delusion.

This recollection, too, constitutes one element of "Mieczysław Rosenzweig."[24]

For Sandauer, the "sharp dissonance" of one person rejecting the collective prayer constitutes a "double refusal," not only in the sense that he is refusing both sides of an old cultural opposition—representations of small-town Jewish life in Central Europe in the nineteenth and early twentieth centuries often hinge precisely on this opposition between a rising class of secularists and traditionalists who are increasingly regarded as backward—but also in the sense that he will not allow himself to be a cliché, to be absorbed into "all the cannons of occupation poetics." That the lone figure here happens to be the author's father, a detail that he deliberately suppresses until the moment when it will have the strongest dramatic effect, then strikes its own dissonance.

There is certainly cause for the reader to be skeptical. How, after all, could Sandauer's father hold himself above conventional representations of events that were still ongoing? This is perhaps less perplexing than it appears. For Sandauer declares that his father's refusal to join the collective is a constitutive feature of the author's parabiographical double—that, in effect, this small act of defiance taught Sandauer an essential lesson about ghetto life *as paradox*, as simultaneous belonging and non-belonging, sameness and otherness, individuality and collective identity, and that life writing could not hope to be truthful if it did not rebel against the autobiographical "I."

Parabiography, Autothematism, Veridiction

Notes from the City of the Dead opens with an epigraph that Sandauer has drawn from his own earlier reflections on autobiography:

I am imagining a tale [*opowieść*]—preferably an autobiographical one, in which it is not so much the styles and facts that would be altered, but the tonalities. One and the same event from one's own life could be served with a flavor that is by turns lighthearted or tragic, realistic or grotesque. This would establish a distance and freedom in regard to one's own experiences, treated solely as material that can be given any shape, and such a "parabiography" would seem to run not so much along time as across it; there, the sequence of events would yield to their interchangeability [*oboczność*].[25]

Readers who approach this book expecting a famous literary interpreter's account of surviving spaces of open confinement are likely to find Sandauer's programmatic statement just as strange as Ginzburg's opening gesture in *Notes of a Blockade Person*. After all, both books would at least appear to offer truthful accounts of their respective authors' lived experiences, yet both open by underscoring the essential role of fiction in creating "distance and freedom in regard to one's own experiences." How can these and similar texts claim to represent the experience of a ghetto or besieged city truthfully while simultaneously drawing our attention to those aspects of the account that are invented?

The question, though honest and intuitive, answers itself. In fact, it is the authors' consistent delineation of where fact meets invention that guides the reader in understanding the authors' experiences. Metatextual reflections leap from nearly every page, with the authors telling us explicitly and repeatedly that the very act of exposing the interplay between fiction and nonfiction in the text underpins the text's claims on truthful representation. Ginzburg and Sandauer use these gestures not only to justify their use of fictional avatars, but more importantly to show how the fictional elements of their narratives reveal paradoxes, both external/circumstantial and internal/psychological, that autobiographical convention cannot help but resolve, thereby misrepresenting the paradoxical experience. Sandauer's intention, he tells us at the outset, is to create a "tale" or "telling"—*opowieść*—and not necessarily a "novel" or "autobiography," since he does not trust the interpretive conventions surrounding those genre designations to lead us to an understanding of what he has endured. The way we might arrive at such an understanding, or at least at an effective simulation of the real as Sandauer experienced it, is by placing invented and historical events side by side so that their "alternation"—*oboczność*, their "side-by-side-ness"—allows the reader to interpret their congruencies and disjunctions.

We can now see how the reading strategy that I have been calling "parallactic" throughout this book is not my own appeal for us to approach this literature in a particular way. It is, rather, the interpretive method that, at least in parabiographical writing, the literature demands for itself.

The text conveys this demand, and it also offers instruction in how to meet it, through consistent references to the very acts of writing the text and grappling with its content. Sandauer calls such metatextual gestures "autothematic," the term he used to mark modern texts in which the author's struggle with the challenges of representation become the very thing that the author represents: "It is as if the autothematic work cannot decide whether its action should be mental or actual," Sandauer writes. "It tries to situate the author on the same plane [*plan*] as the heroes and, in this way, to resolve the kinds of epistemological challenges that were posed by the nineteenth-century concept of narrative."[26]

One of Sandauer's central concerns as a literary theorist was how literature, beginning with Romanticism's enthusiastic embrace of irony, evolved from the mere staging of characters' inner psychology in the nineteenth century to the more robust enactment of mental processes, complete with inner vacillations and self-contradictions, in the twentieth. His characterization of the "author on the same plane as the heroes" ties in with that idea of staging, since the theorist is imagining the author's self-representation and his characters literally on the same *plan*, "stage" or "ground," where they might coexist as equals, making the "epistemological challenges" of representation as such a primary focus of the text. Elsewhere, Sandauer specifies that autothematic writing is not a "reflection on literature," which is how we might characterize a vast body of work reaching back almost to the foundations of Western literature, but rather "a work that arises from reflecting on a work that has not arisen."[27] Instead of representing events as realities independent of their author's struggle to represent them, autothematism reconfigures the struggle as the event to be represented. It renders the incommensurability of reality and representation the very object of representation.

Sandauer's postwar reputation is closely tied to his interpretations of Bruno Schulz and Witold Gombrowicz, readings that elevated these authors to the canonical status they enjoy today in part by foregrounding their autothematism, which Sandauer describes as "exposing the element of mystification present in the very fact of offering fabrications as actual events [*zdarzenia prawdziwe*]," so that "the whole reality of the story becomes mental, as in a dream; the difference between truth [*prawda*] and delusion fades away."[28] In no way does this mean that Sandauer rejects literature's capacity to access the truth of human experience. He does not cynically equate invention with "authentic" or "actual events"—*zdarzenia prawdziwe*, which announce their allegiance to *prawda*, "truth." He simply rejects the notion that a text can afford such access to truth when it has erased the traces of its own becoming. Authorial "mystification," when revealed, no longer mystifies. Once exposed, the lie becomes truth's index.

Beyond the conspicuous similarities between how Ginzburg and Sandauer write about their war experiences, the two theorists' attentions to literary evolution were broadly, if independently, aligned. Both sought to understand the mechanisms by which twentieth-century literature strove to represent the individual's experience of the world— that is, how subjects represent the world to themselves. In this project, Ginzburg focuses on how the text stages psychological processes, especially unconscious and semiconscious experiences (as of time), fissures, and lacunae. Sandauer is more intent on formal devices, such as intertextual references and metanarrative commentaries, that make the text's own becoming integral features of the text itself.[29] Sandauer and Ginzburg, in both their personal accounts of open confinement and in their decade-spanning reflections on literature's relationship to the realities it represents, are fundamentally concerned not with the positivist project of defining an objective reality, but with what Michel Foucault called "veridiction," the articulation of representations that are understood to be true reflections of reality within a given discourse community or "regime." As Foucault tells us, "The reality of the world is not its own truth to itself."[30]

Sandauer's definition of parabiography aptly describes authors' motives in fictionalizing their real-life experiences of open confinement. The idea is that in normalizing the events after the fact, by describing insecure spaces from a position of security, one is in fact misrepresenting them. It is only by fictionalizing the experience that the author can place himself in tension with the reality he represents, thereby giving a more honest sense of the experience.

This fictionalization also creates genre confusion, a deliberate effect of these texts' design. Ginzburg's brief preface to *Literature in Search of Reality*

(*Literatura v poiskakh real'nosti*, 1987), which includes the first printing of *Notes of a Blockade Person* as a unified text, and which is quite absent from its English translation, notes that the author makes little distinction between those parts of the book that are scholarly and those that are essayistic or inflected with fictional elements. "Essayistic writing for me," she tells us, "has sometimes crossed naturally into storytelling [*povestvovanie*], even with conventional, invented characters. I find them necessary as objects of analysis for these or other facts of spiritual experience."[31] In calling her text *zapiski*—and in this respect, too, the English translation, *Blockade Diary*, is strikingly counterproductive—she is using a word that she herself has described, in reference to Alexander Herzen, as "merely a provisional term, . . . convenient precisely because of its vagueness, its lack of definite generic content."[32]

The responsible reader approaches a novel differently from a newspaper article, posits a different relation between each text and the facticity of what it represents. What that relation is or should be when it comes to "notes," however, remains unfixed. The reader will not necessarily know how such a text's content aligns with historical reality, with the author's unique, lived experience. One needs clear instructions. This is why Imre Kertész, whose camp-themed novels are frequently characterized as "autobiographical," categorically rejects the "autobiographical novel" as a genre:

> A book is either autobiography or a novel. If it's autobiography you evoke the past, you try as scrupulously as possible to stick to the recollections; it's a matter of extraordinary importance that you write everything down exactly the way it happened, as it's usually put: that you don't varnish the facts one little bit. A good autobiography is like a document: a mirror of the age on which people can "depend." In a novel, by contrast, it's not the facts that matter, but precisely what you add to the facts.[33]

So stark a generic separation may be curious coming from an author so frequently observed to have violated it. Even the text in which Kertész makes these remarks has a fictional construct: it is written as a long interview that never took place. Kertész's words should nevertheless be taken at face value, as a defense of genre and of how genre shapes readerly expectations and interpretive practices. Ginzburg, meanwhile, could hardly be regarded as Kertész's adversary in this, since both exploit genre expectations to portray aspects of their lived experience.

As a genre, parabiography foregrounds the reader's confrontation with genre.

Genre Trouble: Notes on *Zapiski* from Dostoevsky to Ginzburg

Ginzburg provides the interpretive rules for her augmented representation of a besieged city throughout her book, beginning with the genre designation in the title. These are *zapiski*, she tells us—"notes." The word alone suggests that the book consists of sketches and impressions without a narrative or argumentative telos, and this is largely true. To the Russian reader, however, the word also hearkens back to a textual predecessor—namely, Dostoevsky's *Notes from the House of the Dead* (*Zapiski iz mertvogo doma*, 1862), the first novel that the author published following his return from four years in an imperial prison colony near Omsk. That is, the genre conventions exploited in Ginzburg's text about the experience of open confinement are already well established for her readers—not only by Tolstoy, whom she introduces as a measure for calibrating one's *senses*, but by Dostoevsky, who provides a set of representative norms.

Foremost among these norms is that the protagonist and the author of the "notes" are not coterminous. Dostoevsky's novel draws on the author's own experience in a prison camp, a trauma that helped shape the remainder of his life and career and that was especially formative of his essential critique of Nikolai Chernyshevsky. But it also announces itself immediately as fiction: not only is the protagonist, Gorianchikov, *not* named Dostoevsky, but unlike the real author, whose crime was intellectual—he had belonged to the banned Petrashevksy Circle—Gorianchikov is guilty of uxoricide, an act that Dostoevsky abhorred. The narrative is furthermore encased in the kind of framing device that had been typical of late Romantic fiction a generation earlier, creating an ironic distance between the narrator and the actual author, whom the text now situates as the editor of Gorianchikov's notes. As the novel opens, Dostoevsky therefore appears as his own avatar to receive the manuscript that contains Gorianchikov's story, itself a kind of anthropological study of the life of a prison colony.

In this way, Dostoevsky's book is at once personal, conveying details of his own suffering and deprivation, and general, offering a glimpse into a basic institution of Russian society that few of his readers would otherwise see. (Unlike most of the prison camp's population, Gorianchikov is a member of the nobility, as was the real author and many of his readers.) *Notes from the House of the Dead* also preserves the narrative tension around the question of the hero's survival even as we know that Dostoevsky survived his sentence to write the book. After all, we have no assurance about Gorianchikov's future, which even the novel's conclusion leaves in question. By focalizing the narrative on a character whose survival is uncertain, the author is able to perform an end run around the paradox of writing a survival tale about a figure—the author himself—whose survival we must assume from the beginning.

At the time Dostoevsky wrote his novel, the term *zapiski* would already have signaled to Russian readers that the author was fictionalizing autobiographical material. A decade earlier Ivan Turgenev had finished serializing his celebrated *A Hunter's Notes* (*Zapiski okhotnika*, 1847–1851, usually presented in English as *Sketches from a Hunter's Album* or *A Sportsman's Sketches*). Nikolai Gogol's short story "Diary of a Madman" ("Zapiski sumashedshego," literally, "Notes of a Madman"), first published in 1835, was already part of the literary canon by the time Dostoevsky's book was published, and while it could not be argued that Gogol's story is autobiographical, the text does assume the form of a diary and ultimately proved, in an unsettlingly Gogolian way, prescient. Readers of *Time* (*Vremia*, 1861–1863), the thick journal that Dostoevsky produced with his brother Mikhail, and where *Notes from the House of the Dead* was initially serialized, saw the term deployed frequently in the journal's table of contents, whether referring to biographical or historical documents, personal reveries, or something in between. Dostoevsky would apply the term *zapiski* more famously two years after *Notes from the House of the Dead*, in *Notes from Underground* (*Zapiski iz podpol'ia*, 1864), a philosophical polemic written in the form of a fictional journal.[34] It is to this tradition that Ginzburg attaches her account of besieged Leningrad.

At its point of origin, the *zapiski* genre designation signals to the reader which set of conventions to use in interpreting the text. But this tradition is obscure to the anglophone reader. Indeed, the first edition of *Notes from the House of the Dead* to appear in English (in 1881, the year of Dostoevsky's

Figure 2.1 Establishing a precedent that would become standard for translated fiction based on real-life camp experiences, the first English editions of Dostoevsky's *Notes from the House of the Dead* give no indication that this is fiction. Source: Google Books / New York Public Library

death) had all the paratextual markers of nonfiction (figure 2.1). It bore the title *Buried Alive, or: Ten Years of Penal Servitude in Siberia*, and it gave no indication of being fiction whatsoever.[35] A subsequent translation published in London in 1911 as *The House of the Dead, or: Prison Life in Siberia*, likewise presents Dostoevsky's novel as an autobiography. It was only with Constance Garnett's 1915 version that the subtitle *A Novel in Two Parts* would specify the book's genre for English-language readers as fiction.

Such genre confusion is understandable. In the anglophone literary tradition, certainly, we have no stable conventions for reading "notes," and our natural default may in fact be to treat them as evidentiary, since the word implies an instantaneous recording of experience, more reflexive than reflective, unmediated by the authorial manipulation of the material. The word *zapis* (in Russian and Polish; *zápis* in Czech), for which *zapiski* is the plural diminutive, means "record" or "recording." But *zapiski* are effectively beyond fiction and nonfiction, a generic divide that is, as I have already indicated, more loosely defined outside of the English language. The European reader approaches these texts with the expectation that they correspond to lived experience *without* transcribing it.

That the texts themselves repeatedly draw attention to their own fictional devices can only cause confusion for readers of English-language editions, for whom the outward signs of genre instability have typically been stripped away and replaced with the paratextual markers of memoir and autobiography. This is certainly true of early editions of Dostoevsky's novel, and it has been a standard, consistent feature of the reception of its literary descendants, including Ginzburg's *Notes of a Blockade Person*.

Reality and Its Double: Theatricality and Camp Representation in *Notes from the House of the Dead*

Dostoevsky conceived of *Notes from the House of the Dead* explicitly as a dramatic reenactment of camp life, not a report on his personal experience, which he would nevertheless draw from in creating his portrait. The novel can likewise serve as a primer for interpreting the ever-present theme of theatricality in camp representation.

The practice of reading Dostoevsky's novels through the critical lens of their theatricality is already more than a century old. It begins with the poets, philosophers, and dramaturgs of the Russian Symbolist tradition, achieves its first sustained treatment in Viacheslav Ivanov's 1911 *Dostoevsky and the Novel-Tragedy* (*Dostoevskii i roman-tragediia*), and, for many interpreters of Dostoevsky and philosophers of literary representation, reaches its apotheosis a generation later in Mikhail Bakhtin's *Problems of Dostoevsky's Creative Work* (*Problemy tvorchestva Dostoevskogo*, 1929).[36] Theatricality is an intuitive point of entry into Dostoevsky's fiction, not only because of the formal features that reminded these early twentieth-century readers of dramaturgy in the guise of a novel, but also, and perhaps especially, because Dostoevsky frequently presents his characters struggling against the performance of social scripts they have adopted. That attentiveness to social form is so dominant in *Notes from the House of the Dead* that Didier Fassin credits it with inspiring and, more than Foucault or Erwin Goffman, shaping *Prison Worlds*, his ethnography of modern carceral institutions in France, "not that a nineteenth-century Russian labor camp and a twenty-first-century French prison have much in common."[37] Yet Fassin fails, like so many others, to distinguish between the novel Dostoevsky wrote and the factual testimony that the anthropologist believes he has read. "Dostoevsky's *memoir*," Fassin writes, "and his detachment and reflexivity, descriptive power and analytical lucidity, withholding of judgment and concern for truth were, for me, a source of inspiration."[38] Dostoevsky's novel is undoubtedly a powerful dramatization of the "truth" of his experience of an imperial prison colony, but it is just as certainly *not* a "memoir" setting out the facts of that experience. Time and again, we find that the "descriptive power" of the representation underwrites our assumption of its facticity.

It so happens that Dostoevsky was initiated into the world of the camp through a theatrical staging. Arrested for taking part in clandestine discussions of liberal politics, which the czarist authorities had outlawed as seditious, members of the Petrashevksy Circle, including Dostoevsky, were sentenced to death and placed before a firing squad in 1849. The commutation of their sentence to eight years' penal servitude (later reduced to four) arrived just in the nick of time, the would-be execution having been staged in advance, unbeknownst to the actors or their audience, to send a powerful message.[39] Again, a successful dramatic staging is powerful by design. Facts alone, whether of a case or of a past event, rarely are.

No wonder, then, that Dostoevsky chooses to represent his years in the prison camp by staging it as someone else's experience, all the while thematizing the theatricality of life in the camp. Gorianchikov, the novel's protagonist, is immediately fascinated by how his fellow inmates make a show of their escalating aggression, despite it rarely leading to actual violence: "All this was new to me, and I watched with curiosity. But then I learned that all scenes like this were extraordinarily innocent and played out like in a comedy, for everyone's pleasure; they hardly ever came to blows. It was all fairly typical and portrayed the manners of the camp."[40] The culture of cursing in the camp is likewise theatrical: "The dialectician of cursing was esteemed. They would almost applaud him, like an actor."[41]

As if to drive the theatricality of this environment home, part 1 (of two) culminates in a much-anticipated theatrical production staged by the convicts themselves. (According to a fellow inmate, in actuality it was Dostoevsky himself, already an author of some reputation, who was called upon to direct the camp theater.)[42] And because the effort to stage their comedy is not forced—and because the pleasure of the farce *consists in the farce of staging a farce in the camp*—even the anticipation of the theater becomes theatrical: "With still a week to go before the performance, [the inmate] Baklushin would boast to me that they didn't see such theater even in *Saint* Petersburg. He would parade around the barracks, brag unmercifully and shamelessly, though at the same time good-naturedly, and it happened that sometimes he would suddenly let slip a bit of 'thee-ATE-er,' that is, from his role—and everyone would have a laugh whether what he had said was funny or not."[43] The author's emphasis on how Baklushin specifies the "Saint" in "Saint Petersburg," as well as on his exaggerated mispronunciation of "theater," points to the would-be actor's lack of sophistication. The braggart is, after all, not a big-city actor, but an inmate *acting* like an actor.

The theater that these nonactors present is likewise not an actual theater, but a theater of a theater, a collective action that simulates a theater without presenting any coherent narrative: "An entire act was presented, though it was apparently an excerpt; the beginning and ending were missing. It didn't have the slightest point or sense."[44] In the camp's ironic *mis en abîme*, the episodic nature of the camp text is echoed in an episode of episodic playacting *within* the text. Presenting a coherent narrative, however, was never the point of the theater within the camp: that's what an *actual* theater is for. In the prison camp, by contrast, the prisoners are attempting to manufacture a fleeting and ultimately illusory reconnection with the world they have lost in their "world apart," even at the risk of losing themselves within their own illusion. In his description of this scene, Dostoevsky emphasizes the distinction between life outside the camp, "to live like a human being," and life inside, "in the camp way," as well as the ephemeral nature of the illusion of having stepped from one form of life into the other:

> [Our folk] disperse happy, satisfied, they praise the actors, they thank the petty officer. Not a peep of argument. Everybody is somehow unusually satisfied, as if happy even, and they fall asleep not like always, but almost with a peaceful spirit—but how could that be? And still, it's not some dream I've imagined. It's real, it's the truth. [*Eto pravda, istina.*] All they had done was allow these poor people to live like themselves, to have fun like a human being, to live, if only for an hour, not in the camp way [*po-ostorzhnomu*]—and a person changes morally, if only for a few minutes.[45]

Authors who represent their experiences of open confinement through parabiography and real-life fiction are well aware that their descriptions of the "world apart" sound otherworldly, like "some dream." Their texts, with their often fetishistic fascination with the strange idiolects and inverted social forms typical of camp life, read like science fiction because these authors have embraced the paradoxes of these spaces, the uncanny ironies layered into the experience itself. At the same time, because these authors have cast an ironic regard on institutions and circumstances replete with irony, they can see how "unbelievable" the "unbelievable" true story can be. Accordingly, they frequently express their own skepticism about what they have only just relayed ("And still, it's not some dream I've imagined."), only then to insist that they haven't made it up. "It's real," Dostoevsky's fictional proxy insists, "it's the truth." The Russian language observes a clear distinction between what is true as a matter of fact (*pravda*, an earthly truth) and what is true on a higher metaphysical or spiritual plane (*istina*). Dostoevsky's hero insists that his account is both.

Even more striking in this brief passage about the seduction of theatricality, however, is how the author characterizes the peculiar form of life engendered by the camp space, *ostrog*, which literally means "stockade" but by the nineteenth century had become almost synonymous with "prison camp," the purpose that the Russian Empire's stockaded Siberian forts had long since come to serve. Dostoevsky deploys the marked phrasing *po-ostorzhnomu* to designate the strange way of being that becomes the only one left to the camp inmate.[46] The novel's narrative frame makes clear that, even after he is released, Gorianchikov's fate is tragic, since he can never stop living *po-ostorzhnomu*, anticipating a pattern often attested in survivor testimonies and highlighted by authors of parabiographical accounts: even if one manages to get out of the camp, one never fully leaves the "world apart." Recognizing this means accepting the moral burden that subjecting individuals and entire communities to the conditions of camp life or besiegement constitutes an exile, often permanent, from the possibility of living "like themselves," "like a human being."

At the same time, by revealing the social forms peculiar to life in the camp, Dostoevsky provides a common touchstone not only for how these kinds of spaces will be represented, but also for how they will be experienced. Just as readers in besieged Leningrad would read *War and Peace* to confirm the authenticity of their own lived experience, future authors of parabiography and real-life fiction readily compared what they endured to

Notes from the House of the Dead, as if Dostoevsky's novel could define what it means to live *po-ostorzhnomu*, "in the camp way." One of the most notable real-life fictions of Soviet labor camps, Gustaw Herling-Grudziński's *A World Apart* (*Inny świat*, 1951), which bears the telling subtitle *Sowiecki zapiski*, or *Soviet Notes*, explicitly models its narrative structure on Dostoevsky's novel and repeatedly refers to its predecessor in ways that obfuscate the line between fiction and nonfiction, a technique that would become a signature of Herling-Grudziński's postwar career.

For some of Dostoevsky's literary descendants, his emphasis on the theatrical could in fact stray too far from the social reality of the camp. Varlam Shalamov, for example, laments how the portrayal of role-playing masks the reality of criminality in prison colonies, a key source of inmates' torment: "In *Notes from the House of the Dead*, Dostoevsky affectionately observes the actions of the unfortunate ones who behave like big kids, enjoy the theater, argue childishly among themselves without anger. Dostoevsky did not encounter and did not know people from the real criminal world."[47] Elsewhere, however, Shalamov offers the same text as a key instance, alongside Solzhenitsyn's *One Day in the Life of Ivan Denisovich* (*Odin den' Ivana Denisovicha*, 1962), of the author-survivor succeeding in a twofold task: "in overcoming reality, in struggling with memoir, the memoir did not lose its power."[48]

Even as Dostoevsky's novel became a model for camp representation, it also served as a reference point for the lived experience of the camp. For example, describing the use of meaningless labor as an instrument of torture in Nazi camps *before* the war, Roman Gul, a Russian liberal intellectual who spent six months in Oranienburg, simply refers his readers to *Notes from the House of the Dead*.[49] At the same time, as Emily Johnson observes, because letters written home from within the Soviet Gulag system could not contain any references to the violence that prisoners endured there, the lacunae within these testimonial documents, which we might otherwise enfold with the brightest aura of authenticity, required readers to seek a more complete truth in texts that *model*, rather than merely report, the camp experience:

> Works of fiction and, indeed, memoirs that describe Stalin-era labor camps rely so heavily on literary models that one cannot take them as an exact, factual account of past events and conditions. In writing about their camp experiences, the first great chroniclers of the Stalinist

labor camp system, including Gustaw Herling[-Grudziński], Solzhenitsyn, [Varlam] Shalamov, and [Evgeniia] Ginzburg, made use of descriptive and structural clichés drawn from earlier literary texts set wholly or in part in prisons, including the most important prison text for Russian authors, [*Notes from the*] *House of the Dead*, the novel that Fyodor Dostoevsky wrote based on his experiences at hard labor in the 1850s. Similarly, later generations of Gulag chroniclers tended to hew closely to the models established by Herling, Solzhenitsyn, Shalamov, and Ginzburg: in memoirs and interviews produced during the late Soviet and post-Soviet periods, survivors often explicitly reference descriptions of the camp system by their best-known predecessors or unconsciously interpolate sections of earlier accounts into their own memories.[50]

For the vast majority of people who suddenly found themselves in a camp, ghetto, or besieged city in the middle of the last century, the "camp" occupied much the same place in the social imaginary as it does for us today, as an institution that is fundamentally present while, for most of us, beyond our immediate experience. Like Lidiia Ginzburg's friends in besieged Leningrad, those who entered the camp or ghetto or who found themselves in comparable spaces of open confinement could rely on only the textual models of the spaces and experiences to know whether they were now living "in the camp way." At the same time, this feedback loop always presents the potential for fraud. The same models of space and experience that would confirm the "truth" of survivors' experience, and that they would later recycle in their own accounts or "unconsciously interpolate . . . into their own memories," remain equally available to those who have not lived through comparable catastrophe but seek to convince us that they have.

The Theater of Cruelty (1): Self-Alienation

The repeated emphasis on theatricality in the literature of open confinement—its relentless staging *of* staging—advertises to the audience that the conventions of the autobiographical pact do not apply. Even if one allows for stylistic flourishes and manipulations of fact "for dramatic effect"—and the James Frey case would seem to illustrate how reluctantly "the triumph of the fact" will make such allowances—the very construction of the text refuses the simple identification of the hero with the author. Gorianchikov is not Dostoevsky. N., the titular hero of *Notes of a Blockade Person*, is not Lidiia Ginzburg.

But if the main character is *not* the author, then how are we to know how to read the text in the first place? Is it a novel? An autobiography? An ethnography? Which genre conventions allow us to understand what Ginzburg calls a "conventional person?" And why does the author choose to represent herself as a nonself, a collective personality drawing details from her own life, the lives of her friends, and from what she witnesses around her, as though these different degrees of intimacy were equivalent in the representation of historical trauma?

Ginzburg, for whom the textual representation of real human psychology was a lifelong fascination, provides strong responses to these questions within the text and throughout her wartime writing. N., she insists, is a fractured self, not to be contained in the unitary autobiographical "I." N. is first of all a body in pain, a body "alienated" from itself by the physical transformations of hunger and injury, and therefore producing "new sensations, not its own."[51] "Ultimately," Ginzburg writes in *Notes*, "everything doubled in a strange way: the emaciated wrapping—from the class of things belonging to the inimical world—and the soul set apart somewhere within the ribcage. A vivid embodiment of philosophical dualism."[52]

Read strictly with an eye toward factual representation, this is absurd. How can a composite character have a body at all? Yet it is through this paradox, and not in spite of it, that the reader arrives at a heightened awareness of the real beyond the text, much as Antonin Artaud sees a figure for the operations of the theater in the story of a man acting on the premonitions brought to him by a violent dream. "Even destroyed," Artaud observes, "even annihilated, organically pulverized and consumed to his very marrow, he knows we do not die in our dreams, that our will operates even in absurdity, even in the negation of possibility, even in the transmutation of the lies from which truth can be remade."[53] Ginzburg's aim in offering us N. is just such a transmutation. N.'s condition is universal: no one has N.'s body, not even N., yet N.'s body is everyone's. In this we can already discern the truth claim of such a representation, insofar as N.'s condition reflects the physical self-alienation that, according to Ginzburg, was indispensable to the experience of the siege, which is why to ascribe the condition to any single individual would be not only unnecessary but potentially falsifying. For Ginzburg, individual persons look all kinds of ways under normal historical conditions, but the "blockade person" has a consistent appearance that suggests its own paradox: while every body is immediately recognizable as that of a "blockade person," one's own body is unrecognizable to oneself.

This self-alienation extends well beyond outward appearance, however. N. is both Ginzburg and not. The intellectual remains an intellectual by nature, yet his or her social utility has become, like that of most everyone else in the besieged city, purely performative. Like cooks without food to prepare or doctors without medicines or supplies, those in the business of knowledge production continue to behave as though they are still producing knowledge, even as their material conditions make such labor impossible. In this, members of the intelligentsia are no different from anyone else in the city, which Ginzburg repeatedly describes as a simulation of what it had been before the war, a "synthetic reality" whose inhabitants perform their former lives for each other.[54] Buildings rent by bombs provide the occasional reminder that all this performance—shopping for nonexistent food, seeing to immaterial formalities in a nonfunctioning office—occurs in an expansive and elaborate theater: "There are cross sections of houses that persistently recall a Meyerhold set."[55]

We can remark additional layers of theatricality in accounts of purely performative labor used as a means of torture in both Soviet and Nazi camps,[56] as well as in the pretense of juridical procedure that frequently enshrouds arbitrary violence in predictable, performative scripts. We find this in both nonfiction reflections, such as Artur London's 1968 book *The Confession* and its 1970 dramatization for film, and in, say, Yuri Dombrovsky's 1975 novel *The Faculty of Useless Knowledge* (*Fakul'tet nenuzhnikh veshchei*), which frequently compares the elaborate charade of investigating invented crimes to theater, so that at one climactic moment toward the end of the book the victim being interrogated informs his tormentor, "Even now you're playing a part, not conducting an investigation. You should have been an actress, not an investigator."[57]

The theatricality that one encounters so frequently in the literature of concentration camps, ghettos, and besieged cities is, as these diverse examples indicate, not merely a trope of camp representations, but also an intrinsic feature of camp experience, and that experience often approaches situational extremes that amplify the camp's theatricality. In *Inhuman Land* (*Na nieludzkiej ziemi*, 1949), for example, Józef Czapski presents the absurdity endured by two prominent Jewish socialists, Henryk Ehrlich and

Wiktor Alter, as the accusations leveled against them changed repeatedly; their accusers could not be challenged because they had already been executed; and Ehrlich and Alter were themselves sentenced to death, then *not* executed, and sentenced to death *again* (and not executed again), only to be murdered later on Stalin's orders.[58]

The spaces of open confinement that have generated so many representations from the last century are already highly ironized: one need only be aware of the paradoxes built into the camp as an institution to experience their ironies theatrically.

Why fictionalize? Why theatricalize one's real-life experience? To communicate a sense of self-conflict that might be obscured by a conventional recital of facts and dates. One must theatricalize to make the experience of the text visceral in a way that echoes the bodily experience of open confinement: in the "dramatic reenactment," the act would be lost without the drama. These explanations, essential though they may be to an understanding of the narrative dynamics of real-life fiction, gloss over a more fundamental fact of historical understanding—namely, that it operates on a scale far beyond the reach of individual human experience. The numbers are simply too big.[59]

Marek Edelman, the last surviving Jewish combatant of the Warsaw Ghetto Uprising and an invaluable source of information about life and death in the ghetto, recalled the problem of scale decades later:

> If four hundred thousand people can be locked away and eaten by lice, if they can die of hunger and can't do anything about it, then they're subhuman. . . . Roosevelt said *expressis verbis* to the delegation that came to him: yes, it's true they're murdering them, but don't write that they've murdered a hundred thousand, because that's a figure that no one cares about. Write that little Masha with the long braids and the big eyes was killed by two Germans. That will speak to society. But when thousands perish, thousands daily, it becomes banal in people's eyes.[60]

Roosevelt, in Edelman's retelling, understands naturally that people are more likely to be moved—emotionally, certainly, and perhaps also to action—by an individual story than by numbers, and in his reference to "Masha with the long braids" he was himself echoing such an emblem. Notices posted by the Gestapo in Warsaw had urgently sought *die kleine Wanda mit den blonden*

Zöpfen, "Little Wanda with the blond braids"—actually Niuta Tajtelbaum, a young Jewish assassin fighting the Nazis in the Warsaw Ghetto before she was caught, tortured, and murdered in 1943. Edelman, who experienced the atrocities he describes firsthand, reaches for an emblem or type, "Masha with the long braids," that itself refers to an emblem that has replaced its holotype, the historical Tajtelbaum, whom Edelman may well have known personally in the ghetto.[61]

To make the "world apart" real, Edelman tells us, one must turn to real-life fiction.

CHAPTER III

Real-Life Fiction

> Simply dreaming of surviving—even crippled, destitute, defeated—would already have been crazy enough. Nobody would have cherished such a dream, it's true. Yet suddenly, as in a dream, it was true.
> —JORGE SEMPRÚN, *LITERATURE OR LIFE* (TRANS. LINDA COVERDALE)

Marek Edelman's later sense that forceful storytelling was more powerful than the recitation of cold facts and figures, however accurate they may be, was already recognized during the war by Jan Karski, a Polish spy whose daring infiltration of ghettos and concentration camps brought the English-speaking world some of its first direct accounts of the fate of Poland's Jews, published in 1943 as *Story of a Secret State*. There, already despairing of nonfiction's inefficacy in mobilizing states and armies, he informs us that he had initially turned to novelists to tell the truth of what he had seen with his own eyes. "I told what I had seen in the ghetto to some of the world's great writers," Karski writes, "to H. G. Wells, Arthur Koestler, members of the P.E.N. Club—as they could describe it with greater force and talent than I."[1]

The "greater force" sought by Karski is precisely what precipitated Jerzy Kosiński's turn from social science to the novel in *The Painted Bird*, one of the most notorious specimens of fiction based on its author's real-life experience of open confinement. Born in Łódź as Józef Lewinkopf (1933–1991), a name that marked him unmistakably as a Jew, Kosiński's family did not share the fate of most of his city's Jewish residents, surviving the war under an assumed identity and forged papers in a small village in central Poland. As was sometimes the case with others whose survival depended upon their playing a role, Kosiński continued to play his role long after the circumstances that had necessitated it had ended, keeping his assumed name and gaining renown not only as an author, but as a public obfuscator of his own biography and literary influences.[2]

Kosiński's effort at dramatic self-representation begins with *The Painted Bird*, wherein the first-person narrator depicts hiding out among peasants in the countryside. Unlike the author, the novel's protagonist has been separated from his parents, finding himself in unfamiliar surroundings and in the care of strange and incomprehensible people. Unlike the peasants and parish priest who had actually kept the Lewinkopf family safe, the country folk in Kosiński's novel are brutal and depraved, freely given to fits of violence and bestiality. In his introduction to the novel's second edition, Kosiński explains his motivation for portraying his survival with a sadism bordering on caricature, emphasizing his dissatisfaction with how a broad, top-down survey of historical facts failed to capture how "millions like my parents and myself, lacking any chance to escape, had been forced to experience events far worse than those that the treaties so grandiloquently prohibited": "The extreme discrepancy between the facts as I knew them and the exiles' and diplomats' hazy, unrealistic view of the world bothered me intensely. I began to reexamine my past and decided to turn from my studies of social science to fiction. Unlike politics, which offered only extravagant promises of a utopian future, I knew fiction could present lives as they are truly lived."[3]

The graphic nature of Kosiński's narrative created an intriguing split in its public reception. Polish readers regarded its representation of the peasantry, unrelentingly brutal and prone to animistic superstition, as offensively false.[4] Audiences in English regarded the novel's disorienting brutality as a mark of its authenticity. In April 1967, the American man of letters Lewis Galantière, himself both an eyewitness to the aftermath of the war in Europe and a notorious fabricator of his own biography, wrote to Kosiński that *The Painted Bird* "ought to be a nightmare but it isn't; it is a work of art (all your reviewers agree on that), as credible as a fairy tale (which is either credible or nothing), with a hero who is beyond sentiment, beyond heroics, a hero of myth who tells his story as [Leopold von] Ranke said (impossibly) history should be written, *wie es eigentlich gewesen* [as it actually was]."[5] Roger Baldwin, another friend of the author and a founding member of the American Civil Liberties Union, wrote to Kosiński that "the book stands on its obvious genuineness as experience, not art," and that "its strength derives from what was dug out of memory, however treated by later insight."[6] Yet the author, who obsessively collected and archived press clippings and letters pertaining to his own quest for fame, was also sensitive to the ease with which readers equated intensity with facticity. After Henry Allen published an especially hagiographic profile of Kosiński in the *Washington Post* in 1971, Kosiński felt compelled to compose a letter to the editor in which he points out, "as I have often done in the past," that the work "is not my autobiography; it was written and published as a novel," and that the author "consciously avoided any names of people or places that would suggest a definite locality."[7]

The omission of most historically verifiable information is conspicuous in *The Painted Bird*, so much so that at times the author's evasions only serve to underscore themselves. Once the invading army has been defeated, for instance, the narrator is taken to an unnamed city by a Russian sergeant, "who had some military business in the town where there was a center for lost children. This industrial city, the country's largest, was where I had lived before the war."[8] Biographically, the city that Kosiński is refusing to name is Łódź. The author's ostentatious withholding of the names of the city and the entire country around it should signal that, inasmuch as Kosiński may be aiming for truth, he is less concerned with fact.

How can we characterize the truth that Kosiński wishes to portray, if not in terms of fact? For one thing, facts are an atomization of the data of experience; if they could reveal their own patterns, we would have no need of the human sciences.[9] This is why Kosiński's protagonist realizes, in a moment of epiphany, that the superstitious behavior of the simple folk around him is demonstrating the foundational structure of reality: "Suddenly the ruling pattern of the world was revealed to me with beautiful clarity. I understood why some people were strong and others weak, some free and others enslaved, some rich and others poor, some well and others sick."[10] In observing the peasants' rituals and prayers and their seemingly direct impact on lived reality, the narrator comes to appreciate how superstition might be an elemental form of *narrative* reason, not because of its manufactured causality, but because it draws materiality, events, and mind into a unified rhetorical universe. We can read *The Painted Bird* as the author's effort to do the same—that is, to access the real, and even to command and reshape it, through invention. Kosiński says as much in his introduction (playfully entitled "Afterward," hinting at its response to the divided public reception of the novel's first edition), where he declares, "It was therefore very much for their sakes [i.e., those who could not 'describe their anguish'] and for people like them that I wanted to write fiction which would reflect, and perhaps exorcise the horrors that they had found so inexpressible."[11]

The *Real* in Real Life: *Enargeia*

Because life is not text, let alone mere fact, a dispassionate recitation of locations and dates—the names and ages and occupations of the living and the dead—could only fall far short of Kosiński's stated goal, which is not to deliver these facts, but the *visceral sense* of the "world apart" he had entered as a hunted child. Ancient rhetorical theory refers to this *embodiment* of textual detail as *enargeia*, the "bright, unbearable reality," as Alice Oswald puts it, that is irreducible to documentary detail. *Enargeia*, she says, is "the word used when gods come to earth not in disguise but as themselves."[12]

What I call "real-life fiction" might encompass a parabiographical text or even a fraudulent one with a high degree of correspondence to the author's lived experience. In its most distilled form, however, "real-life fiction" achieves this *enargeia* by blurring or altogether obliterating the separation between the actual author and his or her textual avatar. Unlike Lidiia Ginzburg's *Notes of a Blockade Person* or Artur Sandauer's *Notes from the City of the Dead*, these narratives are typically written in the first person. Their first-person narrators often (though not always) share the actual author's name. Even when they do not, as is the case, for example, in Jiří Weil's *Life with a Star* (*Život s hvězdou*, 1949), the information about the author's lived experience provided in peritextual sources (biographical notes, book reviews, etc.) overlaps so notably with the contents of the novel that the reader can easily feel invited to accept narrative details as real-life facts. Lived reality and its double in representation merge. The actor becomes the role.

Real-life fiction can therefore be said to occupy another point along the parabiographical spectrum we have been tracing. From the fraudulent text whose fakeries correspond to biographical truths, as in the case of Wilkomirski's *Fragments*, to the explicitly paratextual reflection that supplies the critical tools necessary for the reader to parse fact from invention, we arrive at fiction that is difficult and at times impossible to distinguish from autobiography.

What motivates the authors to adopt such an approach, which at first glance might easily be mistaken for mere deception or authorial trickery, is the desire to represent the survivor's sense that life under the conditions of open confinement has split experience into parallel tracks, one that consists of everyday expectations, behaviors, and norms—the humdrum, quotidian existence that is easily reducible to narrative information, albeit not very interesting—and the other made up of uncanny inversions of the same, of *enargeia*, of paradoxes and pains that overwhelm the body with their realness while also resisting unambiguous articulation in words. "In other words," Jean Améry writes, "nowhere else in the world did reality have as much effective power as in the camp, nowhere else was reality so real."[13]

Once again, Shklovsky's notion of art comes to mind, as a device that "estranges" the subject from reality in order to return her to it with fresh eyes, only now we see more clearly the idea's troubling potential: What if the estrangement is so shocking, so traumatic, that the subject can no longer reintegrate, or even distinguish, the parallel experiences of reality and representation? The "world apart" demands that there also be a "world," at once familiar and alien, real (insofar as one remembers what life had been before entering the camp, before walls enclosed the ghetto, before the artillery shells began raining down on apartment blocks), yet imaginary (since it belongs to a faraway place and time so much *less real* than the reality of the camp, ghetto, or besieged city). "Nothing really happens as we hope it will, nor as we fear it will," Améry paraphrases Proust. "But not because the occurrence, as one says, perhaps 'goes beyond the imagination' (it is not a quantitative question), but because it is reality and not phantasy. One can devote an entire life to comparing the imagination and the real, and still never accomplish anything by it."[14]

Enargeia: the availability of a term for representation that seems to embody the visceral force of lived experience seems to acknowledge, at the very foundations of Western reflections on representation, a failing of representation as such. Just as Plato admonishes us, representation is never what it purports to represent. "No writer, no poet could ever describe this life," Sima Vaisman, a Jew forced into servitude as an infirmary doctor in Auschwitz, laments before asking, "Is this what hell is?"[15] For Elie Wiesel, whose international reputation grew from his ability to represent the camp experience to those who had never known it firsthand, the impenetrability and inaccessibility of the lived experience turns almost all representation into either a lie or kitsch:

> Auschwitz is something else, always something else. It is a universe, a creation that exists parallel to creation. Auschwitz lies on the other side of life and on the other side of death. There, one lives differently, one walks differently, one dreams differently. Auschwitz represents the negation of human progress and casts doubt on its validity. Then, it defeated culture; later, it defeated art, because just as no one could imagine Auschwitz before Auschwitz, no one can now retell Auschwitz after Auschwitz. The truth of Auschwitz remains hidden in its ashes. Only those who lived it in their flesh and in their minds can possibly transform the experience into knowledge.[16]

This would appear to place the survivor-author in a double bind. In order to appreciate the epistemological split between life and the camp, which "lies on the other side of life," one would have to have already "lived it in their flesh and in their minds." For Wiesel, only someone who has already experienced the "world apart" can tell the "world apart," and then only to someone else who has had the same or similar experiences. More likely, the representation succumbs to sensationalism and sentimental invention: Rosenblat's *Angel at the Fence*, Boyne's *Boy in the Striped Pajamas*, and any number of similar texts. This, for Wiesel, is not the land of open confinement, but "the land of kitsch, where, at the expense of truth, what counts is ratings."[17] Yet an unvarnished representation of the facts would be equally unfaithful to the lived experience, since "memory is more than isolated events, more than the sum of those events. Facts pulled out of their context can be misleading."[18]

Seeing Double: Absorbing and Resisting the Image

Historians, theorists, and literary authors who survived the "world apart" are often in agreement with Wiesel that the truth of the experience cannot be communicated by facts alone. Pieter Geyl, a Dutch historian who was at one time, like Wiesel, a prisoner in Buchenwald, emerged from the camp with the conviction that when it came to historical understanding "the emphasis on technical exactitude is proving the embarrassment to the free use of imagination," and that "imagination has a great part to play if history is to evoke or interpret the past significantly."[19] Paul Ricoeur, who as a reserve officer in the French army spent the entire war in a Nazi POW camp (Oflag II-D), reaches a similar conclusion not by extolling the necessity of imagination, but by underscoring the historical inadequacy of historical facts, "capable of being asserted in singular, discrete propositions, most often having to do with the mentioning of dates, places, proper names, verbs that name an action or state." These, Ricoeur reminds us, are not the events to which they refer, nor can they make those events present through their referentiality: "A vigilant epistemology will guard here against the illusion of believing that what we call a fact coincides with what really happened, or with the living memory of eyewitnesses, as if the facts lay sleeping in the documents until the historians extracted them."[20]

These words of caution could apply to *any* historical representation, not just that concerned with catastrophes such as those exemplified by Auschwitz, the Siege of Leningrad, or the Gulag system. Certainly, the extreme horror of these spaces and events adds urgency to the need for a parallactic interrogation of the convergences and incongruities between the representation and the available historical data that pertains to it, similar to what Georges Didi-Huberman calls "dual action," or reading "in spite of all," when we encounter photographic images that appear to document atrocity directly: "The *all image* of the Shoah, we agree, does not exist, but not because the Shoah is necessarily unimaginable. Rather, it is because the image is characterized by *being not all*. And it is not because the image gives what Walter Benjamin called a *flash* rather than the *substance* that we must exclude it from our inadequate means of broaching the terrible history in question."[21] Didi-Huberman goes on to say that, despite the danger that the image will "transfix" us, as Susan Sontag warned against, "one must still take into account the *dual system* of images, the flux and reflux of truth in them. When their surface of *misrecognition* is disturbed by turbulence, by a wave of *cognition*, we cross the difficult but fecund moment of a *test of truth*."[22] The "dual action" of reading the camp image consists in absorbing its iconicity as evidence and emblem of the camp experience, which is of course far larger than even the most capacious image could contain, while simultaneously refusing that same expansive iconicity, since the image, frozen in time and bound within its frame, can never come close to delivering everything it seems to promise.

The image is at once *of* something and *not* that thing, both evidence and illusion.

Maurice Halbwachs observes this duality in what he calls the "double focus" of collective memory. Concentration camps, ghettos, and besieged cities provide an excellent illustration of the concept. Our shared cultural knowledge of these spaces is sufficient for us to refer to them conveniently by metonymic shorthand: "Auschwitz," "the ghetto," "Stalingrad." This memory is served, as Halbwachs suggests it should be, by the availability of specific artifacts—"a physical object, a material reality such as a statue, a monument, a place in space"—and of emblems and representations—"a symbol, or something of spiritual significance, something shared by the group that adheres to and is superimposed on this physical reality."[23] In some instances, the symbolic meaning attached to the physical object extends the memorialized site or event in space and time, as when, for example, two bricks were removed from the last remaining portion of the wall that enclosed the Warsaw Ghetto (figure 3.1), at 55 Sienna Street, and were used to cast the recreation of the same stretch of wall at the United States Holocaust Memorial and Museum in Washington, DC (figure 3.2)—though there is nothing about the bricks themselves, beyond their tragic history, to distinguish them from any other bricks. In other instances, the physical space and its symbolic image in the cultural memory have little overlap. The mental image of the Dachau concentration camp outside of Munich that emerges from its brief appearance in Art Spiegelman's *Maus* (1980–1991), which emphasizes the danger of the camp's overcrowded barracks, certainly does not comport with the physical space of the camp today, where the footprint of the demolished barracks is marked only by gravel (figure 3.3). Signage at the site, now a museum, features image and text to assist the visitor in visualizing what is *not* there (figure 3.4)—in effect, to foster a parallactic reading of the space, a "double focus" where neither the collective memory nor the documentary evidence suffices on its own.[24]

Moreover, neither the documentary image nor the physical space suffices on its own. The "double focus" of collective memory demands a concomitant "dual action," not only to allow the evidence to mitigate the inadequacies of the narrative and vice versa, but to expose the divergence of event and telling that is inherent in representation and recurs in every instance of retelling. Thus Annette Wieviorka extends the critique of the total image, of its "being not all," beyond the still image to encompass two

Figure 3.1 The last remaining stretch of the original wall surrounding the Warsaw Ghetto, 55 Sienna Street, Warsaw. The plaque explains that the missing bricks were used to cast bricks for the recreated wall at the United States Holocaust Memorial and Museum in Washington, DC. *Source*: photograph by the author

Figure 3.2 The reconstruction of a section of the Warsaw Ghetto wall made from a cast of bricks removed from the section at 55 Sienna Street, Warsaw. *Source*: photograph by the author

Figure 3.3 The Dachau concentration camp today, with pits of gravel showing the footprint of missing barracks. *Source*: photograph by the author

Figure 3.4 Display board at the Dachau concentration camp with photographs and descriptive text in German and English, allowing the visitor to visualize barracks that are no longer there. *Source*: photograph by the author

major collections of video testimonials by survivors: the Fortunoff Video Archive for Holocaust Testimony, which is housed at Yale University, and which she points out exists in part because of criticism of the American television miniseries *Holocaust* (dir. Marvin J. Chomsky, 1978), and the University of Southern California's Shoah Foundation Archive, which was initiated by Steven Spielberg as a direct response to his experience directing the film *Schindler's List* (1994):

> Two fictional films dealing with the genocide that were seen by tens of millions, even hundreds of millions throughout the world were also at the origin of the two most important testimony archives. But whereas the survivors testified in reaction to *Holocaust*, in order to make their voices heard, one could say that they testified in symbiosis with *Schindler's List*, as a complement and not in opposition to the film. The differences do not end there. The emphasis in Spielberg's project is different from that of the Yale Archive. The person of the survivor is no longer at the center of the enterprise. The survivor has been replaced by a concept, that of transmission. Whereas the founders of the Yale Archive insisted on the survivors' sense of having lived on "another planet," as Ka-Tzetnik put it at the Eichmann trial, on their sense of being forever isolated from the world and from their relatives by an extreme experience, the Spielberg project is based, conversely, on the desire to show "ordinary people," people who have returned to "normal," who have survived the shipwreck of war.[25]

Whether one absorbs the videotaped testimonies in these archives or the popular (and, by many estimations, kitschy) films that helped spur their creation, the historical understanding being delivered to audiences is severely limited, not only by the finite frame of the image or narrative, as Didi-Huberman demonstrates, but by the fact that every text arises from, and is inextricably bound to, the time of its creation rather than to the time it refers to. "Testimonies," Wieviorka tells us, "particularly when they are produced as part of a larger cultural movement, express the discourses valued by society at the moment the witnesses tell their stories as much as they render an individual experience."[26]

What may initially strike us as a theoretical description born of Didi-Huberman's and Wieviorka's belated arrival at the image could just as easily characterize the experience of an actual survivor when confronted with visual evidence of the space he had only recently departed. For example, in his parabiographical text *Literature or Life* (*L'Écriture ou la vie*, 1994), Jorge Semprún, who spent nearly two years in Buchenwald, describes the uncanniness of seeing newsreel footage of the camp after the war. He is in Locarno, a lakeside resort in southern Switzerland, only a few hundred miles from Weimar, yet a world away. He decides to divert himself by going to the movies. And that's when he sees the space he has survived, and the void separating experience from representation hits him:

> These scenes had been filmed in different camps liberated by the Allied advance a few months before. In Bergen-Belsen, in Mauthausen, in Dachau. There were also some images of Buchenwald, which I recognized.
>
> Or rather: which I knew for certain came from Buchenwald, without being certain of recognizing them. Or rather: without being certain of having seen them. It was the difference between the seen and the experienced that was disturbing. . . .
>
> In becoming, thanks to the film corps of the Allied armies, a spectator of my own life, a voyeur of my own experience, I felt as if I were escaping the wrenching uncertainties of memory. As if—although this might seem strange at first—the dimension of unreality, the context of fiction inherent in any cinematic image, even the most strictly documentary one, gave the weight of incontestable reality to my inmost memories. On the one hand, of course, they had been taken from me; on the other, their reality was confirmed: I had not imagined Buchenwald.
>
> My life, therefore, was more than just a dream.
>
> Yet although the newsreel footage confirmed the truth of the actual experience (which was sometimes difficult for me to grasp and situate among my memories), at the same time these images underlined the exasperating difficulty of transmitting this truth, of making it, if not absolutely clear, at least communicable.[27]

On the one hand, Semprún discovers, or rediscovers, his own lived experience in the documentary image: Buchenwald "was more than just a dream." On the other, this revelation comes to him not because he assumes that the newsreel has captured a reality that he had witnessed firsthand, providing a kind of objective corroboration of what he knew only through his own subjective, traumatized, and therefore suspect impressions, but rather because he arrives at the documentary footage already with the conviction that "the dimension of unreality, the context of fiction inherent in any cinematic image, even the most strictly documentary one," cannot claim to tell the whole truth. Witnessing the image's struggle and failure, its inevitable falling short of the real experience, Semprún comes away with a confirmation of what he knows viscerally to be the truth of the "world apart"—namely, "the exasperating difficulty of transmitting this truth." He therefore concludes, "One would have had to treat the documentary reality, in short, like fiction."[28]

A Hallucination Soberly Told: Jorge Semprún

Whereas Didi-Huberman would underline the need to read images of the camp "in spite of all," through the "dual action" of trusting and rejecting their representation of the "world apart," Semprún ascribes the same need to *the act of representing*. The demands of parabiographical representation occur both at the moment of immediate testimony and in every moment of recollection thereafter, for it is the splitting of the world into its parallel forms, the familiar and the "world apart," that contains the truth of the experience that both demands and resists representation. Semprún foregrounds this tension in the title of *Literature or Life*, whose original French title, *L'Écriture ou la vie*, might be rendered more accurately as *Writing or Life*—that is, the question of whether what he is representing in his text is the activity of writing, *écriture*, a loaded term in the French philosophical tradition to which Semprún belongs, or life, the conventional subject of autobiography. As a camp survivor, is he offering a portrait of his own life, or is this instead a representation of the impossibility of a truthful portrait, a portrayal of *écriture*, the always faltering effort to portray?

The answer to this question is encapsulated in Semprún's novel *What a Beautiful Sunday! (Quel beau dimanche!*, 1980), a real-life fiction centered on the liberation of Buchenwald. Late in the book, Semprún describes the revelation of Herling-Grudziński's *A World Apart*, to which he had been introduced by Józef Czapski, another thinker about the relationship between reality and representation in the camps. *A World Apart*, according to Semprún, "is no doubt one of the most hallucinatory accounts, in its sobriety, its restrained compassion, in the naked perfection of its narrative shape, that I have ever read of a Stalinist camp," while it is also "a historical document of the first order, providing a detailed description as well as a fully verified general view, of the Stalinist Gulag in the years 1940–1942."[29] How can Herling-Grudziński's text be at once "hallucinatory" and noted for its "sobriety," simultaneously a paragon of "narrative shape" and "a historical document"? Over and against the pragmatic separation of fantastical literature from documentary history that one encounters so frequently in Anglo-American discourse, Semprún sees no contradiction. For the camp is, in itself, a "hallucinatory," contradictory reality, one that can be communicated truthfully only within a narrative that simulates the experience. The sobriety and restraint that Semprún lauds in Herling-Grudziński, and that so frequently characterizes the tone of real-life fiction more generally, also serves the narrative's claim on historical truth, since it allows the reader to ascribe the text's hallucinogenic qualities to the object of representation rather than to idiosyncrasies of the author's voice in representing it. This is just one more example of how authors of real-life fiction consumed the work of their predecessors and contemporaries with an active, comparative interest in how fictional means could depict historical realities that mere fact might obscure. Powerful specimens of real-life fiction return Semprún to the reality of the camp and the relative unreality of the world around him, which is why, elsewhere in *What a Beautiful Sunday!*, the author tells us that, after reading Solzhenitsyn's *One Day in the Life of Ivan Denisovich*, it was "the world around me that seemed unreal": "It was I who seemed unreal. It was my memory that held me in the unreality of a dream. Life was not a dream, oh no! It was I who was."[30]

Semprún's authorial project might be most visible in his frequently beginning a sentence or phrase with "Or rather ... ," "But still ... " He was preoccupied throughout his writing life with how to connect his personal camp experience with the "collective frameworks" described by Halbwachs as "the instruments used by the collective memory to reconstruct an image of the past which is in accord, in each epoch, with the predominant thoughts of the society," which "confines and binds our most intimate remembrances to each other."[31] The fact that the collective memory is grounded "in each epoch," rather than in the time to which the memory refers, is what prompts Wieviorka to warn us about video testimonies. It is also what compels a writer like Semprún to fictionalize his real-life experience, telling us, for example, that "reality often needs some make-believe, to become real. In other words, to be made believable. To win the heart and mind of the reader." "Not that what we lived through is indescribable," Semprún writes; rather,

> It was unbearable, which is something else entirely (that won't be hard to understand), something that doesn't concern the form of a possible account, but its substance. Not its articulation, but its destiny. The only ones who will manage to reach this substance, this transparent density, will be those able to shape their evidence into an artistic object, a space of creation. Or of re-creation. Only the artifice of a masterly narrative will prove capable of conveying some of the truth of such testimony. But there's nothing exceptional about this: it's the same with all great historical experiences.[32]

Semprún's echo of Halbwachs's notion of collective memory is not accidental: Halbwachs had been Semprún's professor at the Sorbonne and was interned with him at Buchenwald (where Wiesel and Kertész were kept among the other Jewish prisoners). In the same text, Semprún describes in nauseating detail holding his dear teacher as the latter is dying of dysentery. If the details provided were not nauseating, could it still be characterized as truthful? Life and death in the camp is *not* "indescribable" (Semprún), *not* "beyond the imagination" (Améry), it is "not necessarily unimaginable" (Didi-Huberman). We describe camps and besieged cities in news reports and imagine them in literature and film every day. The problem is that, without imagination, the factual description loses "this substance, this transparent density"—its *enargeia*—and therefore any claim on the reality it seeks to represent. As Semprún puts it,

> Even if one had given evidence with absolute precision, with perfect objectivity (something by definition beyond the powers of the individual witness), even in this case one could miss the essential thing. Because it wasn't the accumulation of horror, which could be spelled out, endlessly, in detail. One could recount the story of any day at all, from reveille at four-thirty in the morning to curfew—the fatiguing labor, the constant hunger, the chronic lack of sleep, the persecution by the *Kapos*, the latrine duty, the floggings from the SS, the assembly-line work in munitions factories, the crematory smoke, the public executions, the endless roll calls in the winter snow,

the exhaustion, the death of friends—yet never manage to deal with the essential thing, or reveal the icy mystery of this experience, its dark, shining truth: *la ténèbre qui nous était échue en partage*: The darkness that had fallen to our lot, throughout all eternity. Or rather, throughout all history.[33]

Yet Semprún is quick to point out that the inadequacy of even the most detailed description is not just a symptom of distance, of hindsight. He is at pains to emphasize that it is inherent in the experience itself and exposed in even the most proximate representation or recollection. At the same time, as Bela Brodzki observes, "Semprún posits, and in so doing performs, what he claims to be the failure (or irrelevance) of testimony—the accretion of details as the ultimate cataloguing of atrocities," so that he can continuously revisit, rework, and reimagine what those details fail to encompass, the paradoxical simultaneity of death and life, of precarity and survival, that was the daily reality of the camp.[34] This is why he records—or, rather, textually reenacts—his arguments with others about whether the best, most representative telling of these experiences would be testimonial or artistic. He declares to a fellow liberated inmate, "How do you tell such an unlikely truth, how do you foster the imagination of the unimaginable, if not by elaborating, by reworking reality, by putting it in perspective? With a bit of artifice, then!"[35] To another interlocutor, he declares, "So I need a narrative 'I' that draws on my experience but goes beyond it, capable of opening the narrative up to fiction, to imagination. . . . Fiction that would be as illuminating as the truth, of course. That would help reality to seem true-to-life, truth to seem convincing."[36] Imre Kertész emerged from the same camp with much the same conviction, thinking of literary creation as a certain, necessary form of historicism: "Creation is a path to remembrance. When I started to write, my memories of the camps lay dormant. But as you start to create, to write, you bring them out of this obscurity. This is when they begin to seem absurd and you try to understand them, and as you do they pass into fiction. Many of the events that I wrote about in *Fatelessness* happened just as I recounted them but I still can't think of them as reality—only as fiction."[37]

Throughout *Literature or Life*, Semprún also threads an illustrative commentary on how he drew on his own sense of self-splitting in creating the character of his *Jewish* avatar, Hans, in writing his semiautobiographical novel *Fainting* (*L'Évanouissment*, 1967), which is concerned largely with how experiential and historical memory become fractured by trauma. He revisits the novel so frequently that *Life or Literature*, in its parabiographical commentary, thereby provides the paratextual material that would be needed to read *Fainting* as parabiography as well. Here, too, however, simple error can intrude to fictionalize fact, as Semprún, ever obsessive over dates and careful to document his precision by sharing his various mnemonic devices, recollects a crucial injury he sustained when jumping from a commuter train after the war. This was on Monday, August 5, 1945, he insists in *Literature or Life*.[38] In *Fainting*, the same events are fictionalized as having occurred on August 6, not August 5, 1945, though still on a Monday.[39] If one is tracking the representation against the reality to which it refers, it is the novel that turns out to be correct.

The "Gray Zone" Versus the Fascism of Representation: From Primo Levi to Gillian Rose

One need not be making a conscious effort to infuse a recollected memory with *enargeia* to lose track of whether the first Monday of August 1945 was the fifth or the sixth. These kinds of slips can happen to any of us, even when, like Semprún, we imagine ourselves to be fastidious in cleaving to what is objectively verifiable. At the same time, the more the author leans into the effort to infuse the narrative with "density" and visceral data, the more one finds the factual data bending to artistic, narrative demands.

Again, this effect is not a consequence of authorial manipulation, but rather a reflection of how these author-survivors experienced the "world apart" as a contrapuntal reality to the outside. The experience of the camp, the ghetto, or the besieged city is a reality bifurcated into both poles of its many paradoxes. In the camp, cruelty derives its horror not from being the norm, but from how it renders kindness into something shocking. In the chilling short stories of Tadeusz Borowski, based on his experiences in Auschwitz and Dachau, "the concentration camp is the norm, and the world outside is, and will be again, one large concentration camp," to borrow Clifton Fadiman's characterization.[40] In real-life fiction, the author does not inhabit the "world apart" exclusively, but as a reality for which the familiar reality, the world outside the camp or ghetto, becomes a phantasm or shadow. As much as the peculiar reality of the camp, it is this schizophrenic division of realities that the authors of real-life fiction endeavor to represent to those who have not experienced it. Time and again they tell us that the camp is liberated, the besiegement ends, one is no longer confined to a ghetto or hunted through the countryside, but the survivor's awareness of the split in reality into world and antiworld endures.

Once one has entered what Primo Levi calls the "gray zone" of the camp, the physical and moral space where the conventional "bipartition" of social being into "we" and "they," of "friend/enemy," no longer reflects reality as such, it becomes impossible to leave.[41] No matter how long it took for one's body to become recognizable to oneself, Varlam Shalamov writes in his story "Grishka Logun's Thermometer" ("Termometr Grishki Loguna," 1965), "we didn't count on returning to our former souls. And, of course, we didn't. No one did."[42]

Semprún, too, would affirm this split epistemology as a permanent condition in his consideration of Primo Levi's death:

> You find yourself in the middle of the whirlwind of nothingness a nebulous void, murky and grayish. From that moment on, you know what this means. You know what you have always known. Always, beneath the glittering surface of daily life, this terrible knowledge. Close at hand, this certainty: nothing is true except the camp, all the rest is but a dream, now and forever. Nothing is real but the smoke from the crematory of Buchenwald, the smell of burned flesh, the hunger, the roll calls in the snow, the beatings, the deaths of Maurice Halbwachs and Diego Morales, the fraternal stench of the latrines in the Little Camp.[43]

"Nothing is true except the camp." The survivor's eyes have been opened to a fundamental, Platonic truth, that the everyday world is an illusion, only the reality just beyond it is one not of ideal forms, but of parody, inversion, and ambiguity.

A similar conclusion sparked controversy when it was voiced in 1962 by Piotr Rawicz, an assimilated Jew who had survived Auschwitz under a false Christian identity and gained postwar fame for *Blood from the Sky* (*Le sang du ciel*, 1961), his French-language novel fictionalizing the camp experience. In a much-publicized interview with Anna Langfus, who had fictionalized her own survival of the Lublin Ghetto and subsequent imprisonment and torture in her novel *Salt and Suffering* (*Le Sel et le Soufre*, 1960), Rawicz insists that he chose to write about the experience of open confinement during the war not because he had any interest in representing a discrete and peculiar moment in history, but because he found it illustrative of reality as it truly is: "I chose this era because I find it . . . quite representative, and because it lent itself extraordinarily well to my point. Historical or political truth does not interest me. The only thing that matters to me is ontological truth."[44] Taken aback, Langfus presses Rawicz on the appropriateness of using the camp as a setting for "purely literary" purposes, a question that still applies to entire generations of writers and filmmakers born since, as well as to the publics who consume their work. But Rawicz insists that the camp is the real world in all its naked truth, that the "world apart" is a reality without artifice: "I find this era perfectly normal. It corresponds to what is most deeply within us. For me, this war is the very germ of being, being in its pure state."[45]

Meanwhile, it would become a frequent trope of camp literature that the individual who insists on living in illusion, in believing that the world one had known before is the sole reality, that it will be possible to return there after the camp has been liberated and the tyrant defeated, is almost certain not to survive. Such figures live within the fantasy of their own survival, the counterfactual *if only* that places them in the illusory other side of the next ordeal, which they then cannot penetrate. Dostoevsky gives us a dark example, that of a man who arrives in the camp hospital after having endured the first half of a punishment by flogging:

> He arrived in the hospital beaten half to death; never had I seen such sores; but he had come with joy in his heart, with the hope that he would remain alive, that the rumors were false, that they had just let him go from under the rods, so that now, having endured a long trial, he had now begun to dream of the road, escape, freedom, of fields and forests. . . . Two days after his release from the hospital he died in the very same hospital, in the same bunk as before, not having withstood the second half [of the punishment].[46]

The "gray zone" is not only a space of moral ambiguity, though that is Primo Levi's focus in discussing the term. It is also a space where world and antiworld are held in tenuous balance, where the reality of one does not negate that of the other.

In real-life fiction, the infection with the "gray zone" is real, both in the space of open confinement and beyond it. The dramatic reenactment of precarity in text, sometimes decades after the initiation into the "world apart," manifests its ever-presentness, so that the death of a writer like Primo Levi becomes one more layer of narrative commentary to be read, another textual irony to be considered parallactically against the rest. This is how Gillian Rose, like Semprún, interprets the death of the author: "The human, temperate, restrained prose of Primo Levi's representation and witness did not protect or save him from the unexpressed ways in which he felt irrevocably contaminated by his experience, even though he knew that he had been effective in disseminating his witness."[47] There is an ethical imperative, Rose argues, for representation that leans into the "gray zone," and that communicates it to the world as the inconvenient truth of the camp experience: that no one so "contaminated by his experience" ever recovers his innocence, no one returns. Popular representations of the experience of open confinement—particularly those that offer a sentimental vision, where suffering is redemptive and the human spirit unbreakable—stumble perhaps most meaningfully on this point. In the sentimental survival tale, the individual navigating a maze of impossible moral choices and situational paradoxes dissolves into clearly delineated ranks of the wicked and the righteous, with the audience pre-positioned in alliance with the more comfortable of the two.

Gillian Rose has this in mind when she calls for a "representation of Fascism [that] would engage with the fascism of representation."[48] When we view popular representations of open confinement, we enjoy a privileged perspective after and above these phenomena. The sentimental text assumes that we have fully grasped these spaces, that they are unambiguously sequestered in time (a past that becomes increasingly legendary as it recedes), locked in a received significance (where we know just as unambiguously who is the victim, who the perpetrator), and that our regard, directed backward, fully grasps what concentration camps, ghettos, and besieged cities *were*, so that we can be assured that they *will never be*—as the cliché goes, "never again." Clichés in lieu of analysis; asserting a present position of right based on a generalized vision of past wrongs; instrumentalizing suffering as a step toward a better future; demanding unanimity in the qualification of historical victims and victimizers: this is what Rose means by the "fascism of representation." Such representation encodes our presumptions of what the experience is *supposed to mean* from within the privilege of our belated arrival to it. It represents the past in terms of ready-made grievances and easily identifiable enemies, a central feature of the logic of fascism.

An excellent example of this sentimental revisionism, for Rose as well as for Michael Rothberg, is *Schindler's List* (dir. Steven Spielberg, 1993), based on Thomas Keneally's historical novel *Schindler's Ark* (1982). Not because of aesthetic decisions that the unsympathetic observer might deride as kitsch, but because kitsch harbors a poorly concealed Manicheanism, an unambivalent adjudication of good versus evil, a predisposition to see meaning in meaningless events. It is not a question of fictionalization, but of whether the text is true to the reality that it purports to represent—that of the "gray zone," of the paradoxical "world apart."

What Rose calls the "fascism of representation" applies as much to a nonfiction documentary film like Claude Lanzmann's monumental *Shoah* (1985) as it does to *Schindler's List*, which leaves viewers "in a Fascist security of our own unreflected predation, piously joining the survivors putting stones on Schindler's grave," even as we have been moved and entertained by the violence we have just consumed.[49] Michael Rothberg traces this infelicity to Keneally's novel, suggesting that, *because of* the author's "reliance on factual testimonies," he "misses the 'truth' of the events he attempts to describe," since he cannot relate any detail that is not already circumscribed by survival. "Again and again," Rothberg remarks, "the 'Schindler Jews' are put into life-threatening circumstances only to be saved by 'a special and startling deliverance.' The point is not that these all-but-unfathomable stories are not true—the least familiarity with the irrational rationality of the Holocaust confirms their likelihood—but that they couldn't not be true, based as they are on a certain reading of *survivor* testimony."[50] A survivor testimony is necessarily, aprioristically a testimony of survival, whereas the "truth" of the experience of a camp, ghetto, or besieged city cannot be told without the potential for non-survival at its center. The conventional reading of the survivor tale is prescribed by its exclusion of non-survival. The same critique casts a shadow over Terrence Des Pres's reading of survival literature: "Survivors *choose* life," Des Pres declares, but his data set is doubly skewed, (a) preselecting texts by survivors, who (b) present their survival as a choice.[51] Real-life fiction, by contrast, tends to present survival as incidental, an afterthought, happenstance that could just as easily have gone the other way. To enter the "gray zone," which Rose characterizes as the "collusion between executioner and victim," would be monstrous otherwise.[52] She offers Borowski as an exemplar of the literary representation of the "gray zone," not because he did not recognize the distinction between perpetrator and victim, but because he occupies both positions at once while obscuring "from what position, as whom, you are reading," so that "you emerge shaking in horror at yourself, with yourself in question."[53]

Fraudulent narratives of open confinement, we should note, generally avoid this kind of ambiguity. In fact, they exploit the "fascism of representation," because in the "fascism of representation" the victimhood and innocence of the alleged survivor are unassailable. For Misha Defonseca, it is the personal need to ascribe meaning to a meaningless tragedy that justifies the fraud. "I lied, yes, but I did it to save us," she says. "To rehabilitate my father, to give some meaning to my mother's death, and to save myself by giving myself permission to breathe in this world."[54] It is not a coincidence that in the frauds perpetrated by Dösseker, Defonseca, and Rosenblat, the survivor is always a child with a loose, impressionistic understanding of their circumstances. Nor is it surprising that, as unremarkable as it is for someone to adopt a fraudulent narrative of victimhood, it is virtually unheard of for someone to pretend to have been the perpetrator.

But just as *Shoah* can falsify reality by featuring only the voices of the living and their retrospective verdicts about victimhood, a camp memoir can seem just as false for its assumption that the experience *means* anything at all, or that its meaning is already embodied in the event, rather than in the reader's individual encounter with the text. This is precisely how Borowski attacks Zofia Kossak's *From the Abyss* (*Z otchłani*, 1947), in which Kossak, a Polish resistance fighter thrown into Auschwitz, frames her survival as an expression of Catholic martyrology. There is a *meaning* to survival, Kossak declares—"This is why God has permitted certain people to see hell on earth and to return, in order to bear *witness to the truth*"—and "an objective, impersonal style" for conveying that meaning without the intrusion of the personal.[55] Borowski has nothing but derision for the notion that survival in the camps meant anything beyond the camp. To ascribe an overarching significance to that violence would be, for Borowski, to extend it, to make textual signification both the reason for the violence to have occurred and, through mimesis, the prosthesis by which it reaches beyond the violent act.[56]

At the same time as Borowski does not wish to redeem violence by instrumentalizing it as a means toward a higher good, he is particularly insistent that the truth of the camp experience cannot be told impersonally, because the "gray zone" is an interpersonal space: "I believe that a materialistic worldview is the only way, that the meaning of Auschwitz is perfectly resolvable within its own framework, since the problem is ethical: it concerns man and his social conditions, and that's the central problem of Auschwitz, that of one prisoner's relation to another!"[57] For Borowski, the truth of this experience cannot be communicated by Kossak's "objective, impersonal style." It requires a performative reenactment of the slippery interpersonal relations that typify life in the "world apart." To tell her camp experience, Borowski observes disapprovingly, Kossak steps outside, beyond the camp, observing it from a system of norms and values that have no meaning within the "world apart."[58]

At Home in the "Gray Zone": Tadeusz Borowski

As we have seen, in real-life fictional representations of open confinement the person who already sees himself elsewhere, in the now counterfactual universe of his dreamed-of survival, typically has little hope of surviving. He has already succumbed to illusion. "Does one maybe live on hope?" Shalamov asks after describing how forced laborers in Kolyma lived through their starvation. "But after all, he doesn't have any hope. If he isn't a fool, he cannot live on hopes. That's why there are so many suicides."[59] Later in his *Kolyma Tales* (*Kolymskie rasskazy*, 1954–1973), in the story "Seraphim" (1959), the "Engineer" advises the eponymous hero, "And there are good days and bad, days of hopelessness alternating with days of hope. One lives not because he believes in something, hopes for something. The instinct to live protects him, just as it does an animal."[60] In the short story "At Our Place, in Auschwitz" ("U nas, w Auschwitzu . . .," 1946), Borowski is even more explicit in his rejection of hope as a tool for survival: "It's hope that tells people to go apathetically to the gas chamber, that tells them not to rebel, that plunges them into lifelessness. It is hope that rends family ties, tells mothers to renounce their children, wives to sell themselves for bread and men to kill."[61] And Lev Razgon, echoing Solzhenitsyn, indicates that the relinquishing of hope was a commonplace in the Gulag: "The thesis formulated in *The Gulag Archipelago*—'Do not ask, and do not hope'—was not invented by its author, but was worked out by anyone who tried to understand his future with eyes open."[62]

This marks one of the most consistent features distinguishing real-life fiction of survival from popular portrayals written by authors who never experienced a camp or besieged city firsthand. Whereas the latter conventionally emphasize hope as the essential factor in the protagonist's survival, frequently in a kitschy, sentimental mode where hope always wins over despair, the narratives of actual survivors most often attribute their survival to chance while also portraying one's confidence in the "normal" world as a liability. Améry draws this point out explicitly in reference to intellectuals in the camps who found themselves incapable of reconciling their lived experience with the "world apart" they had entered:

> Not only was rational-analytic thinking in the camp, and particularly at Auschwitz, of no help, but it led straight into a tragic dialectic of self-destruction.... Long practice of questioning the phenomena of everyday reality prevented [the intellectual] from simply adjusting to the realities of the camp, because these stood in all-too-sharp contrast to everything that he had regarded until then as possible and humanly acceptable.[63]

The foremost task of real-life fiction is to represent the process by which the would-be survivor enters the "gray zone," absorbing the "world apart" as equally valid to what had been "regarded until then as possible." Whereas, in a more explicitly parabiographical text, the author might choose to present this two-worldness, the sense of negotiating between two mutually exclusive worlds, through the subject's own divided consciousness, in texts where the author is more easily confused with their textual avatar the dominant is on the bifurcation of the world itself and on the impossibility of a permanent restoration of the world's wholeness. In such instances, the writer might *become* their textual self-representation first, in the sense that audiences will identify the actual author with the text's narrator, though also in the sense that the author assumes key features of their own textual persona.

The reader is perhaps most likely to confuse the actual author with their textual self-representation when the two share a name, as is the case, for example, in Gustaw Herling-Grudziński's *A World Apart* and in the camp stories of Borowski and Shalamov. The first edition of *A World Apart*, despite its careful modeling on Dostoevsky's *Notes from the House of the Dead* and explicit use of many of the same fictional devices, bore remarkably nonfictional language on its front cover: "The shocking personal experiences of a man who spent two years in Soviet prisons and labor camps." Subsequent editions designated Herling-Grudziński's book—again, prominently on the book's cover—*The Journal of a Gulag Survivor* and *A Memoir of the Gulag*, though the book is neither a journal nor a memoir. Such paratextual markers signal to the reader that he or she is to interpret the information within the text through the nonfiction paradigm—that is, as factual data reflecting real people, places, and events, at least to the best of the author's recollection. Calling a book a "diary" or "journal" suggests a documentary account contemporaneous with the events described therein. Just as importantly, these genre designations would seem to activate Lejeune's "autobiographical pact," even though what Lejeune calls the "phantasmatic pact" would be more appropriate to the parallactic reading that these texts call for. Given contradictory or altogether misleading instructions, the reader easily mistakes the text's protagonist for a purely factual depiction of the biological entity who composed the work.

The paratextual markers of Tadeusz Borowski's short stories, which are based mostly on his experiences as a non-Jewish Pole in Auschwitz, are especially confusing and provocative. His first two stories about the concentration camp experience, "At Our Place, in Auschwitz" and "The People Who Went" ("Ludzie, którzy szli . . ."), appeared (without any attribution to him individually) in the volume *We Were in Auschwitz* (*Byliśmy w Oświęcimiu*), published in 1946 and authored collectively by three writers whose camp identification numbers appear before their names on the title page. The book is dedicated to the American Seventh Army, "which liberated us from the Dachau-Allach concentration camp." The publisher's note, by Anatol Girs, inmate 191250, declares, "Certainly this book is unnecessary as an artistic act. But as a document it is quite distinctive."[64]

We now know that Borowski—inmate 119198—played a key role in assembling and editing the entire text, which was followed in quick succession by two collections of camp-themed stories, *Farewell to Maria* (*Pożegnanie z Marią*, 1947), which, in omitting most paratext, leaves it to the reader to decide what is fact and what is fiction; and *The Stone World* (*Kamienny świat*, 1948), which includes an admonitory preface that reads in part,

> Some of these short stories are merely realistic, some are trivial, others polemicize with writerly attitudes. The dedications indicate to

whom polemics are addressed, though not always. Some merely pay honor. I am not a positive Catastrophist, I didn't know a *Kapo* named Kwaśniak, I have not eaten human brains, I have not murdered children, I did not remain in a bunker, I didn't go to the opera with Germans, I didn't drink wine in a garden, I don't succumb to infantile daydreams—in general, I'd be very sorry if these stories from *The Stone World* were regarded as pages from their author's personal diary merely because they are written in the first person.[65]

Borowski's protest is remarkably reminiscent of Mikhail Lermontov's 1839 foreword to *A Hero of Our Time* (*Geroi nashego vremeni*), in which Lermontov instructs his audience in how to read long-form narrative fiction in Russian by ridiculing them for having fallen victim to biographical ambiguities the author has himself cultivated. As with Romantic audiences a century prior, a certain confusion on the part of Borowski's readers is likewise to be expected. The "Kapo Kwaśniak" he declares not to have known, for example, is the main character of a story entitled "A Tale from Real Life." Borowski was also an active participant in postwar debates, both in print and in person, on the proper role of fiction in our representation of historical fact. That his own suicide would become an object of literary interpretation, just as Primo Levi's would, merely adds another layer of irony within the discourse.[66]

Ka-Tzetnik in Jerusalem: When the Author Becomes the Avatar

A typical example of such paratextual manipulation is the combination of title and subtitle that Lev Razgon gave to the literary narratives representing his survival of the Gulag: *Not Made Up: A Novel in Stories* (*Nepridumannoe: Povest' v rasskazakh*, 1989). As cofounder of Memorial, the independent human rights organization established to document Stalinist and post-Stalinist crimes committed by the state against its own citizens, Razgon would have lasting influence on the Russian collective memory of the camp system. In an all too typical irony, Memorial was forced to close in April 2022, shortly after the Russian invasion of Ukraine, as part of the state's effort to control information about its own crimes.

But there are also instances where the writer fully embraces the conflation of real and imagined author. Bruno Dösseker, having invented the persona of Binjamin Wilkomirski, who had survived the Shoah to write the memoir *Fragments*, has lived the rest of his life *as* his character, years after the fraud was exposed.⁶⁷ The boy born Józef Lewinkopf *became* Jerzy Kosiński, the identity created to enable his escape from those who would murder him. And in one of the most performative examples of the author becoming his avatar, Yehiel Dinoor *became* Ka-Tzetnik 135633, whose name simply means "creature of the KZ"—*Konzentrationslager*, or concentration camp—and therefore "inmate 135633," the number tattooed on his forearm.

By the time of Adolf Eichmann's infamous 1961 trial in Jerusalem, Ka-Tzetnik was already the author of the Yiddish-language novel *House of Dolls* (*Dos Hoyz fun di lyalkes*, 1955), a notoriously semi-pornographic representation of forced prostitution in Auschwitz. The novel's factual basis was disputed for decades, not only because Ka-Tzetnik's portrayals of sexual violence and wanton depravity in the camps, both in *House of Dolls* and in subsequent works written in Hebrew, were outlandishly extreme, nor because they later served as an inspiration for the explicitly pornographic "Stalag" novels and films that enjoyed an international cult following in the 1960s and 1970s, but also because the author's true identity had been hidden behind his disturbing nom de plume, raising doubts about whether the author had ever been in a concentration camp, let alone whether he had witnessed anything like the sadistic sexual practices he describes in *House of Dolls*.

Ka-Tzetnik revealed his civilian identity as Yehiel Dinoor at the Eichmann trial, where he testified against the accused in a manner as theatrically striking as his prose. His testimony does not touch on Eichmann's guilt but focuses instead on the splitting of the world that forms so consistent a theme of real-life fiction from the "world apart":

> I do not regard myself as a writer writing literature. This is actually a history of the Auschwitz planet, the chronicles of Auschwitz. I myself was at the Auschwitz camp for two years. The time there is not a concept as it is here on our planet. Every fraction of a second has a different wheel of time. And the inhabitants of that planet had no names. They had no parents and they had no children. They were not clothed as we are clothed here. They were not born there and

they did not conceive there. They breathed and lived according to different laws of nature. They did not live according to the laws of this world of ours, and they did not die. Their name was a number, "Ka-Tzetnik" number so-and-so.[68]

Of course, the prosecutors have not asked the witness about the metaphysics of the camp. They have merely asked him to explain his choice of the name Ka-Tzetnik, which he insists is "not a pen-name." The prosecutors then present Ka-Tzetnik with a striped camp uniform and ask him to identify it, at which point his testimony becomes even more mystical:

> This is the garb of those who lived on this planet called Auschwitz. And I believe wholeheartedly that I must carry this name as long as the world will not awaken after the crucifying of a nation to erase this evil. As humanity has arisen after the crucifixion of one man, I believe wholeheartedly that just as in astrology the stars influence our destiny, so is this planet of the ashes, Auschwitz, facing our planet, and influencing, radiating toward our planet.[69]

Ka-Tzetnik rambles uncertainly for a few more sentences, insisting, "I can still see them [the dead of Auschwitz] gazing at me," before the prosecutors and judges try unsuccessfully to interrupt and retract his testimony. He then rises from his seat and collapses face down on the floor (figure 3.5).

Hannah Arendt despised the theatricality of Ka-Tzetnik's testimony. In *Eichmann in Jerusalem*, she describes Ka-Tzetnik dismissively as "the author of several books on Auschwitz that dealt with brothels, homosexuals, and other 'human interest stories.'"[70] She also derides his explanation of his name as a performance "he had done at many of his public appearances" and his description of "Planet Auschwitz" as "a little excursion into astrology."[71] More than anything else, she laments Ka-Tzetnik's substitution of meaning for evidentiary data that would mean nothing on its own, that would approach a cold "banality" equal to that of Eichmann, her subject:

> This, to be sure, was an exception, but if it was an exception that proved the rule of normality, it did not prove the rule of simplicity or of the ability to tell a story, let alone of the rare capacity for distinguishing between things that had happened to the storyteller more

Figure 3.5 The author Ka-Tzetnik (Yehiel Dinoor) collapsed on the floor at the trial of Adolf Eichmann, Jerusalem, 1961 (00:08:54). *Source*: EichmannTrialEN, "Eichmann Trial—Session No. 68, 69," YouTube, March 9, 2011, video, https://www.youtube.com/watch?v=m3-tXyYhd5U&ab_channel=EichmannTrialEN

than sixteen, and sometimes twenty, years ago and what he had read and heard and imagined in the meantime. These difficulties could not be helped, but they were not improved by the predilection of the prosecution for witnesses of some prominence, many of whom had published books about their experiences, and who now told what they had previously written, or what they had told and retold many times.[72]

Arendt is not wrong: Ka-Tzetnik had indeed used the same metaphorical descriptions before. He uses them several times in *House of Dolls*, where he endeavors to explain how, even within the camp, different modes of existing became difficult to grasp to those who had not seen them for themselves: "They had come from another place that was unknown, though you knew that this place was there. Like you know from one star of the existence of another; you know, but in no way could you imagine how it looked there."[73] One cannot quite grasp the "world apart" without having seen it firsthand, in part because the world of the camp looks somehow similar to the one "outside," only its fundamental rules have been inverted: "Outside, in the world of mankind, death is the same, but life is diverse. Whereas, in the camp, life is the same, but death is diverse. . . . Each camp would lie here in the truck, like a separate race, like specimens from various planets. In life they were all the same."[74] And elsewhere in the same novel: "The sun burned from over [the German soldier's] shoulders, and it looked like an enflamed Gestapo-man would descend from a bloody planet and remain standing between heaven and earth."[75]

Arendt wishes for testimony that hews close to the facts—"close" not only in the sense of their proximity to what is independently verifiable, a testimony free from emotional or stylistic embellishment, but also "close" temporally, so that recollections of what had been experienced firsthand would feel *immediate* as evidence, without the patina of twenty years' traumatic repetition. She appears to idealize an unreality. For the survivor in this instance *did* offer narratives, both testimonial and literary, oral and written, over decades, and those narratives were necessarily reified and reshaped by their retelling, just as Semprún suggests all camp recollection is molded by the constant interplay between the survivor's externalization of memory (in each retelling) and absorption of those narratives that have already been externalized (by others and oneself). Arendt prefers the material witness, the survivor who can tie this particular defendant to the specific crimes for which he has been called to answer.

In his admittedly theatrical performance of witness at the Eichmann trial, Ka-Tzetnik bears witness to an equally valid reality, one that his very presence on the witness stand belies: that Yehiel Dinoor *did not survive*. What survives to testify against Eichmann is only an individual precipitate, a lone specimen of the species here reduced to the pluralized third person, the "they" who "did not live according to the laws of this world of ours, and they did not die," but were called " 'Ka-Tzetnik' number so-and-so."

Ka-Tzetnik's slide into the third person demonstrates in language the reality of the diminished self in the camp experience. At the same time, it suggests a fundamental feature of survival under such conditions—namely, that the line separating life and death for these depersonalized, diminished people was blurry and unpredictable. But how does the author represent this condition in real-life fiction? In the representation of one's own precarity, the author of real-life fiction would seem to face much the same epistemological dilemma as the memoirist or witness: the simple fact that the witness has survived to provide testimony assures the audience of their survival, eliminating the uncertainty and terror at the center of the experience. The visceral sense of precarity might be reduced all the more when the narrative offered by the survivor-author is composed in the first person. Again, we know *paratextually* that the person who wrote these words gets out of the camp, ghetto, or ruin.

In real-life fiction, as with parabiographical texts that foreground the "dual action" (Didi-Hubermann) required for their critical interpretation, the author endeavors to construct a "double focus" (Halbwachs), one that reflects the writer's difficult, often painful "double refusal" (Sandauer) to conform to one potentially falsifying discourse norm or the other, in order to show the reality of how, under these exceptional conditions, "everything doubled in a strange way" (Ginzburg). Consequently, even in a first-person narrative, the author of real-life fiction typically displaces herself from the center of the text's most harrowing episodes, simultaneously representing the author's very real sense of alienation from self and heightening the dramatic action, since the reader does not know whether the figure at the focal point of the recentered narrative will survive.

Refocalization: Bringing Precarity Into Focus for Gustaw Herling-Grudziński and Tadeusz Borowski

Among the ways that parabiography and real-life fiction might deviate from memoiristic convention, none is more vital to their impact on the reader, nor more problematic for our parsing of their historical veracity, than their manipulation of point of view, focalization, and narrative arc. Literary memoirs, of course, can demonstrate some variation in all three areas, but there is only so much leeway before we find ourselves in some kind of genre confusion.

At its core, the memoir is an elaboration of testimony, with which it shares generic parameters. Typically, it is composed in the first person, and we identify this first-person point of view with the real-life author. Furthermore, the narrative is focalized primarily or exclusively on the same first person. That is, while the narrator may draw on hearsay or historical data to fill in gaps in his or her own experience, what the reader encounters within the narrative construct is seen through (or over the shoulder) of the narrator.

This is the sine qua non of testimony: the author, narrator, and focal point of the narrative converge. Or rather, as Philippe Lejeune has established, the "I" of the autobiography "masks . . . the gap that exists between the subject of enunciation and that of utterance"—that is, between the deictic narrative voice and its subject: "We are made to understand that the person we are talking about is 'the same' as the one who is speaking."[76] And as Lejeune suggests, this gap can expand and contract throughout the autobiographical text, narrowing in self-referential reflections, but expanding during narrative.

Even in sustained narrative, however, any investment we may have in an Aristotelian arc, which paratextual signals already instruct us to suppress when reading a witness statement, is generally constrained by the historical sequence of events. In other words, things like consistent dramatic development leading toward crisis and resolution are no more operative in testimony than they are in our own everyday lives. "The dialectic of [autobiographical genres]," Lidiia Ginzburg tells us, "lies in their piquant combination of free expression and constrained invention—constrained, that is, by what actually happened."[77] Indeed, when one reads testimonies and memoirs by survivors of concentration camps and besieged cities, especially by nonprofessional writers—and the volume of these is staggering, this being perhaps the most thoroughly documented period in human history—one finds that their interest is much more historical or psychological than narrative.

Not so with parabiography and real-life fiction, in which we either cannot identify the narrative point of view with the author, or we do so at our peril. Instead of using the "I" to mask the difference between the deictic voice and the "subject of utterance," as happens in memoir, or else establishing an absolute distance between the deictic voice and the subject of utterance, as we find in narrative (whether factual or fictitious), the author blurs the distinction altogether, frustrating the reader's attempt to understand the generic parameters for reading the text. The text is compelling in part because it is simultaneously otherworldly and, somehow, real.

A very simple way of accomplishing this is to filter the author's experience through a third person point of view, an instance of illeism foregrounded in parabiography. A more subtle device frequently encountered in real-life fiction is refocalization. Even when the author has chosen to preserve the first-person point of view, refocalization allows her to be at once within the story and off to its side, effectively mitigating the autobiographical paradox that I described at the beginning of this book. It also helps us account for the moral discomfort often noted by readers of these texts, not in reference to the brutalities committed by textual perpetrators, but in response to their authors' apparent emotional and/or circumstantial distance from the events being described.

An especially powerful example of this is the "Night Hunts" ("Nocne łowy") chapter of Herling-Grudziński's *A World Apart*, the first set within the Yertsevo labor camp proper, where the author also reveals that his main reading during his time in the camp was Dostoevsky's *Notes from the House of the Dead*.[78] This chapter, which serves as an introduction to the topic of violence in camp life, recounts two instances of gang rape to illustrate the inversion of values in the camp: the victim, a young Ukrainian woman, falls in love with the ringleader of the attack, then begs his forgiveness when he allows his fellow inmates to rape her a second time.[79] Throughout this episode, the reader is left to worry over the fate of Marusia, the young woman, upon whom Herling-Grudziński focalizes this portion of the narrative, fostering a heightened sense of drama. What this refocalization does not reveal, however, is the position of the author himself vis-à-vis the events he describes: the first rape, which occurs on a snowy bench outside the barracks, or the second, which takes place in the barracks that Herling-Grudziński shared with the perpetrators. Is the narrator imagining an event and reporting it with the exacting detail of an eyewitness? Is he an eyewitness, one who observes the crimes attentively and reports on them without intervention or judgment? Did the author participate in the rape and reconstruct it in such a way as to obscure his culpability or wish away his shame?

Refocalization not only directs the reader to invest emotionally in third parties whose survival is not guaranteed; it can also cast the author-survivor in an ethically ambiguous light, one where the victim is also a perpetrator, the witness also a participant. The author draws the reader into the "gray zone." Through third parties, we sense the precarity that had been an essential feature of the author's own lived experience, and we also see the bifurcation of world and self that is rendered more explicitly in parabiography. Focalizing on a third person, or, in some instances, having the first-person narrator assume a name that is not the author's own, the writer enacts what Giorgio Agamben calls "heteronymic depersonalization." By reentering, through text, the paradox of witnessing, where those who have been robbed of personhood have everything to say and no way of saying it, the author-survivor reasserts their personhood:

> Testimony appears here as a process that involves at least two subjects: the first, the survivor, who can speak but who has nothing interesting to say; and the second, who "has seen the Gorgon," who "has touched bottom" [quoting Primo Levi], and therefore has much to say but cannot speak.... Testimony takes place where the speechless one makes the speaking one speak and where the one who speaks bears the impossibility of speaking in his own speech, such that the silent and the speaking, the inhuman and the human enter into a zone of indistinction in which it is impossible to establish the position of the subject, to identify the "imagined substance" of the "I" and, along with it, the true witness.[80]

This blurring of the line between survivor and witness, author and character, is part of what makes Tadeusz Borowski's camp stories particularly disturbing, enough so that, in the preface to *The Stone World*, he would feel a need to defend his real-life self against accusations leveled against his textual avatar. Most of Borowski's camp stories are narrated in the first person by a figure who shares his name and the documentable details of his biography, though with modifications that elevate the drama of his narratives. For example, at the end of the title story of *Farewell to Maria* we learn that Maria, Borowski's fiancée, was murdered: "As I later learned, Maria, as an Aryan-Semitic *Mischling*, was taken away with a Jewish transport to an infamous camp on the sea, gassed in a crematorium chamber, and her body no doubt made into soap."[81] The fate of Maria, told in the third person and based on hearsay ("I later learned," "no doubt"), has been held in suspense until the very last sentence, where the first-person narrator's matter-of-fact detachment from the horrors he is conveying, a signature stylistic feature of Borowski's camp stories, elevates the otherness of the "world apart." Borowski has chosen his details to resonate with an initial audience—postwar Poland's war-traumatized readership—that would find in them confirmation of what they had, for the most part, only heard about through news reports, rumors, or other texts. The "infamous camp by the sea" would be Stutthof (Sztutowo), near the Baltic, which was already well-known to Borowski's audience as a site where large numbers of the Polish intelligentsia had been concentrated and liquidated. The notion that Maria's body was "no doubt made into soap" refers to the popular belief that the Nazi occupiers manufactured soap from the fat of civilians who had been murdered in concentration camps, with the effort led by Rudolf Spanner at the Danzig Anatomical Institute.[82] (While there is some evidence that Spanner experimented with making soap from human fat misappropriated from anatomical specimens, there does not appear to have been anything akin to a plan to use concentration camp victims to produce soap on an industrial scale.) Borowski knows that many of his readers have no firsthand experience of the camps, so he exploits their dark imaginings of what might have transpired there to elicit real horror. In order to accomplish this, however, he has to fictionalize. The real Maria Rundo survived the war, and she had been married to the author for nearly half a year at the time he first published the story.

A Fractured Point of View: Jiří Weil

The "Tadeusz" who tells us these stories is only exceptionally their main character. While the author draws us into identifying the deictic voice with his own, he simultaneously distances us from him by focalizing on third parties. This necessarily confounds readerly expectations, leaving the audience to wonder what in the text reflects biographical fact and what arises from an authorial imagination, which is what prompted Borowski to furnish his admonitory preface to *The Stone World*, as a sort of instruction manual for the book's use.

An even more striking instance of genre confusion, however, comes in Jiří Weil's real-life fiction *Life with a Star*, published in 1949. The book's Czech title, *Život s hvězdou*, is ambiguous, insofar as the Czech *život* can also signify "a life"—that is, a biography, a *životopis*, especially of a holy figure. The book's congruencies with the facts of the author's life were already easily discernible, and the genre confusion it provoked then fueled official attacks that followed the author for the rest of his life.

Life with a Star is, like Borowski's stories, narrated in the first person, and it relates many details drawn directly from the author's personal experience in occupied Prague, but here the narrator does *not* share the author's name. Instead, the novel's speaker is called Josef Roubíček, a generic moniker: "Roubíček" is the stock name for the "Everyman" in Jewish jokes told in Czech ("Roubíček meets Kohn," etc.). And the name does come into play as a major plot device, one that also displays Weil's dark humor: as Jews are being summoned for deportation, Josef consoles himself with the notion that there are so many Roubíčeks that it will be some time before the Nazis get to him. It is only at the end of the novel, when the protagonist is finally summoned and decides instead to live completely in hiding, that he burns all his writings and papers, thereby erasing his identity: "It was then, as the stove burned with the last pages of my scribblings, through which the name of Josef Roubíček was to be erased, that I grasped that there was not and would never again be a Josef Roubíček who wanted to evade, dodge, squirm, only in order to avoid freedom."[83]

The freedom he is referring to here is his ultimate embrace of death, of the reality that he can no longer pretend to be living as himself when he is merely hiding in the shadows of the "world apart," the inverse world of the Jew in occupied Prague. This had been Weil's own existence. Having been summoned to join a transport to Theresienstadt in 1942, he avoided it with a marriage of convenience to a non-Jew and, when the Nazis eliminated that exception, faked his own death by jumping from a bridge in February 1945. He spent the rest of the war, like his textual avatar, as a nameless Jew avoiding capture.

Until the end of *Life with a Star*, Roubíček moves through Prague as if in a separate space, a space whose phantasmagoric quality is augmented by arbitrary, seemingly nonsensical conventions, as well as by an increasingly uncanny deictic gesture—namely, that Weil never writes "German," "Nazi," or "Czech," and the word "Jew" appears only once in the entire book, and then only in an insult shouted by a third party. (This echoes an oddity I will discuss later: the fact that in Ernst Lubitsch's classic 1942 comedy *To Be or Not to Be*, the film itself is at pains not to allow the word "Jew" to be spoken, a discretion that becomes increasingly ridiculous as the film refuses to give obvious difference its proper name.) In effect, Weil pushes the reader to experience his Prague as Roubíček sees it, as an absurd storyworld where certain boundaries are over-defined, while others are not defined at all:

> I had particular streets forbidden on different days, I couldn't set foot on some on a Friday, but for others not on a Sunday, on some I had to move quickly and never dawdle, I mixed up the names of the streets

and the days and some of the streets I didn't even know, I imagined that one day I'd chance upon some street that would be called Hermelin [a popular Czech cheese; Roubíček's imagination often turns toward the food he does not have], that a policeman would jump out of nowhere and arrest me, because Hermelin Street is on some new list of forbidden streets that I haven't read yet. I was informed that I am not allowed to go to parks, but I knew that I wouldn't know what's a park and what isn't, there were paths lined with trees that could be taken for gardens but, then again, didn't have to be.[84]

The description of space here is tragicomic: New York City parking rules rendered as a matter of life or death.

Even more bewildering is what Weil does with focalization. Whereas Borowski speaks in the first person while diverting our attention to the third, Weil's avatar speaks in the first person while redirecting us to a third party whom he addresses in the second person. Roubíček has to speak to someone, so he speaks in apostrophe, whether to Růžena, his absent lover from before the war; to Tomáš, a stray cat who sometimes shelters with him in the abandoned, derelict attic where he lives; and, when these two are unavailable, he simply speaks to Death. Roubíček is fully aware that none of these figures can answer him, and he suggests more than once that Růžena, in particular, may be no more than a figment of his imagination: "Růžena could not answer me, she was not in the room, she wasn't with me at all. I didn't know what had happened to her, I hadn't seen her in so long. Maybe she wasn't even in the world, maybe she never even lived."[85] Although Roubíček continues to address Růžena and to talk about her to the reader, he is also at pains to emphasize her fictive nature, or, more accurately, the fact that within the novel's storyworld Růžena is an imaginal projection based on a central figure from Roubíček's own biography: "And I also speak with Růžena, who is a shadow, who maybe was never in the world, it seems I created her out of smoke, vapor, and fragrance as I was tossing and turning all night in my sleeping bag, that she would be the ray of light that penetrates the blackout shades."[86] Růžena, it turns out, is an element of real-life fiction within the real-life fiction that Weil is presenting to us.

These deviations from the point-of-view and focalization conventions of the memoir have a decisive effect on narrative arc. With a conventional memoir or testimony from spaces of open confinement, our primary investment as readers may be historical or psychological, but it is rarely narrative per se. After all, the overwhelming majority of such texts have been composed by nonprofessional writers whose primary investment is documentary, and who are neither interested in cultivating identification and suspense, in "drawing the reader in," nor practiced in doing so. But for Weil, Borowski, or Herling-Grudziński, who had already launched literary careers before the outbreak of the Second World War, the recourse to literary devices is natural in the texts' composition, certainly, but perhaps also in shaping the experiences that those texts represent. For the literary author intent or representing the otherworldly experience of the "world apart," one must confront the very practical problem of how to create suspense when the expressive unity of the retrospective memoir—the "I" that Lejeune tells us unifies the real author, the narrator, and the deictic subject—renders survival a foregone conclusion from the outset. A conventionally autobiographical text that announces itself as the story of how its author survived already projects the narrator's certainty regarding the subject's survival, since the "I" ties the narrator and the subject together.

We might reasonably ask why the same isn't true of a third-person narrative, including a reliable biographical account of someone else's survival. The answer here is the same as for prose fiction narrated in the third person. A number of theorists, notably Seymour Chatman, have observed that what makes a narrative suspenseful is not our ignorance of what will happen; were that the case, we would never experience suspense while reading a text or watching a film for the second or third time, whereas we may feel just as much narrative tension anticipating something that we already know is going to happen. Instead, Chatman argues, the reason we experience suspense is because we have come to empathize with characters whose knowledge is often less than our own.[87] We know what they do not know. Moreover, we know *that* they do not know.

While this principle is most clearly operative in third-person narrative, we can also find hints of it in certain life-writing genres, especially in diaries and notebooks composed in real time during the events they depict. Elena Kochina's diary of the Leningrad blockade, or else Anne Frank's diary written in hiding, can be remarkably suspenseful, if only because we know that the "I" of the diary entry on one day does not know what will happen on the next.[88] Borowski and Weil, like Herling-Grudziński, Shalamov, and others, achieve this in their retrospective accounts of survival by turning our attention to third parties whose fates are not known in advance. This allows them to build narrative suspense by structuring their texts around smaller arcs, what Chatman calls "kernels," shorter instantiations of the Aristotelian "episode."[89]

Taken together, these episodes constitute an elaborate, multipart performance. They convert testimony as to the course of historical events into a spectacle of survival, and they do so using a method that has become so ubiquitous in our contemporary media culture that we easily overlook it altogether. For this deflection of the first-person testimony into a third-person spectacle—an instance of what Franz Stanzel describes as the movement from "figural" to "authorial discourse"[90]—is analogous to what we now call "dramatic reenactment," a staple of news programs, documentary films, and television shows whose sole purpose is to turn survival into a spectacle. "Autobiography, when it is not autobiographical, consists precisely in not saying Me but He, as in fiction," Jean-Luc Nancy writes. "In saying He, one has already modified the personal position of subjectivity. This assemblage of thought under the sign of *eros* is definitely nothing other than exit from oneself and access to the other."[91] Nancy is reflecting, appropriately, on Levinas's writings from the years he spent as a prisoner of war, mostly in the Stalag XI-B camp in western Germany. There, Levinas, not otherwise deeply practiced as an author of fiction, attempted to represent his experience in a novel, eventually abandoned, called *Eros*.

Narrative Distance: Representing Violence Violently

Once again, the terminal paradoxes of the camp spaces are subsumed into the task of representing them. Somehow, the endless monotony of daily life in a concentration camp or city under siege must maintain the reader's interest without misrepresentation. Somehow, the world of open confinement, where the hero is neither confined to a cell, nor able to leave the tightly circumscribed antiworld to which he or she has been assigned, must convey its strangeness without losing the sense that there is no other world than the camp itself. "And though we would go out beyond the great *Postenkette* [camp sentry gate] to the 'real' world," Borowski writes in an anonymous commentary to his story "A Day in Harmenz" ("Dzień na Harmenzach," 1946), "we were still followed by our real 'world'—the camp."[92] Thus the author will often focalize the narrative on a third person, whether remembered, imagined, or composited, in order to assume thoughts, feelings, and impressions that cannot belong to the author's lived experience—at least, not as presented.

The same is true of consequence. In real-life fiction, the sequence of events *means* something within the episodic "kernels" of the narrative, even as the author's survival was never predestined, never "plotted" as a narrative. The actual daily experience of the spaces discussed in this book, as we know from countless testimonies, was misery, discomfort, horror, fear, and abject boredom—and even these were regimented in the extreme. In satisfying the readerly expectation for building action, real-life fiction exploits the discourse norms of fiction to communicate those experiential paradoxes that, though features of real life, cannot simply be told without smoothing out the paradox.

Real-life fiction is not journalism, but what Dwight Macdonald calls, in a useful parallel to parabiography, "parajournalism." Macdonald tells us that parajournalism is marked by its "exploiting the factual authority of journalism and the atmospheric license of fiction," a tradition he traces to Daniel Defoe, "one of the fathers of modern journalism," whose odd place in the literary canon was secured by fiction long assumed to be fact.[93] Defoe is likewise a textual touchstone for the literature of concentration camps, ghettos, and besieged cities; as we will see in our discussion of "horror" toward the end of this book, this literature refers not infrequently to *Robinson Crusoe* (1719), whose first printing didn't even acknowledge that it was anything more than its hero's personal account, and *A Journal of the Plague Year* (1722), which Macdonald praises as "a hoax so convincingly circumstantial that it was long taken for a historical record," though the text's veracity as a "journal" is easily disproven: its author was a young child during London's Great Plague of 1655. Beyond the more proximate model provided by *Notes from the House of the Dead*, Gustaw Herling-Grudziński consciously turns to *A Journal of the Plague Year* as a potent example of how to give readers a visceral experience of the camp.[94]

What these models provide our authors is a path for remaining within the represented experience and outside it, at the center of the storyworld and slightly off-center. Herling-Grudziński describes his turn to Defoe as following a lesson he had already begun to intuit immediately after the war had ended: "The lesson rested on the fact that certain chapters of humanity's 'dark history'—cataclysms, epidemics, exterminations, barbarian conquests, genocides—are performable [*odtwarzalne*] only with the chronicler's maximally impersonal pen."⁹⁵ The word that Herling-Grudziński uses for the text's capacity to represent a "dark history" that has occurred outside of text, *odtwarzalne*, is revealing: the verb *odtwarzyć* refers to the reconstruction of an event or a space based on available facts or scripts, the performance of text on stage, or the playing back of an audio or visual recording. Defoe's "chronicler" *plays back* the horrors of plague-stricken London with a detachment that amplifies their horror, in no small part because it emphasizes the narrator's simultaneous access to the world he depicts and distance from the world (elsewhere, another time) his readers inhabit.

This is why Herling-Grudziński would later single out James Joyce's characterization—that, in Defoe, "the star of poesy is, as they say, conspicuous by its absence"—as the best sentence he had ever read about this text, though with the caveat that "one would have to take it more or less literally: the dead light of the star of poetry consciously pushed aside; the narrative key [is] in the descriptions of cataclysms and plagues."⁹⁶ Here, indeed, is a genre-based explanation for the unsettling matter-of-factness that typifies much real-life fiction. By refocalizing the narrative on third parties and arranging the tableau and dramatic arc of each episode, the text focuses on "descriptions of cataclysms and plagues." The narrative voice of real-life fiction is often closely observant of horror while eerily distant from it.

The result is a text whose reading the reader might experience as violent. The title alone of Borowski's "This Way for the Gas, Ladies and Gentlemen" ("Proszę państwa do gazu," 1947) is enough to shock us with its ironic distance toward what it explicitly promises. But there is similar power in Herling-Grudziński's frightening description of day blindness, or in his difficult and prolonged explanation of the effects of the hunger strike that ultimately resulted in his being released to Władysław Anders's army in 1942. It's in Kosiński's visceral depiction of a man gouging out another man's eye, or in Borowski's chilling comments about removing infants' corpses from a box car. This is a literature that consists of memorable moments, of instances of grotesque and unnerving violence *played back* for the reader in full, often relentless detail by a narrator who barely acknowledges that there is anything out of the ordinary in what we are being exposed to. All testimonials about the experience of concentration camps, ghettos, and besieged cities depict violence, but the authors of real-life fiction insist on making the reader experience those depictions *violently*.

It is because of the visceral experience of violence in reading that some real-life fiction, notably *The Painted Bird* and *House of Dolls*, have been attacked as pornographic or sadistic. This characterization is not incorrect, insofar as these and allied texts coax the reader into experiencing detail within the body, as the quick oscillation between titillation and disgust. And because bodily experience feels immediate and authentic, the textual world to which the representation refers feels immediate and authentic too. Time and again, from Jerzy Kosiński to James Frey, it is the most shocking violence—the eyeball hanging from its socket, the root canal without anesthesia—that seduces us as a mark of authenticity.

Thus, for example, Serge Klarsfeld tells us that "the documentary value of the sketches and paintings of David Olère is exceptional," because "he drew only from his memory and looked only for truth," and that, there being "no photographs of what went on in the interior of the crematories" (an oft-repeated inaccuracy), "only the hands of David Olère reproduce the horrible reality."[97] Olère was one of the few survivors of Birkenau's *Sonderkommando*, the team tasked with moving bodies from the gas chambers to the crematoria.[98] His compositions are highly stylized, and their most impressive elements are those that stylistically differentiate them from other camp illustrations. Olère's portraits of Ilse Koch, for example, rely heavily on caricature (figure 3.6) to depict a figure whom Olère never saw (she was stationed at Buchenwald, not Auschwitz) engaged in the making of lampshades out of prisoners' tattooed skin, a powerful (if likely apocryphal) legend that arose around Koch before her 1947 trial. Even a casually critical consideration of Olère's artwork must acknowledge that, for all their unsettling force, these stark images are neither immediate nor, in the strict sense, evidentiary. Instead, they are figurative representations of their author's experience and memory, more a communication of pain than a documentary of specific acts or events. The viewer experiences that violence viscerally, as the simultaneous attraction to the image and the desire to look away.

It would be a vast oversimplification, however, to suggest that the reason authors of real-life fiction aim to have their audience experience depictions of violence violently is because they want to *seem* authentic, or else to assume that it is the events being depicted, and not the quality of their representation, that is violent. One can read dozens of survivors' firsthand accounts without experiencing the body blow of a short story by Borowski or Shalamov. The orchestration of violence in

Figure 3.6 David Olère, *Elsa (Ilse) Koch and Her Victims*, 1946. Ink wash on paper. Source: Collection of the Yad Vashem Art Museum, Jerusalem, Israel. Gift of Mr. Serge Klarsfeld and Mr. Alexandre Oler, France. Photo © Yad Vashem Art Museum, Jerusalem

real-life fiction is a means to a different, more simulative end. These authors do not merely wish to tell their audience about the violence of the "world apart"; they want them to experience the apartness of their world, its counterfactuality, as real, and for that one must feel violence.

Time and again, those who have passed through the camp or ghetto tell us that the effect of violence therein was epistemological, that it shunted them into a new experience of the real, one built on uncanny inversions, paradoxes, and performances. Subject to torture, Jean Améry tells us, he pitched headlong into a world of fiction: "I accused myself of invented absurd political crimes, and even now I don't know at all how they could have occurred to me, dangling bundle that I was."[99] Herling-Grudziński likewise regards violence as the indispensable initiation into the world of the counterfactual. In *A World Apart*, he writes,

> Tortures are applied in interrogation not for their own sake, but in an auxiliary capacity. The real aim is not to force the accused to sign an invented and fictitious confession, but rather the complete disintegration of his personhood.... One can regard the prisoner as "prepared" for the final act [of signing his confession] only when one can clearly see his personhood breaking down into tiny constituent pieces: among his [mental] associations, gaps appear; thoughts and feelings pop out from their principal bearings.... The machine keeps spinning in its wider rotations, but it no longer works as before: everything that had seemed absurd to the accused just a moment before becomes a likelihood, though it is still not true; feelings change their color; power slowly fades.[100]

Herling-Grudziński portrays a situation in which the violence inflicted on the human organism causes it to work—body and soul—in a different way, much as a machine can be retuned or retooled for a new purpose. In torture, "everything that had seemed absurd to the accused just a moment before becomes a likelihood, though it is still not true." The violence that initiates one into the inverse world of open confinement produces a dual consciousness—the same divided subjectivity that we see in parabiography— that then demands a parallactic reading, Didi-Huberman's "dual action" of being simultaneously credulous and critical. Herling-Grudziński illustrates this duality with memorable episodes that show how essential it is to the experience of the "world apart," as when he describes a dying prisoner's confession that he had murdered Stalin:

> Before [his death], as last rites, he wanted to take upon himself a crime he had not committed, an act he had not performed. For so many long years he did not know why he suffered. Today he wanted to confess, he wanted to lodge himself in the cruel and incomprehensible verdict of his fate, which had been presented for his signature seven years earlier. Guarding himself from an uncertain future, struggling in the snares of the present, he ratified the past that had been imposed on him. So as to save, if only for a moment before his demise, some sense of reality and of the value of his fading existence.[101]

Of course, not only had this man not murdered Stalin, but at this time (1940–1942) Stalin was still very much alive. This is how we know that the violence has done its job, that it has effectively pushed the victim into a counterfactual existence. If I had murdered Stalin, the inverse logic of the "world apart" tells us, they would have cast me into hell. I *am* in hell, so I must have murdered Stalin.

Just as factually verifiable circumstances undergird real-life fiction—these places are real, their violence is real—their fictional elements bleed back into, and might easily be mistaken for, fact. They suggest what K. K. Ruthven calls "substitutional supplements," details that are congruent with established history while also not attested within it, forming the kinds of counterfactual narratives favored by "creative writers" and treated with suspicion by professional historians.[102] Where this assessment falls short vis-à-vis the literature of concentration camps, ghettos, and besieged cities is that the authors of these texts already regard themselves as having been initiated into counterfactuality—an inverse, cruel, theatrical reality running parallel to civilization as they have known it till now, and which continues elsewhere.[103] For the authors of real-life fiction, the goal is not merely to *represent* violence, but to *inflict* it on the reader, to initiate them, simultaneously, into the counterfactual existence of the "world apart."

The Theater of Cruelty (2): Picturing Terezín and Gurs from Inside

The theatricality that we see so frequently as a central feature of open confinement, of being imprisoned in open space, begins with the violent splitting of the world, and of the survivor's experience of the world, into inside and outside, factual and counterfactual. Under such circumstances, existence becomes an elaborate performance, layered with ironies and paradoxes, and the camp or ghetto or besieged city becomes a theater of life and death, sometimes one that contains a literal theater.

The Nazi camp at Theresienstadt (Terezín), northeast of Prague, presents one of the most colorful examples of this theatricality, if also one of the most tragic, given how children were especially used there as props, performers, and victims.[104] In Theresienstadt, theater and plastic arts flourished for a time, fostered by the large population of Jewish artists, composers, and craftsman who had been deported there from Prague and surrounding towns, as well as by the fact that the camp's physical layout, encompassing a former Austro-Hungarian garrison and its adjoining town, made it easier to replicate the appearance of civil society within the confinement of the Nazi concentration camp system.[105] "In spite of the inhuman conditions in Theresienstadt, the cultural life was rich," writes Helga Weissová. "Literary evenings, concerts, theatre performances and lectures were held in the dormitories, in the lofts, and in the courtyards."[106] This simulative function was deliberately conceived. In response to Allied accusations of mass murder, the Nazi regime presented Theresienstadt as a "model" of how Jews were being treated in German-occupied lands. In reality, the vast majority of the more 150,000 persons kept in Theresienstadt died, whether there or following deportation to other camps, particularly Auschwitz. While only 23,000 or so survived Theresienstadt, the "model" was convincing enough that the delegation of the International Committee of the Red Cross that visited the camp in 1944 declared the conditions there to be humane.

One can see why in the few minutes that have survived from *Theresienstadt: A Documentary Film from the Jewish Settlement* (*Theresienstadt: Ein Dokumentarfilm aus dem jüdischen Siedlungsgebiet*, dir. Kurt Gerron and Karel Pečený, 1944), also known as *The Führer Gives the Jews a City* (*Der Führer schenkt den Juden eine Stadt*), a propaganda film shot in Theresienstadt with staged scenes of Jewish life. In its theatricality, its staging of life, *Theresienstadt* echoes *Das Ghetto*, albeit with the meaningful distinction that the footage and staged vignettes shot in Warsaw were intended to show a sharp contrast between Jewish prosperity and poverty, whereas *Theresienstadt* offers a fantasy of universal happiness in the camp—even as the camp's creative energy was real, for a time. What remains of the original film is clearly marked as "Staged Nazi Film," lest the unsuspecting viewer misinterpret its theatricalized version of life for reality, much as the Red Cross delegation did. Several clips of entertainment tend toward uncanny simulation, as the theatrical performance is itself theatricalized to create a substitute reality (figure 3.7).

The duality of the "world apart," which consists in its fundamentally belonging to the social and spatial fabric of modern society and its being simultaneously alienated from it, necessitates the staging of the space as "model." For it is only in reading the model that we—those of us who are forever and fortuitously excluded from the camp or besieged city—can appreciate it as a space. We enter the camp without really entering it; we

Figure 3.7 The performance of a children's musical in the Nazi propaganda film *Theresienstadt* (1944) (00:07:39). *Source*: Kurt Gerron and Karel Pečený, dirs. *Theresienstadt: Ein Dokumentarfilm aus dem jüdischen Siedlungsgebiet* (Berlin: Nazi Schutzstaffel, 1944)

see the camp from above, in a map, diagram, or scale model, and animate its inhabitants and their social interactions by absorbing narrative data, the simulations offered by stories, drawings, and films.

Film is also how we know the North Compound of Stalag Luft III, for example, a POW camp located near what is today the western border of Poland. The camp's remoteness from any major city or tourist site makes its actual physical space that much less familiar than sites like Auschwitz and Birkenau, which receive millions of visitors annually to what is largely a postwar reconstruction. And yet Stalag Luft III, as an imaginal simulation, is deeply embedded in the fabric of popular culture: it is the setting of the 1963 film *The Great Escape* (dir. John Sturges), starring Steve McQueen, which fictionalizes Paul Brickhill's 1950 firsthand account of a daring, mostly unsuccessful attempt to escape the camp through three tunnels. The would-be escapees' fourth tunnel, built as the "successor" to the other three (and therefore left out of the classic film), was situated beneath the "theater," which the prisoners of war had built for themselves, and where they did rehearse and perform actual plays while also using their theater theatrically—that is, as performative cover for yet another escape attempt.

Texts that endeavor to provide a truthful representation of their authors' real-life experiences of the camp—truthful not only in their representation of circumstances, but also in their tracing of experiential paradoxes that defy reduction to dates and locales—often thematize their own theatricality, the sense that they are "staging" tableaux that, in keeping with the behavioral norms and institutional scripts of the camp, are themselves experienced as staged. Thus the title of one of the most exceptional artworks to emerge from the Shoah: Charlotte Salomon's *Life or Theater?*, a numbered sequence of gouache paintings and transparencies that Salomon produced in the eighteen months or so between her release from the Gurs concentration camp, a French-administered camp in the Pyrenees, and her murder in Auschwitz. In that work, concentration camp life is treated only obliquely, not as a special episode in the life of the artist, but as one organically intertwined with a lifetime of suicidality and sexual victimhood (figure 3.8). Gurs appears initially in this sequence as a respite, the openness of her confinement relieving Salomon briefly from being raped by her grandfather, whom she would eventually murder before her own death (figure 3.9). The most explicit camp violence represented in *Life or Theater?* is not that visited upon Charlotte, but her imagining of what was endured by her father in Sachsenhausen (figure 3.10) before Charlotte was sent to live with her grandparents in southern France.

That quasi-fictive violence—*quasi-fictive* because it is simultaneously real and rendered and, in a way that Salomon's thick, smudgy technique emphasizes, general: the experience of countless people, yet of no one person—looks much as we would expect it to look, echoing the kinds of eyewitness sketches that one can find on display today in Sachsenhausen's museum. These representations confront the viewer with the familiarity of their idiom—they partake of a visual iconicity that makes the situation readily accessible despite, if not through, the abstract composition—and they also confront us with our alienation from the experience, with the fact that, for the vast majority of us, what we "recognize" in the representation is the model of what it is *supposed* to look like, a staging that flaunts its own theatricality.

Figure 3.8 Charlotte Salomon, *Life or Theater?*, plate 558, summarizing the entire sequence by declaring its title. *Source*: Joods Cultureel Kwartier, Amsterdam

The Model and Its Double: The Comparative Space of Real-Life Fiction

Such theatricality, though essential to the communication of the camp experience to those who will never know it firsthand, naturally contributes to the persistent anxiety about the authenticity of camp representation and the exceptionalism (or comparativity) of camps, ghettos, and besieged cities. One appropriately dramatic staging of this worry can serve as a model of this consternation. In 1995, two prominent international voices among concentration camp survivors, Elie Wiesel and Jorge Semprún, were

Figure 3.9 Charlotte Salomon, *Life or Theater?*, plate 540. "God, it's so beautiful here." *Source*: Joods Cultureel Kwartier, Amsterdam

invited to Buchenwald for a conversation about the camp experience and its place in our collective memory. Though both had been interned at Buchenwald, their status in the camp had conditioned different experiences. Wiesel, a Romanian Jew, was transferred from Auschwitz with his father to be worked to death; Wiesel's father died there. Semprún, a Spanish Communist, was held as a political prisoner, which afforded him slightly less precarious conditions and a higher likelihood of survival. Already, we cannot begin to discuss this exchange without comparing its participants. Which makes their exchange that much more remarkable:

JORGE SEMPRÚN: I wonder whether, in order to address young people and their curiosity, their need to know, we shouldn't try, instead of going

Figure 3.10 Charlotte Salomon, *Life or Theater?*, plate 430. "Here one works and doesn't laze about." *Source*: Joods Cultureel Kwartier, Amsterdam

back in time fifty years, we shouldn't start with the present. That is to say, take examples from what is going on today, not confuse . . .
ELIE WIESEL: Nor compare. One should never compare.
JORGE SEMPRÚN: Nor compare. We must not fall into the trap of May '68, where they used the slogan "CRS-SS," which is absurd.
ELIE WIESEL: Or talk about Auschwitz in Serbia today.
JORGE SEMPRÚN: Or talk of Auschwitz in Serbia. But still, just one example: Ethnic cleansing permits [us], without making a comparison or amalgam, or trying to say that Auschwitz is already there, because that is . . . it's simply monstrous to say that, to try to comprehend the

totalitarian mechanisms that were at work and which rear their heads again in various places, from time to time. I wonder if it would not be better to go further back—I don't know, it's a question I ask myself—so that the lesson could be more effective. So that commemorations are not simply a ritual of remembrance but a concrete act—political, in the larger sense of the term—for the young people of today.[107]

The exchange stages—dramatizes—the anxiety of comparison, a comparison that Wiesel rejects programmatically, even as doing so apophatically affirms the inevitability of comparison. Leon Wieseltier observes this caveat astutely, writing that "when Elie Wiesel insisted in a refugee camp at the border of Kosovo that the fate of the Jews was different, his presence there suggests that it was also the same."[108] And one could argue that, in seeking each other out and referring repeatedly to one another's work, survivors are already drawing these comparisons themselves, as Bella Brodzki suggests: "If much of Semprún's literary performance is characterized by a kind of defiant pride in his 'fatal singularity'—his existential solitude—it is no less defined by his sense of fraternity and solidarity with other survivors of this massive collective catastrophe, despite differences in their individual experiences."[109]

Since the kind of comparisons I have been discussing occur in literary and artistic representations, where they are always already present (and where the comedic approach, as we will see, foregrounds the ironic distance between the individual experience and its theoretical model) it is essential that we acknowledge that such comparisons are also baked into history on the ground and philosophical reflection from above. "At a great distance in time," Timothy Snyder points out in *Bloodlands*, "we can choose to compare the Nazi and Soviet systems, or not. The hundreds of millions of Europeans who were touched by both regimes did not have this luxury.... These Europeans, who inhabited the crucial part of Europe at the crucial time, were condemned to compare."[110] Similarly, Jeffrey Veidlinger demonstrates in his recent work how Jewish communities in Eastern Europe regarded the systematic violence perpetrated against them over decades by different actors, whether Cossacks, Nazis, Bolsheviks, or Ukrainian nationalists, not as discrete waves of injustice, but as an ongoing, continuous, and communal experience.[111]

This continuity is readily discernible in literary and cinematic representations, for those who are willing to see it. As one illustration, I would

Figure 3.11 Rozalie Lautmannová (Ida Kamińska) understands the roundup of Jews in her small Slovak town as a "pogrom" in *The Shop on Main Street* (01:54:18). Source: *The Shop on Main Street*, dir. Ján Kadár and Elmar Klos (Prague: Barrandov Studios, 1965)

point to the dramatic moment near the end of the Academy Award–winning tragicomedy *The Shop on Main Street* (*Obchod na korze*, dir. Ján Kadár and Elmar Klos, 1965), where we see the elderly Rosalie Lautmannová, played by Ida Kamińska, trying to understand why she would be required to join her fellow Jews gathered on the town square for deportation to concentration camps. Though the film was made over two decades after the events it depicts, Lautmannová's realization that she was about to be swept up in a "pogrom" (figure 3.11) clearly reflects the lived experience of the artists: Kamińska, a Polish Jew and legend of the Yiddish theater in Warsaw, had spent the war being shuttled repeatedly around the Soviet Union; Ján Kadár, the codirector, was a Slovak Jew who spent most of the war in a labor camp; and Ladislav Grosman, the author of both the Slovak-language screenplay and the Czech-language text upon which it is based, was a Slovak Jew who spent the war as a forced laborer and, following the events depicted on the margins of the film, in hiding. For these survivors, open confinement is always and necessarily a space of comparison, one where individual subjectivity was subordinated to a shared circumstance. Thus Hannah Arendt suggests that suicide was much more commonly chosen by people *before* they entered the camp than when they were in the camp, because, she says, it was considered inappropriate to assert the individuality of your fate after that fate had become collectivized.[112] And she says this not in, say, *Origins of Totalitarianism*, but rather in her notes on her own, brief time in a camp, which happened also to be in Gurs, alongside Charlotte Salomon. Kosiński would reach a similar conclusion in his turning to fiction in *The Painted Bird:* "Autobiography emphasizes a single life: the reader is invited to become the observer of another man's existence and encouraged to compare his own life to the subject's. A fictional life, on the other hand, forces the reader to contribute: he does not simply compare; he actually enters into a fictional role, expanding it in terms of his own experience, his own creative and imaginative powers."[113]

The movement from particularity to model is fraught because it invites precisely the kinds of additional meanings and associations that people like Wiesel find troubling. On the one hand, one might argue that being a Jew in a Nazi concentration camp differed fundamentally from being a *zek* in the Soviet Gulag, since the Soviet camp was at least nominally a "correctional" institution, projecting the assumption that the inmate could be reformed, whereas the Jew's condemnation to eradication is as irrevocable as the racial designation that serves as its basis.[114] On the other hand, comparisons between the Nazi and Soviet camps are part of the texts' genesis. Writing of Buchenwald, Semprún thinks of Solzhenitsyn and Herling-Grudziński in Soviet camps. Editing the first edition of Shalamov's *Kolyma Tales* (*Kolymskie rasskazy*, 1978, published in London "without the author's knowledge and consent"), Mikhail Geller turns to Borowski's stories from Auschwitz, calling the two authors "unanimous" in their representations.[115] Semprún's allusions to *A World Apart* then compel Herling-Grudziński to reaffirm the appropriateness of Geller's comparison.[116]

From Model Camp to Camp Model

Even if the author-survivors might be making these comparisons themselves, both in their lived experience and while grappling with how to represent it, how do we understand the more distant comparisons that

Figure 3.12 Zbigniew Libera, *Lego Concentration Camp*, 1996 (detail). *Source*: *Zbigniew Libera: Work from 1984–2004* (Ann Arbor: University of Michigan School of Art and Design and Center for Russian and East European Studies, 2005)

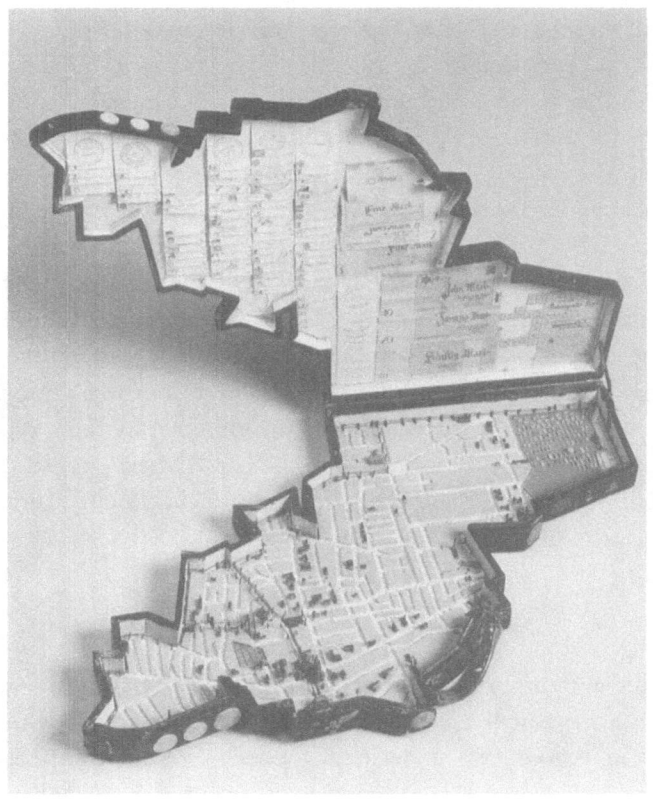

Figure 3.13 Leon Jacobson, *Scale Model of the Łódź Ghetto*. *Source*: United States Holocaust Memorial Museum

encountering a model inevitably generates? How do we go from the reality of, say, Stalag Luft III to the film *The Great Escape*? Or from the concentration camp as such (already a comparative placeholder, "Auschwitz" as metonym) to contemporary artworks that sometimes shock or offend with their irony, as we see in Zbigniew Libera's Lego concentration camps (figure 3.12)? Why might we find these challenging in a way that, say, Leon Jacobson's scale model of the Łódź Ghetto (figure 3.13), produced *within* the ghetto, is not?

A major reason for the anxiety, I believe, is that representations that theatricalize their own representation do exactly what Semprún argues they *should* do—that is, they connect the past explicitly with the present, which necessarily disrupts the judgment of that past by reestablishing its continuity with the now. When one visits the United States Holocaust Memorial and Museum in Washington, DC, one sees Leon Jacobson's scale model of the Łódź Ghetto as a referential artifact: it informs us of a particular place and time that is far from Washington, far from today. The same can be said of the scale model of the Auschwitz Crematorium II in the same

Figure 3.14 Scale model of Buchenwald concentration camp with the largely empty camp terrain in the background. *Source*: photograph by the author

museum, or of the scale model of the Warsaw Ghetto at the Mémorial de la Shoah in Paris. These are informative, three-dimensional texts.

But viewing them is very different when they are located at the site to which they refer. The scale model of Buchenwald *at* Buchenwald is uncanny: it represents the space right outside the window, which looks nothing at all like the model (figure 3.14). The same is true at Dachau. Or Treblinka. If you go to Stalag Luft III, you'll find a very similar scale model, one that looks nothing like the site, but that does look very much like the space where Steve McQueen mouths off to his Nazi captors in *The Great Escape*. That's because the scale model at the site's museum is not of the entire camp: it is actually the model that was constructed for the filming of *The Great Escape*. The model in situ confronts us viscerally with the ironic distance between reality and representation and demands a comparison between them.

Recognizing this distance is, I argue, ethically necessary. First, it means acknowledging that there is no privileged position outside of the discourse from which one could say that we can (or cannot) compare the experience of, say, the Nazi concentration camp at Sachsenhausen with that of the Soviet NKVD Special Camp Number 7. For one thing, they were the same site: as in several other instances, the Soviet security apparatus was not going to waste a perfectly good concentration camp.

CHAPTER IV

Comedy

It isn't a fact. It actually happened.
—IL'IA SEL'VINSKII, QUOTED BY LEV RAZGON[1]

On a bright Sunday afternoon in June, while visiting the kinds of sites I discuss in this book—or, rather, while visiting the spaces where these sites once stood—I overheard a conversation between a Polish father and his young son. They were taking a break from mountain biking through the Kraków city park that had formerly been Konzentrationslager Płaszów, which is most familiar as the setting for much of what is depicted in *Schindler's List*. Standing in the shadow of the main camp monument (figure 4.1), the boy, perhaps six or seven years old and visibly straining to parse the signage, asked his father, "Hitler had a camp here?"

"He did," the father replied solemnly. My contemporaneous notes record a contemplative pause.

"Was Hitler his first name?" the boy asked.

"No," his father explained patiently, "it's a last name. His first name was Adolf."

Now there was a much longer pause. The boy was struggling to understand. Finally, he came upon the question that would clarify everything.

"Did he have a tent?"[2]

The boy's father seemed very much aware of my presence as a foreigner, albeit not in the sense that my appearance or demeanor would suggest that I am not Polish. What made me a foreigner in that immediate context was that I treated the park not as a park, but as an important historical site.

Figure 4.1 View of the main monument To the Martyrs Murdered by Hitler's Agents of Genocide, 1943–1945, Płaszów concentration camp, Kraków, Poland. *Source*: photograph by the author

Everyone else was using the space as generations before them had, strolling, cycling, pushing a stroller, setting out a picnic. As is frequently the case with former concentration camps and ghettos, the needs of living generations overwrite the sufferings of the past, sometimes completing the efforts of perpetrators to obliterate the physical infrastructure of mass murder.[3] The father reacted with a sharp, flustered "No!!!" and ushered his child back onto his bike.

I quickly turned away upon hearing the exchange between father and son, both to hide the impropriety of my eavesdropping and the potentially greater impropriety of my own stifled laughter. The boy's confusion, however, was funny. His father's reaction was funny. Funny, too, is the sense of mismatch between subject and affect, that life and death in a concentration camp *cannot* be treated with humor, that the very notion of a comedic representation of the "world apart" is taboo.[4]

Here is yet another paradox within the representative norms that shape our image of the camp, ghetto, or besieged city. As we have seen throughout this study, the writers of real-life fictions based on their experience of these spaces—individuals who were very often literary authors before their violent initiation into the "world apart"—were acutely sensitive to the layered ironies of their circumstances, from the dark theatricality of camp life to its strange inversion of everyday norms. They knew some of the extensive body of one-liners and narrative jokes ("anecdotes") that circulated among the confined or hunted, and that can be illuminating as critiques of both the camp as an institution of culture and of the social differences that are by turns reified and exploded whenever people from different countries, backgrounds, and walks of life are trapped in the same space.[5] "How do you describe the ideal Hitlerite?" asks a famous prewar joke that later circulated widely in Nazi concentration camps, especially among Poles in Auschwitz: "blond like Hitler, slim like Göring, solid like Goebbels, manly like Röhm, and he should be named . . . Rosenberg." Another one, which circulated among Jews in the Warsaw Ghetto, again trivializes the differences between the German occupiers and the people they were hunting. It said that the way to get caught outside the ghetto was to be wearing a moustache and high boots and carrying a *Kennkarte.* Whereas you can easily walk around "looking like a whole synagogue." The police would never suspect!

It is telling that both jokes, and a great many more from the same diffuse corpus, play on appearances, theatricality, and "looking the part." But it is the *structure* of situational humor that will interest us in texts by those who have reshaped their real-life experiences and circumstances using literary techniques, especially in representations of the Nazi camp, where, according to a German character in Ernst Lubitsch's 1942 comedy *To Be or Not to Be*, "We do the concentrating, and the Poles do the camping." (*Poles*, not Jews. More on that momentarily.)

The phrase "concentration camp comedy" may strike many of us as counterintuitive, confusing, or even distasteful, a violation of the sanctity that surrounds traumatic narratives in general and the subject of the Shoah most insistently. Attempts to represent the concentration camp experience in comedy for a popular audience have yielded controversial results, from Roberto Benigni's 1997 film *Life Is Beautiful* (*La vita è bella*), which received the Academy Award for Best Foreign Film despite widespread derision for its sentimentalism and, for some, insensitivity, to the universally panned 1999 film *Jakob the Liar* (itself a remake of an East German film based on Jurek Becker's 1969 novel). In these instances, the criticism of sentimentality does not take into account whether the authors have a personal connection to the stories they are telling. Benigni's film is the purely fictional narrative of an Italian Jew who manages to convince his son that their fraught journey through a ghetto and concentration camp is an elaborate game, whereas Becker's tale, about a Jew in the Łódź Ghetto who regales his neighbors with dispatches heard over a radio he does not have, reflects Becker's firsthand knowledge of the Łódź Ghetto, Ravensbrück, and Sachsenhausen. Other concentration camp comedies, like the 1972 Jerry Lewis project *The Day the Clown Cried*, which Lewis wrote, directed, starred in, and then shelved, have become emblems of poor taste despite never having reached audiences. Lewis's film, which survives only as a partial rough print *sans* soundtrack, was embargoed from public screening until 2024.

Artists' palpable discomfort with using comedy to represent the experience of oppression and precarity goes back to the war itself. Consider, again, Lubitsch's *To Be or Not to Be*, starring Jack Benny and Carol Lombard as actors trying to survive the Nazi occupation in their Warsaw theater. Although a major plot point involves Greenberg, a Jewish member of the acting company who is hiding among them, and who provides frequent comic relief based on his ethnic difference, the film scrupulously, one might say acrobatically, avoids mentioning the words "Jew" or "Jewish." For the contemporary viewer, part of the comedy stems from the contortions the characters then must perform in order to avoid stating what, to us, is obvious.

Situational Comedy in a Tragic Situation

Such glaring avoidances and lacunae are especially ironic in the context of postwar popular media, insofar as the predominant format for comedy in the television era—the situation comedy—may meet its real-life apotheosis in the concentration camp, ghetto, or besieged city. These spaces of open confinement accommodate the sitcom's simple structure exceedingly well: a number of individuals with highly disparate temperaments and backgrounds are thrust together by a situation that is very often beyond their control. As a rule, the sitcom has no plot and little or no narrative progress. Nothing is effectively represented in this representation beyond the purely formal arrangement of contrasts offered by the characters themselves, contrasts that generate the humor that is, for the audience, the genre's only draw.

But we need not speculate. One of the most successful sitcoms in television history, *Hogan's Heroes*, was indeed set in a Nazi prisoner of war camp, where inmates of various nationalities, each of whom played up different American stereotypes of the foreign Other, had to band together to undermine their German jailors. When this show, which originally ran from 1965 to 1971, enjoyed a second life on German television in the 1990s, not only were direct references to Nazism omitted from the dialogue, but an extremely popular reissue of the series redubbed the German characters with thick regional accents so that they, too, could be fully integrated into the economy of ethnic ridicule. All of the principal German characters on the show, incidentally, were played by Jewish actors, some of whom had been refugees. Several members of the cast were concentration camp survivors in real life.

If the very notion of "concentration camp comedy" strikes us as incongruous to the point of taboo, it is not because there was no comedy in the camps and ghettos, or because those who survived these experiences did not regard them through a comedic or ironizing frame, as several of the texts I have just mentioned attest.[6] The reason lies instead in the critical clichés most frequently employed in rejecting these representations: that they "trivialize" the experience, that they are "distasteful" approaches to deep trauma.

In other words, they violate the *model* of the camp—the preconception of what a camp is supposed to look like, what it's supposed to feel like—and the model of the prisoner as a suffering body and spiritual martyr. And there is something still more unsettling here: comedy, ironic play that exposes the structure of the representation, challenges the audience's need for authenticity, for reassurances that the authentic emotional response had been rooted in authentic, *real* occurrences. Comedy makes a show of the show, it performs its magic only to show us the trick behind the trick. No wonder many will find it disillusioning: it is self-consciously designed to expose illusion, which consists in the ironizing superimposition of the collective over the individual, the general over the particular. That ultimately, is what we mean when we object that a text "trivializes" the Shoah or the Gulag or the ghetto. We are saying that it takes a specific tragedy and turns it into a generic situation, a space of adventure.

Here, however, we must draw a sharp distinction between frivolously generalizing a situation and theorizing it, as is overtly the case when real-life fiction collides with comedy. In theorizing the experience of open confinement, these texts offer a meticulously ironized "world apart," a stripping bare of its nihilistic machinery. They extrapolate the irreducible individual experience into the space of comparison. This is the stuff of art and literature, certainly, but it also reflects how historical particularity enters circulation in broader cultural discourse. It is how Nazi sites of imprisonment, torture, and extrajudicial execution—over forty-three thousand of them across occupied Europe—come to be known metonymically as "Auschwitz," eliding not only the distinctions between different camps, but also the different Auschwitzes—its main constituent camps and factories—and its many subcamps. The same metonymic operation obtains in the Gulag, which consisted of over four hundred camps spread over thousands of miles. In the movement from particular experience to model, however, there is the persistent anxiety that the unique individual trauma is also elided.

These examples point again to the simulative quality of camp representation, which, as representation, must be understood broadly, generically, encompassing texts that are not set strictly in a camp, but instead in a besieged city, or even in an occupied city where the protagonists live in hiding and are therefore cut off from the institutions and social norms that had defined their behaviors before their initiation into a new, alternative, precarious "world apart." In that reality—in the camp, in the besieged or occupied city—the characters perform elaborate simulations of the lives they had known before, often nesting performances in increasingly elaborate, delicate layers of irony. For example, several imprisoned actors might cope with the unbearable intersection of terror and boredom in the camp by creating a small theater, simulating the very site they have been deprived of within the site of their deprivation, and the play they perform in that small theater would then simulate yet another stratum of the simulation. Each layer ironizes the others: a ghetto café with nothing to serve its patrons is an ironizing simulation of an actual café, and the cabaret performance in the ghetto café alerts those patrons to the performance they are also providing themselves and each other.

This construct can repeat itself through an indefinite number of representational layers; one can easily imagine, and in fact we have specimens of, the camp play within a play, and so on. Having entered a storyworld that is a warped inversion of the world of everyday experience, it is unsurprising to find, both in the historical record and in literary representation, a Dantesque descent through worlds within worlds. And while this movement can easily precipitate tragedy—the literature is rife with instances in which the failure to recognize the camp as real life guarantees that the victim will never leave it—it also lays the groundwork for treating the camp as a setting for comedy in a neoclassical vein: the circumstances already impose a classical unity of space, time, and action, and the reader's privileged position, his or her surfeit of historical knowledge relative to what is known by the characters in the text, is mirrored back to us by characters who themselves know more than their companions. This is obvious even in the examples I opened with: *To Be or Not to Be* is set in a theater where the performers pull their captors into the performance; both *Life Is Beautiful*, based loosely on the writings of camp survivor Rubino Romeo Salmonì, and *Jakob the Liar*, inspired by Jurek Becker's ghetto experience, focus on protagonists who create elaborate performances to help their fellows accommodate the new reality they have entered.

First as Tragedy, Then as Farce: Ladislav Grosman

For some, the incongruity of life inside and outside the camp, between the past and a present without future, would be too much to bear without such an accommodation. Even the initiation into the "world apart" of the camp, the ghetto, the life in hiding, is frequently presented as an admission into the theater. For example, early in his autobiographical novel *Lucky as Hell* (*Z pekla štěstí*, literally "from the hell of good fortune," written in the late 1970s and published posthumously in 1994), Ladislav Grosman's child protagonist, Robert, often compares his own movements from hideout to hideout, caretaker to caretaker, and eventually into a ghetto, to watching a play or a film. A typical instance is when Robert describes watching through a glass door while arrangements are being made for his safety as being like "in a theater of the mute, since everyone was talking with their hands and mouthing, and you couldn't hear them."[7] As he is preparing to be smuggled from Slovakia into Hungary, even the circumstance of the child in hiding becomes a lovely joke about the opacity of Jewish ways as seen by non-Jews: "I told [my friend] Jožko Naščák through the window that he should be sorry he's not a Jew, because if he were we could now be having a magnificent adventure together, though I didn't mention the rabbi's wife, who was sneaking me over the border. Jožko said he knows all about it anyway, even if we hush it up, yeah, you hush everything up, he said, because you're Jews, and you turn everything into secrets."[8] Robert is an adolescent naïf with an insatiable thirst (or lust) for knowledge of the world, which he has acquired through the only means available to him: seemingly unrestricted, uncontextualized access to trashy romance novels. And because the overblown adventures he knows from these bodice rippers resonate readily with the dangers and intrigues to which he is now a party, Robert sees everything that is happening to him through their lens.

Grosman, a Slovak Jew who eventually came to write primarily in Czech, had spent much of the war in hiding, much like his young hero, eventually winning fame as a novelist and screenwriter. He is best known for his novel and screenplay for the 1965 film *The Shop on Main Street*, which similarly takes a comedic, albeit ultimately tragic, approach to the Shoah in a small Slovak town, generating humor from the persistent miscommunication between a bumbling Slovak laborer and the elderly Jewish woman whose sewing shop he has been assigned to Aryanize. Here, at the beginning of Grosman's brief literary career, the humor is much as it will be at the end, in *Lucky as Hell*, consisting not in one-liners, but in situational set pieces that expose the ridiculousness of ethnic tribalism among those who ultimately find themselves in the same boat. The effect is particularly powerful when it plays with the absurdity of *intra*-ethnic differences, as when, in a flashback in *Lucky as Hell*, Robert's mother complains that his father has brought a professor from Hamburg and his two sons home for lunch. Robert's family doesn't have anything to eat as it is, and they are much too diminished to host others. Not to worry, Robert's father assures his mother, because the professor and his sons are even poorer. Robert's family are unwanted in Slovakia, but the professor and his sons are refugees, unwanted in Slovakia *and* Germany. And the professor "is a vegetarian anyway, I mean, just give him a bit of carrot and he'll eat that."[9]

One may wonder whether such humor, in this case about real starvation, could enjoy popular appeal in English. Not only does the idea of a Holocaust comedy run against the grain of our historical consciousness, as several critics and scholars pointed out after the release of Benigni's film, but the differences that form the joke's basis are largely illegible within that consciousness. As a rule, popular representations of Jewish suffering in Nazi-occupied Europe homogenize Jews into a monolithic ethnic collective—Jews, or even "the Jew," as distinct from non-Jews—whereas the social spaces of concentration camps and ghettos were defined by their forced mixing of languages, mutually unintelligible or derided dialects, social and professional classes, origins, religious practices, and perhaps most notably political leanings: in a great many of the jokes told in concentration camps political ideology, and not race, is the primary identity marker. These differences are compounded by the presence of other ethnicities and nationalities, each having their own internal distinctions and tensions; thus the ethnographic attention that is a staple of camp narrative. When one filters that data through a naive narrator, as Grosman does, encountering every difference as a bizarre curiosity, the effect is likely to be humorous.

The Comedy of Difference: The Animal Fables of Horst Rosenthal and Jiří Robert Pick

The practice of exploiting the comic potential of ethnic differences in representing the camp experience goes back to the camps themselves. Sander Gilman has identified Jurek Becker's 1968 novel *Jakob der Lügner*, the basis of the two *Jakob the Liar* films, as "the first novel since 1945 to represent the Shoah in a comic vein or, at least, not to rely on pathos as a way of understanding those murdered in the Shoah."[10] But this is inaccurate. In addition to the many hand-drawn caricatures produced and circulated in the camps—much of the ethnic humor in the camps was visual, as one might expect in such a densely multilingual environment—there were also longer narratives composed in illustrated panels. Notable among these are the three short books made by Horst Rosenthal, a Breslau Jew, during his time in the French-administered Gurs internment camp, in the Pyrenees. The first, and best known, *Mickey in Gurs* (*Mickey au camp de Gurs*, 1942; "Published without Walt Disney's Authorization," the handwritten lettering on the cover declares), follows a skillfully rendered Mickey Mouse (figure 4.2) as he wanders among the heartless gendarmes, mechanical bureaucrats, and emaciated inmates of the Gurs camp, all the while trying to understand their bizarre ways.[11] Like his author, this Mickey is constantly being asked his nationality and insists that he has none: he's "international"—and is therefore accused of being a communist! Rosenthal's second two compositions, meanwhile, aim sharper satirical barbs at the brutality of camp life: they are presented as tourist brochures explaining how one might approach a visit to Gurs. "But do not assume that we are losing our grip," he writes at the end of *A Brief Guide to the Gurs Camp* (*Petit guide à travers le camp de Gurs*, 1942). "Far from it! We even have a

Figure 4.2 Horst Rosenthal, *Mickey au camp de Gurs*, 1942, featuring a drawing of Mickey Mouse reacting to a photographic postcard of the camp. *Source*: public domain

permanent theater company whose Director is named Nathan. He's been presenting the same program for a year and a half. He only changes the titles. He shows the French in the camp what true Parisian spirit is. It's, well . . . As one says in German: *Schall und . . . Rauch!*"[12] Theatricality again: the pièce de résistance of Rosenthal's tour of Gurs is a theater (figure 4.3)—or rather a theater of a theater; there are no plays, only the one performance with changing titles—where a Jew, "Nathan," tells the French what it means to be Parisian.[13] Theater is presented as the means for remaining cultured, not "losing our grip," where the French verb *s'embêter*, "to get bored," contains the antithesis of culture, *bête*—"beast," "animal," the former human stripped of civilization and reduced to bare life in the camp—though one can retain a grip on humanity only through illusion, summed up in the name of Max Reinhardt's Berlin cabaret, "Sound and Smoke." Delayed by an ellipsis, the word "smoke" in Rosenthal's text carries a much more ominous suggestion.

Unlike his Mickey Mouse, who doesn't like Gurs and eventually has himself erased from the page, Rosenthal did not survive; he was murdered in Auschwitz shortly after producing these texts. But Rosenthal was not alone in reimagining life in the camps, and the events of the war more generally, through anthropomorphized animals. The use of animal imagery in ethnic satire is self-evident and so deeply rooted in Western art as to be a cliché. Art Spiegelman's *Maus* also famously observes this scheme, drawing several of its animal-ethnic equivalences directly from Nazi

Figure 4.3 Horst Rosenthal, *Petit guide à travers le camp de Gurs*, 1942. *Source*: public domain

propaganda, to both comic and tragic effect. The practice was already widely visible, however, in 1944, in Edmond-François Calvo's *The Beast Is Dead!* (*La bête est morte!*, started in 1942), a substantial, two-volume graphic history of Nazi brutality in France drawn as an assault of German wolves, supported by industrialist pigs and propogandist weasels, against peaceful French rodents.[14]

The animal fable also makes its way into literary fiction about the camp, again to comedic ends, notably in *The Society for the Protection of Animals: A Humorous Novella from the Ghetto, Insofar as That Is Possible* (*Spolek pro ochranu zvířat: Humoristická—pokud je to možné—novela z ghetta*), written in the late 1960s by the Prague satirist and playwright Jiří Robert Pick. As a teenager Pick had lived in Theresienstadt with his parents; his father was sent onward to Auschwitz, where he died. In *The Society for the Protection of Animals*, Pick uses details and experiences from his own life to compose the first-person account of Tony, a boy who, hearing about the existence of societies for the prevention of cruelty to animals in the outside world, resolves to establish one in the camp. The only problem is that there are no animals in the camp, and when a prolonged search wins Tony a single mouse, which he names Helga, he has to protect her from circumstances that are in fact much more menacing to the boy than to his pet. Told, again, from a naive perspective, the book is densely packed with jokes that expose how the distinctions that people live by in the outside world—the differences between Jews and Germans, rich and poor, communist and capitalist, animal and man—undergo various instances of reductio ad absurdum within the camp:

> "When it is ze resting time," Mr. Kurt Brisch said, "zer should be no dying. Ze dying iz for betveen ten und noon. Zese are ze visiting hours."
>
> Even though he said this ironically, it didn't strike the men as so strange. So many illogical orders had been issued in the ghetto. For example, Mr. Löwy claimed, it wasn't long ago that the commandant's office gave the order that no non-Aryan could walk his dog along the embankment in the ghetto. And that despite the fact that, first, Jews were not allowed to have a dog; second, Jews were not allowed to walk along the embankment; third, all Jews were required to do labor, and even if they could walk along the embankment and had a dog they wouldn't have time to; fourth, no Jew, even if he did have the time, could walk his dog there, since he had enough trouble keeping himself on Jewish rations, let alone keeping a dog; and, fifth, there was no embankment in the ghetto. (There was no river.) So why would the men be surprised if they were to give the order that in the ghetto one had to die between ten o'clock and noon?[15]

The humor here is symptomatic. The German Jew's difference is marked by his cartoonish accent and ungrammatical Czech. The difference between the Jew and the non-Jew is marked by the latter's need to impose ridiculous and humiliating restrictions on the former. (These jokes often touch upon death, as when Tony's friend Ernie is shot trying to escape, and the men are about to bury the body: "There it is, that stupid German logic of theirs. Die in peace and quiet, they burn you in the crematorium. But if you get up to something, they give you a proper burial.")[16] Most importantly, the joke follows a standard pattern of one-upmanship that, in an inflection that is especially common in Jewish humor, inverts the expected hierarchy of value, so that the point that would render all the others irrelevant is assigned the least significance, almost as an afterthought: that there is no river in the ghetto, or that the family has no food for themselves, let alone for guests.

Most of the secondary literature on humor in the camps focuses on its function as a psychological coping mechanism. While there is no reason to dispute this claim—When is humor *not* a coping mechanism, if not for assimilating a specific circumstance, then for assimilating reality itself?—we may be misled by assuming that these textual representations simply attempt to rebel against tyrannical authority through a carnivalesque inversion of hierarchies, a strategy that, as theorists from Bakhtin to Foucault to Agamben have repeatedly demonstrated, ultimately reasserts the very hierarchies it seems to subvert. What the comedies I have mentioned do instead is to expose the arbitrariness, pettiness, and ridiculousness of social hierarchy as such, to reveal it as roles created to serve the performance rather than the performers—a cruel performance that is always the same, even if the titles keep changing.

The Tain of the Mirror: Representing the Limits of Representation in *Undzere Kinder*

The simulative nature of camp representation, as I have argued throughout this study, always implies an ironic distance, an authorial oscillation between life in the precarious space as experienced from within and the self-reflection required to represent that space from an outside—beyond the camp, after the war—that had been invisible and, at times, perilous to imagine as the experience unfolded. Just as the representation clearly forms a commentary on the lived praxis, the praxis places constant pressure on the possibility of its representation, resisting and delimiting it while also anticipating and demanding it. In this way, the same ironic space that shapes the tragic in parabiographical narratives and fictionalizations also anticipates the comic in texts like those by Grosman and Pick. One could even argue that comedic representation of the concentration camp or life under siege—whether collective, as in the city under bombardment, or individual, as in the Robinsonade of evading pursuers in the ruins of civilization—is of necessity parabiographical, since it requires the author to examine his own lived experiences from an ironic distance. This is certainly the case with *Lucky as Hell* and *The Society for the Protection of Animals*, which reflect the lived experiences of Grosman and Pick, respectively, but through protagonists whose vulnerability is signaled by their being younger than the authors had been when they entered the camp (Pick) or hiding (Grosman), with the authors' personal tragedies—the murder of Pick's father in Auschwitz, for example—omitted from the textual representation. Grosman's parents and three of his siblings were killed in the German attack on Ružomberok during the Slovak National Uprising in 1944, which precipitated the mass roundup, deportation, and execution of Jews that forms the situational backdrop of *Lucky as Hell,* though not its content.

If ironic distance is the sine qua non for a comedic representation of tragic experience, the thematic preoccupation with performativity and theatricality is its natural consequence. As we have seen from the very beginning, theatricality is deeply embedded across literature that represents real-life experiences of life in extremis, or that even purports to be, since a fraudulent text perpetrates its deception by assiduously observing received scripts for what such a representation is *supposed* to look like. Parabiography and real-life fiction, meanwhile, beginning with the pivotal theater scene that closes part 1 of Dostoevsky's urtext *Notes from the House of the Dead,* repeatedly draw our attention to instances of theatricality within the camp or besieged city, generally to represent the uncanny simulation of those social forms that the conditions of interment or siege have rendered impossible or absurd, and often underscoring the danger of confusing the "world apart" with the world as such.

As the ironic distance expands, however, we move from representations of how performance operates within, and is integral to, the experience of open confinement, to the metanarrative reflection on representation, on how best to perform the experience after the fact, particularly for an audience that may not have its own living memory to resonate with the narrative, without leveling its inherent paradoxes into a recitation of unconflicted facts. Grosman and Pick, like Jurek Becker in *Jakob the Liar,* make the performance of a received or wished-for counterfactuality the central theme of their comic representations. They accomplish this by exploiting the inferiority of the hero vis-à-vis the audience, insofar as the audience enjoys a far more expansive historical awareness of the events surrounding the protagonist than the hero can access. We know what the hero does not, which allows us to delight in the disjuncture between what the characters perceive from their limited purview and what we see from our broader historical perspective. In *Jakob the Liar,* in fact, this inequality is a key feature of the narrative: Jakob's knowledge of circumstances is superior to that of his own audience in the Łódź Ghetto, and our knowledge is superior to his. In true Aristotelian fashion, the inequality that elevates the tragic dimension when the author focuses on a third person whose fate is unknown to us just as effectively amplifies the comic when we know much more than the naive or ignorant character.[17] We ourselves are not deceived, but we enjoy watching others being deceived—so long as the stakes are not too high.

It should come as no surprise, then, that the first film comedy about survival in spaces of open confinement, *Our Children* (*Undzere kinder*, 1948), can be more accurately characterized as a film about the question of whether a truthful representation of such experiences, let alone one that relies heavily on comedy, is even possible. The last Yiddish-language feature film to be made in Poland, *Our Children* stars Shimon Dzigan and Israel Shumacher, the most famous comic duo in the Yiddish theater of interwar Poland and, later, in Israel. They play themselves. The film opens with documentary footage of Nazi oppression during the war and of the film's own cast and crew after the war has ended standing before Natan Rapoport's Monument to the Heroes of the Warsaw Ghetto. This use of documentary footage to ground the fictional narrative in a concrete historical reality is typical in both comedy and horror films about the "world apart." The opening credits then accompany the eponymous children, all Jewish orphans who have survived the war, as they take a horse-drawn carriage from the countryside into Łódź, where they see a poster advertising a matinee performance by the celebrated actors. After needling the orphanage's director to allow them to attend, the children end up disrupting the performance just as Dzigan and Shumacher are performing a scene as starving beggars in the Łódź Ghetto.

The children visit the actors in their dressing room to apologize for their rambunctiousness, but they end up critiquing the veracity of the representation: "That's not how it was in the ghetto," "That's not what the poor looked like in the ghetto," "In the ghetto no one gave challahs to the poor," etc.[18] The children offer their own performance for the actors, singing "My Ration Card" ("Di bone," 1940s), a song about starvation from the Warsaw Ghetto: "Oh, my ration card, / I won't give away my ration card, / I still want to live a bit more, / Not give up my ration card."[19] Shumacher is impressed, calling the children "a genuine source": "No actor can depict this material like these children can." He then turns to Dzigan and tells him, "We need to learn from the children how to perform the ghetto."[20] The comedians take the children and their teacher up on their invitation to visit them at their orphanage in Helenówek, in the countryside just outside of Łódź.

It is important here to emphasize that what the film depicts is not any single point of view. Rather, as in the camp stories of Tadeusz Borowski and Varlam Shalamov and the shorter episodes embedded in the narratives of Lidiia Ginzburg, Gustaw Herling-Grudziński, and others, our attention is drawn to a variety of experiences retold episodically from different child perspectives. Dzigan and Shumacher had no personal experience of the Łódź Ghetto, having spent most of the war in the Soviet Union, first as Yiddish-language comedians, then as prisoners in Soviet camps, returning to Poland in 1947. In his memoir, *The Power of Jewish Humor* (*Der koyekh fun yidishn humor*, 1974), Dzigan describes the horror of their arrival in Warsaw after the war and realizing that, in "a city where we had a hundred and one friends, there wouldn't be any place for us to sleep." They do manage to find friends in Łódź, but "the city's ruins, its misery, crushed us":

> We decided to travel out to a children's colony on the outskirts of the city, in Helenówek, to convalesce a bit. The colony had collected rescued Jewish orphans. They had been scattered among goodhearted Christians, in churches, or else merely cast into barns and silos during the German occupation. So they were running across the grassy grounds, playing hide-and-seek—like children. As if they hadn't yet had enough of hiding. I stood in a corner, observed our little hoi polloi, our pride-and-joys, and the sadness gnawed at my mood. They were the only ones left from their families. . . . These children, I thought, are our continuation—despite [idiom: *af tsu lehakhes*, "in mockery of"] the enemies and destroyers. For them, the children, it was worth it to keep going on and to build life anew. The little ones had given us strength to shake off our own terrors, insofar as such a thing was possible.[21]

In the closing words of this passage, we hear a clear echo in Yiddish—*af vifl dos hot zikh gelozt* (insofar as such a thing was possible)—of the ironizing subtitle of Pick's *Society for the Protection of Animals*—namely, *humoristická—pokud je to možné—novela z ghetta* (a humorous novella from the ghetto, insofar as that's possible). It is a telling phrase that signals the limit point of what can be achieved by telling, of what can be told "in spite of all." The lived experience is such that no narrative can accomplish what these authors self-consciously present as the putative aim of narrativizing experience in the first place—that is, a *catharsis*, "to shake off our terrors," or else at least to amuse us. The representation thus represents its own limit, theatricalizes it, asserting the simultaneous need to know and the impossibility of knowing. "And how, in fact, can one accept not to know?" Blanchot asks. "We read books on Auschwitz. The wish of all, in the camps, the last wish: know what has happened, do not forget, and at the same time never will you know."[22]

This effort to represent the experiences of being hunted, confined, threatened, and mistreated while also questioning the very possibility of representing such an experience truthfully is explicitly the subject of *Our Children*. That is, the real-life experience of Dzigan and Shumacher presented in the film is not the actors' own survival in Soviet camps, but rather their experience of trying to understand and represent *others'* experiences that are in certain respects comparable: Dzigan and Shumacher have also been in camps, have also been in peril, and Dzigan clearly states that they reach out to the children in order to aid the adult actors in their own recovery, their own convalescence, *tsu kumen a bisl tsu zikh*—literally, "to return to oneself a little."

In this way, the comedy duo play a dual role in the film. They are simultaneously an audience to the narratives of others and tellers of their own tale, which is not about surviving their ordeal in the Soviet Union but about how one can use theater to survive one's own survival, "insofar as such a thing was possible," and whether it is a self-deception even to try. This real-life crisis, in which the crisis of survival fuses with the crisis of representation, suffuses the film. Note that there is no mention of the film in the passage I have quoted, nor anywhere else in Dzigan's memoir. While Dzigan and Shumacher did have modest film careers in Poland before the war and more success after their emigration to Israel, he relays their experiences at the orphanage in Helenówek purely as autobiography, as a trip he and Shumacher undertook, not a film they made. Likewise, Natan Gross, the film's director, describes the film's initial concept as arising from his own inner conflict when Saul Goskind, the producer, approached him about making this film with Dzigan and Shumacher:

> I was one of those who had been saved from the Shoah, and I lived among those saved from the concentration camps: how could we be thinking of comedy? But—how could you imagine a film with

Dzigan and Shumacher that *isn't* a comedy? I was neither thinking about, nor interested in, a film set before the war. Ultimately we came up with a concept that we later developed with Rachel[a] Auerbach, and I worked it out with Saul Goskind, as well as Dzigan and Shumacher. The idea referred to current events.[23]

Gross, the director, had survived the Kraków Ghetto before living in Warsaw clandestinely under a false identity. Auerbach, who wrote the film's dialogue, had escaped the Warsaw Ghetto, where she was a member of Emanuel Ringelblum's Oyneg Shabes, the conspiracy of historians and documentarians that is the source of much of what we know about life in the Ghetto, and she spent much of the rest of the war hiding in the Warsaw Zoo. (The history of Jews and their allies, "people lost between worlds," finding refuge in the Warsaw Zoo became the subject of Diane Ackerman's *The Zookeeper's Wife* and of a sentimental 2017 film "based on the true story.")[24] Dzigan and Shumacher had lived through Soviet camps. The children who appear in the film as orphans were the actual residents of the Orphan's Home in Helenówek. What the film depicts is not any one biographical account of the past, but the contemporaneous effort of multiple survivors, each having had unique experiences of atrocity, to find some common language in which to represent those experiences to each other. It is a film about individuals coming to terms with the totality of their collective experience by comparing their personal experiences. This negotiation plays out in the ironized space of real-life fiction—again, the filmmaker's struggle with the crisis of representation, as well as the actors' trip to the orphanage in the film, are *reenactments* of the real—and this ironic framing allows for both the comedic meta-commentary on the film's dilemma and the tragic possibility that the dilemma itself is irresolvable.

The film's tone wavers between these poles. Many of its set pieces are typical of family cinema from the middle of the last century: amusing song-and-dance numbers performed by the comedians or the children in turn, the most prominent of these being Dzigan and Shumacher's staging of "Kasrilevke Is Burning" ("Kasrilevke brent"), based on Sholem Aleichem's story about a shtetl that burns because none of its inhabitants has the wherewithal to put out the fire. The two actors delight the children with their versatile performance, in which they play all the roles (except that of the old nag pulling the water cart). Afterward, the children announce that they know the subject of Sholem Aleichem's satire firsthand—not, of course, from having lived in a shtetl in the Russian Empire, but from having survived the burning of the Warsaw Ghetto in 1943. The comedians respond by challenging the children to come up with their own representations of what they lived through or witnessed during the war. The children go to bed, while the actors and teachers have a contentious and inconclusive discussion of whether there is any value in representing these experiences at all, whether the effect of such theatricality is salutary or merely masochistic. Then, at night, sleepless and exhausted, the actors wander the corridors of the orphanage, eavesdropping on the young wards and their older caretakers as they relate to each other horrors whose memory has been reactivated by the actors' provocation.

This brings us to what effectively serves as the film's climax, which seeks to represent the crisis of representation visually. The orphanage, the orphans, the actors, their visit, the effort of the adults and children to relate to each other's experiences—these are all real-life elements within a film that, we must recall, opens with documentary footage. Yet this last section of the film relies instead on reenactment, the first instance of which is wholly paradoxical: as the comedians are carrying on their conversation with the remaining staff—still before they've started stalking through the dark building on their way to bed—the film cuts to the director of the orphanage, who has retired to her room, and we, the audience, hear the cries of her dead child as non-diegetic sound. This is given to us directly, unmediated by the comedians' presence. When Dzigan and Shumacher do begin making their way up the stairs, the lighting and camera movements take an unsettling, decidedly expressionist turn, and what the comedians overhear from the orphans talking in their bedrooms fades into disturbing reenactments. We hear three tales in succession, in each instance with the storyteller playing him- or herself in the reenactment. What is heard at the door by the actors playing themselves is performed for us by the storytellers playing themselves. The effect is so horrifying that, still unable to sleep, Dzigan denounces the orphanage as a *hoyz fun koshmarn*, "a house of nightmares," and the audience is likely to agree.

It is unclear how any film could recover its comedic bearings at this point. Nor does *Our Children*. Dzigan and Shumacher awaken to the sounds of the children in the courtyard reenacting the performance of "Kasrilevke Is Burning" from the previous evening. With this gesture, the film seems to say, and Dzigan explains to the orphanage's director, "The morning proved that the children are healthier than we are." One could even interpret the children's game as a corrective, restorative reenactment: whereas the residents of Kasrilevke in Sholem Aleichem's story cannot cooperate, the children work together to confront a common threat. But this would require some willful misreading. In the actual film, the children, too, become distracted by their own fun, and in the end they leave the hose spewing water into the mud, the fire in the sandbox still burning.

Though staged as merriment, the children's reenactment of "Kasrilevke Is Burning" can also be read as a daytime extension of the nightmares that have preceded it. The audience does not need to make an imaginative leap from the mythic Kasrilevke to the burning of the Warsaw Ghetto and other Jewish habitations, since the film has already drawn the synecdoche from the burning set to the burning city: the children point it out immediately following Dzigan and Shumacher's performance. By acting out the same narrative in the courtyard as a game, the film rather suggests that the only way for the children to understand their own ordeal is through simulacrum, the traumatic repetition of the received traumatic narrative. Though the tragedy is repeated as farce, the farce inevitably refers us back to the tragedy.

Read in this way, the film leaves its central dilemma unresolved. It does not offer any conclusions about the power of narrative and performance to overcome real-life trauma. On the contrary, it drops its audience into so dense a thicket of mimetic chains that the film's more affirmative, hortatory gestures—this is, after all, a film made under the authority of Poland's postwar Communist regime—cannot offer any reassurance. Other viewers, notably Lawrence Langer, have seen this as a failure to resolve the schematic dichotomy that the film's climactic section appears to present: "By day, *we* seem to triumph over the Holocaust; but at night, *it* seems to triumph over us. The cinematic art of [*Our Children*] seeks to resolve the dilemma but may merely magnify it."[25] I agree that the film amplifies its own dilemma, but it assumes too much to say that it "seeks to resolve the dilemma." Such a reading focuses too narrowly on the film's expressions of hope for the healing power of narrative, which are usually voiced by Shumacher and repeatedly counterbalanced by demonstrations of how representing spaces of open confinement can only amplify the paradox and confusion that are inherent to the real-life experience. This reading also tests the film's structure against too narrow a goal, that of achieving a "triumph over the Holocaust," whereas the film is, from start to finish, a meditation on whether the lived traumas of its creators can be represented truthfully in performance, and, if so, whether they should. Those lived experiences represent the full range of circumstances treated in this book: concentration camps, ghettos, life in hiding. And the trauma most obviously foregrounded in the film is perhaps not that of the children, but the trauma of the comedians themselves. It is they who have come to the children for help, and they are the ones most aggrieved by the irresolution of their dilemma. In this respect, the film succeeds beautifully.

But is it funny? Not as much, I think, as the real-life fictions of Grosman, Pick, and Becker. These authors never relinquish the ironic distance with which they treat their subjects, and this allows them to maintain generic stability throughout their respective texts. Consequently, their novels easily conform to readerly expectations of the comic bildungsroman, picaresque, or trickster tale. The protagonists' historical circumstances, while bound tightly to the authors' lived experience, could be replaced with analogous precarities without an irrecoverable disruption of narrative content. Accordingly, while the themes of simulation and theatricality suffuse texts like *The Society for the Protection of Animals*, *Lucky as Hell*, and *Jakob the Liar*, as they do most real-life camp fiction, any anxieties the authors may have about whether fiction can tell the truth of reality is sublimated into the heroes' innocence and good intentions. In *Our Children*, that ironic distance is always threatening to collapse. The past is once again present, at once inescapable and ungraspable; recall Gross's insistence that the film be about what the filmmakers were facing in their own day, and not about the past. The representation *becomes real* in the nightmarish reenactment, foreclosing any potential for an ironic jibe or sneer.

None of this is to say that *Our Children* lacks for lighthearted musical numbers, physical comedy, or biting one-liners. These comedic elements nevertheless remain incongruous with the film as a whole. Not because the film features genuinely upsetting scenes of violence perpetrated against children, or not only because of this, but because the film's dominant theme is anxiety about, and often outright distrust in, the very possibility of truthful representation as such.

Both the incongruity of affect and the ambivalence regarding its own narrative project likely contributed to the film's fate. Screened once in Poland upon its completion, with a handful of later screenings in France and Israel, *Our Children* was shelved and believed lost for decades, which may explain why Dzigan never even mentions it in his memoir. The last Yiddish-language feature film made in Poland never reached more than a few viewers.

That Joke Isn't Funny Anymore: On Our Awkward Laughter

Virtually all camp-themed comedies face challenges in reaching an audience. Yet, as the examples I have discussed clearly demonstrate, this is not because the survivors of concentration camps or the hunted life did not regard their own experiences with humor, whether in the experiences as they unfolded or later, when facing the task of representing them. The impediment here is squarely on the receiving end of the representation. If the pairing of laughter and persecution in spaces of open confinement is incongruous, it is because it is almost always incongruous *to us*, which is to say that we automatically assign tragic affect as an integral generic feature of camp narratives, regardless of whether such an assignment fits an actual survivor's lived experience or later strategy for representing that experience. Laughter does not occur to us as a potential response because we have decided—or, more accurately, the reception paradigm has decided for us—that we are not *supposed* to find this funny. Major studies of the literature of open confinement generally ignore comic effects, let alone comic texts. When facing life in extremis, comedy simply falls beyond our horizon of expectations.

Yet it is telling that this statement is *least* accurate when the creators of the text have no personal experience of the circumstances they are representing, as is the case with the films *Life Is Beautiful* and, more recently, *Jojo Rabbit* (dir. Taika Waititi, 2019). In such instances, opposing parties might argue over the ethics of appropriating historical tragedy to tell stories that are fundamentally about parental love or the courage of children, themes that can and are treated in any number of interchangeable settings, historical and invented. There is, on the other hand, little question of appropriation in a film like *Our Children* and in books like *The Society for the Protection of Animals* or *Lucky as Hell*, since it is the creators' own experiences that they seek to represent through fiction. This confronts us, the audience, with yet another representational paradox: We can take the joke only when it comes from someone who has no authority to make it, allowing us to enjoy the joke's structure while dismissing its content, which may even heighten the comic effect by violating a taboo. When the joke comes from someone speaking from personal experience, on the other hand, it is too close to events and experiences that, in our own predetermination, are no laughing matter.

We could let the matter rest there. One shouldn't joke about the Nazi genocide of European Jewry. One shouldn't laugh about the Gulag. In Ferne Pearlstein's 2017 documentary *The Last Laugh*, Mel Brooks, who over a long career has frequently poked fun at Nazi iconography (not least in Alan Johnson's 1983 remake of *To Be or Not to Be*), maintains that for him the Shoah itself has always been, and will forever be, out of bounds for comedy. One can accept this position with little objection. And we would, were it not for the fact that some of the most successful real-life fictions of camp life use humor liberally, but that humor is no longer read as humor.

This is the case, for example, of Solzhenitsyn's *One Day in the Life of Ivan Denisovich*, the cynical humor of which was readily legible to the author's Soviet-era readers, including other authors, like Varlam Shalamov, who had similarly fictionalized their own camp experiences. Few today, I think, would count comedy among that novella's principal registers, let along characterize the book as "humorous" in the way that Pick declares his own text to be.[26] There is no question that humor played an essential role in survival; this is richly attested across the full range of accounts from the "world apart," from the Soviet Gulag to Nazi death camps to the experiences of bombardment and hiding. The problem is that humor in these circumstances serves a very different function from humor in their representation—so different, in fact, that a joke cannot simply be transposed from one to the other. Within the camp or the city under siege, humor serves readily identifiable psychological and social needs. The ironic distance in which humor subsists instantly expresses a distance between the teller of a joke and the authority that has placed him in precarity, a distance that no authority can tolerate, as Tzvetan Todorov tells us: "One of the most unforgivable of errors is humor—telling of political jokes, or simply having a sense of humor. Humor is a mark of distance from authority, and thus a proof of individual autonomy."[27] Or, as Dzigan explains in reference to his decision to abandon Poland shortly after the completion of *Our Children*, "humor and satire would be unsaleable goods in the new regime."[28] Telling a good joke, in other words, is a reassertion, however limited, of one's authority over oneself, even if it lasts only as long as the laughter does.

Unlike most other referential features of narrative, humor depends largely on a precognitive operation. We laugh because we "get" the joke before we understand it, which is why the explanation of a joke is rarely, if ever, as funny as a telling with good comic timing. Spontaneous laughter demands that recognition arrive one beat ahead of cognition. At times, we may even laugh twice, first upon "getting" the joke, and again later when we have really thought about it.

With camp literature, those who are intimately familiar with the realities to which the author's jokes refer are most capable of "getting it." That leaves the rest of us with only our horror.

CHAPTER V

Horror

> There will be no other end of the world,
> there will be no other end of the world.
> —CZESŁAW MIŁOSZ, "A SONG ON THE END OF THE WORLD"
> (TRANS. ANTHONY MIŁOSZ)

The poet Miron Białoszewski recalls that, from the relative and tenuous safety of the so-called Aryan side of the ghetto wall, the doomed uprising in the Warsaw Ghetto began with the incongruity of Easter celebrations in the city and, in the "other" city, the city within the city, flames. "And the inferno culminated on Easter," Białoszewski would write twenty years later, in an immersive effort at mnemonic reconstruction. "Up to the sky—fire":

> It had begun. But on Krasiński Square there was this amusement park. Carousels. Swings. And, well, some of our public had a go on the swings, on the whirling chairs. In the thick smoke. Because it rose. And rose. From Bonifraterska Street. And Nowolipki. And Dzielna. Świętojerska. Przejazd. After all, the uprising in the ghetto went on and on. The first harbingers. I had peered into that smoke for the first time in May, and I heard it whistling. Around the tenth, I recall. That was already two days after the mass suicide of the Jewish leadership. In the bunker on Miła Street. The Germans had discovered them.[1]

This passage comes early in *A Memoir of the Warsaw Uprising* (*Pamiętnik z powstania warszawskiego*, 1968), and it establishes, in its accumulation of incongruous details, a sense that, for the Poles of occupied Warsaw, the ghetto had become a "world apart," even as those who read about occupied Warsaw encounter that space as a slightly wider "world apart." "The first condition of extremity," Terrence Des Pres writes, "is that there is no escape, no place to go except the grave. It is like a city under siege, Paris in 1870, Leningrad of the 900 days, or like the town of Oran in [Albert Camus's] *The Plague*."[2] The "world apart," the world in a state of extremity so dire that it becomes a separate world where "there is no escape" *back* into the world one has known, exists in its own sphere, according to its own rules. Białoszewski offers his microcosmic image of urban social collapse because it anticipates, with difference, what Białoszewski and others would experience in the Warsaw Uprising. As Krzysztof Ziarek observes, "*A Memoir* [*of the Warsaw Uprising*] depicts the isolation of Warsaw during the Warsaw Uprising of 1944 as a repetition, a reminder about the seclusion and abandonment of the Jews of the Warsaw Ghetto during their uprising over a year earlier . . . and indicates a pivotal difference between them: the difference between hopelessness and the possibility of hope."[3]

This "possibility of hope," as we have seen, is what the more simulative specimens of real-life fiction withhold, focusing instead on the visceral horrors of the experience. But because the camp or besieged city remains beyond the experiential horizon of most readers, the literature of concentration camps, ghettos, and besieged cities comes generically closest to science fiction and, specifically, the "possible worlds" narrative. As such, among literary paradigms it is most closely related not to biographical or historical genres, but to speculative fiction and fantasy.

This kinship can be felt keenly on both the structural level (in the progression of plot points, from the hero's initiation into the "world apart," his or her assimilation into it, and the eventual emergence from it) and at the close textual level, such as in an author's anthropological attention to the terms, procedures, and technologies that distinguish the "world apart" from the reader's own experiential expectations. The author's task, in yet another rearticulation of the representational paradox, is to familiarize the reader with the "world apart" without allowing the reader to sense that world as familiar. It must be strange and knowable at the same time, echoing within the readerly experience that same sense of the unaccountable, the unassimilated, or the uncanny that Kertész defined as inherent in the camp itself.

This is why, when watching certain cinematic representations of survival in urban ruins, such as the second half of Roman Polanski's *The Pianist*

(2002), I cannot shake the sense that I am watching a modern zombie film. And it is hardly fanciful to suggest that contemporary postapocalyptic fiction, which uses the "possible worlds" model to represent societal collapse and civilization in ruins, draws heavily on the imagery of the Second World War. What the present chapter asks the reader to consider seriously is how that imagery is already anticipated by survivors as they are experiencing societal collapse, that they see it cinematically as science fiction they are living through. That the "world apart" is a horror is obvious. My point is that postapocalyptic horror in the postwar period continues to menace us with the "world apart" in the middle of the last century.

The Literary Attention to Cinematic Detail:
Czesław Miłosz's Warsaw

Białoszewski's description of downtown Warsaw at the beginning of the ghetto's destruction reads almost like a sequence of camera movements. "Carousels. Swings." Sentence by sentence, we cut back and forth across the ghetto wall, trying (and failing) to make sense of the contradictions. "In the thick smoke. Because it rose. And rose." How can this be?

Given how powerful the image is as an emblem for the separation of two worlds, we might just as easily ask whether, if there had *not* been a carousel in Krasiński Square, one would need to invent it, to tell the story of a "little Masha with the long braids" in order to convey the *reality* of these worlds' separation. In fact, there is contradictory evidence regarding whether the carousel set up on Krasiński Square for Easter ever ran, but its (cinematic) image has assumed a (textual) life of its own, in Jerzy Andrzejewski's novel *Holy Week* (*Wielki tydzień*, 1964), in Andrzej Wajda's film *Generation* (*Pokolenie*, 1955), and elsewhere.[4] For Czesław Miłosz, the carousel becomes the emblem of the ghetto uprising and Polish Varsovians' indifference to it, as he says in his contemporaneous poem "Campo dei Fiori" (1943):

> I thought of the Campo dei Fiori
> in Warsaw by the sky-carousel
> one clear spring evening
> to the strains of a carnival tune.
> The bright melody drowned

the salvos from the ghetto wall,
and couples were flying
high in the cloudless sky.

At times wind from the burning
would drift dark kites along
and riders on the carousel
caught petals in midair.
That same hot wind
blew open the skirts of girls
and crowds were laughing
on that beautiful Warsaw Sunday.[5]

    Miłosz's lyric technique has long been described in terms of cinema, with the poet typically opening with a tight focus on an object that interests him and that is initially deprived of context. He then pulls back from that object, revealing the complexity of various intersecting details. "Campo dei Fiori" is no exception. The image of young people catching "petals in midair" is romantic fancy until we consider the context, that these "petals" are the "dark kites" of ash drifting over the wall. The point of this technique is to force the kind of uncomfortable comparison that occurs whenever the "bigger picture" is revealed, so that the detail that is at first familiar and easily welcomed ("The bright melody") becomes an object of horror and disgust ("drowned / the salvos from the ghetto wall").

    Among the poems Miłosz composed in occupied Warsaw, the best example of this technique comes in the first two stanzas of the poem "A Poor Christian Looks at the Ghetto" ("Biedny chrześcijanin patrzy na getto," 1943):

Bees build around red liver,
Ants build around black bone.
It has begun: the tearing, the trampling on silks,
It has begun: the breaking of glass, wood, copper, nickel, silver, foam
Of gypsum, iron sheets, violin strings, trumpets, leaves, balls, crystals.
Poof! Phosphorescent fire from yellow walls
Engulfs animal and human hair.

Bees build around the honeycomb of lungs,
Ants build around white bone.
Torn is paper, rubber, linen, leather, flax,
Fiber, fabrics, cellulose, snakeskin, wire.
The roof and the wall collapse in flame and heat seizes the foundations.
Now there is only the earth, sandy, trodden down,
With one leafless tree.[6]

The poet could surely have described such a scene without enumerating its minute and gruesome details, but his purpose is not merely to describe a circumstance. Rather, Miłosz is tuning the reader's visual imagination so that it grasps matter in the very moment of its transformation. Kazimierz Wyka draws readers' attention to the "filmic" quality of Miłosz's poems as early as 1946, writing that the poet is a *"plastic realist,* one who discerns colors, proportions, and shapes in their potentially objective arrangement."[7] Helen Vendler has made a similar observation, noting how, "beholding twentieth-century reality, he devised the cinematic montage that we call the Miłoszian manner."[8]

Isn't this Miłoszian manner precisely the stock technique of zombie apocalypse cinema, which also fetishizes the before/after of transformed bodies and cities? Isn't the purpose of such entertainment to frighten us with images of our world recast as a "world apart?" What is remarkable here, however, is not how much apocalyptic horror draws on and allegorizes war; rather, it is how much the challenge of representing war sets the stage for the zombie apocalypse.

No Other End of the World: Czesław Miłosz and Jerzy Andrzejewski Write the Zombie Apocalypse

Czesław Miłosz used film as a metaphor at various moments of his life and for various purposes, in disputes about metaphysics, lyric methods, and history, and he did so in two contrary ways. First, for Miłosz film represents the reduction of moral dilemmas: the cheap Hollywood ending. Second, and more importantly for our purposes, film offers a metaphor for spatiotemporal continuity, and thus also for the difficulty of separating the subject from the object, good from evil. Miłosz's meditation on the Western in *Visions from San Francisco Bay*, for example, represents both sides, for it is rooted in his interpretation of Blaise Cendrars's 1924 novel *Gold: Being the Marvelous History of General John Augustus Sutter (L'Or)*. According to Miłosz, Cendrars's novel demonstrates how "the Western itself passed entirely into fable, formalizing its own motifs, arranging them in nearly algebraic equations to divide the characters into good and bad, with the inevitable triumph of justice," whereas Cendrars's book provides "sufficient indication of the distance between the facts and the Western fable drawn from them."[9]

Yet Miłosz's point is to talk not about film genres, but rather of Sutter's character in the novel, where Cendrars presents him as a social outcast living in the open desert, as a man in waiting who strives to create some semblance of civilization and is forced either to revise his moral codes or to cast them aside, since they turn out to be useless or ridiculous in his new context. Writing along these lines in California in 1969, Miłosz is echoing, if perhaps unconsciously, his failed postwar film project about a "world apart."

Miłosz formulated his idea for a film in conversations with Władysław Szpilman, the celebrated Jewish pianist whose experiences during the war later inspired Polanski's *The Pianist*. It was in the wake of these conversations that Miłosz decided to write a screenplay with his friend, the novelist Jerzy Andrzejewski, about a *Robinson warszawski*, a "Warsaw Robinson Crusoe," the postwar term for a person who, like Cendrars's Sutter, had found him- or herself in the ruins of civilization, in this case in a shattered and depopulated area of occupied Warsaw, completely alone, hunted, and striving, insofar as it was possible, to create a version of life as it had been in the world before. (The epithet "Robinson" appears quickly after the war and assumes an aura of legend and reverence. Though the number of people who actually survived as "Robinsons" is difficult to determine—estimates range from four hundred to one thousand individuals—the "desert" in which they lived is easy to identify among specific devastated sites within Warsaw.)[10]

The film that Miłosz had wanted to make was never realized as such. Instead, another production, now titled *The Unvanquished City* (*Miasto niejarzmione*, 1950), was directed by Jerzy Zarzycki, who not only knew Warsaw well, but also had a firm grasp of how cinematic effect could serve propaganda purposes: during the war, Zarzycki had worked in the clandestine Motivational Propaganda Unit. By the time Zarzycki's film appeared in Polish cinema houses, Miłosz had long since resigned from the project and was already living in Washington, DC, as a cultural attaché of the Communist government. "I had my name removed once I found out about the miraculous increase in the number of characters," he wrote almost forty years later. For it was precisely the idea of one person's loneliness and solitude while living among the ruins of civilization that had most fascinated him in Szpilman's account of survival. He had wanted to present the tragedy of an isolated individual trying to rebuild fragments of a lost society.[11]

There is a clear resonance here between the film Miłosz had envisioned and what he would later laud as the "fable" of survival in Cendrars's *Gold*. But in Miłosz's imagination, it is not just the survivor who is the hero of such a tale; the setting becomes a central character as well. We engage this kind of narrative not only to see how the protagonist survives the impossible, but to see the world without us, to reimagine human spaces in which no human could be expected to survive, and in this the story's hero serves as witness and guide. "The main character," Miłosz explained in 1955, "was supposed to be the city, which counted over a million residents before the war and was subsequently turned by common bombs and dynamite into a desert of burnt-out streets, twisted iron, and scattered barricade: Warsaw."[12] It was the poet's own intention that the film "show the terrifying landscape of a dead city and warn people against their own madness".[13]

> The original idea had hardly anything to do with what is understood these days as "action." It was about placing an equal sign between nature, where Robinson Crusoe found himself, and with which he had to contend, and the ruins of a civilization that has been reduced to a state of primal savagery. Therefore, only *survival*, and the gift for improvisation that it requires; an emphasis on the *details* of living (water, sustenance, a place to sleep), as well as on evading constant dangers.[14]

Seeing through the poet's "cinematographic" eye, we discern not the grand metanarratives that have dominated discussions of the war to this day, and that evaluate an entire complex of distantly related phenomena from a bird's-eye view, but a point of view that is closer to that of a camera, of a person who, through overwhelming terror, is trying to register everything he can, both what he sees and what he is thinking, while also fully aware that the perspective of one individual is awfully limited, that the movie camera is more an instrument of exclusion and omission than of inclusion. In this respect, we may point to what Miłosz says in his essay "The Legend of the Monster-City" ("Legenda miasta-potwora"), which he composed in Warsaw in 1942:

> The observer is master. The average passerby, so long as he dreams up conjectures and supplies stories for every eye and mouth noticed on the bus. He dominates with the power of the story he invents. The appeal of the cinema may rest precisely on this. Over a couple of hours, human lives play out before the viewer that reveal to him all the mysteries of the *detail*, that make themselves his own, that incite him to weave every detail into a web of dreams, and each detail opens perspectives onto the past and future of a house, an object, a person.... There is a deep connection between film and the myth of the city/monster/Leviathan.[15]

For Szpilman, as well as in Miłosz's work from this period, that point of view is provided by the person who survives while the city dies. And it must die. For civilization—that is, the idea whose materialization is the city as polis—has collapsed. Thus the original title of Szpilman's wartime memoir is *Death of the City* (*Śmierć miasta*, 1946), though it was written not by Szpilman, to whom it remains widely attributed, but by the music critic Jerzy Waldorff, who composed it "partially from Szpilman's stories, partially from his own meticulous notes."[16] The cinematic quality of Szpilman's account of survival wasn't lost on Waldorff, just as it hadn't been lost on Miłosz while the poet and the pianist were working together at Polish Radio. Waldorff remarks on this specifically in his preface, echoing once again the anxiety that no one would believe that such fantastical adventures were not a literary contrivance: "I would like to stress that there is not a single fact that I have invented myself. They are all authentic, though it could seem that they had been composed by a talented screenwriter and a director of sensational movies."[17]

The title of Zarzycki's film, in the form it assumed as it developed from Miłosz's initial effort, sounds markedly different from what Miłosz and Andrzejewski had come up with, and it is that much more distant from the title of Szpilman and Waldorff's book: instead of *Death of the City*, we have *The Unvanquished City*. The proliferation of characters that Miłosz describes, as well as the embellishment of heroic and patriotic plotlines and the emphasis on the survival of Warsaw (and, by extension, all of Poland), suited the propagandistic goals of People's Poland, yet it was completely contrary to Miłosz's interests (or, one might suggest in light of the catastrophism that dominates his work in the 1930s and into the war years, his obsessions).

Miłosz, however, had envisioned the kind of scenario—in both the cinematic and the situational senses of that word—rather differently. And this, finally, is where we find something extraordinary: the film treatment that Miłosz wrote with Andrzejewski perfectly captures the principal features of the postapocalyptic horror films that have been a staple of world cinema since the war ended. More specifically, the text for *Warsaw Robinson Crusoe* constitutes an extraordinarily effective generic description not of films depicting the struggle against Nazism, but of zombie apocalypse.

Postapocalyptic Cinema: The World as Camp

Adopting Miłosz and Andrzejewski's text for our guide, let us now take a closer look at this instance of genre dysphoria, the suggestion that zombie films are merely a reworking of the tropes of real-life fiction about concentration camps, ghettos, and besieged cities. For the postapocalyptic urban scenario featured prominently in zombie films constitutes an allegorical expression of postwar fears that a monolithic, totalitarian force, whether fascist or communist, will sweep away human civilization, leaving individuals to hide in the ruins while evading those who seek either to destroy them or to absorb them into the collective.

Postapocalyptic zombie films often begin with a prologue, textual or dramatic, that explains the events that have brought about the end of the world. Among the more frequent causes are the radiation left over from a global nuclear catastrophe, whether a war or an accident, or else a disease developed as a biological weapon. Whether the triggering event is political, environmental, or very often unspecified, the scenario leaves the trigger aside. The story does not become about how to stop nuclear war or cure disease. It becomes about how to avoid being caught by the undifferentiated masses and turned into one of them. Still, there is more often than not a direct link between militarism and civilizational collapse. We see this already in the opening titles of *The Last Man on Earth* (dir. Ubaldo B. Ragona and Sidney Salkow, 1964), starring Vincent Price, the first film adaptation of Richard Matheson's 1954 novel *I Am Legend*, the book that introduces the now familiar global zombie apocalypse. In a telling visual cue, we see Price passing the time with a copy of Defoe's *Robinson Crusoe*. There is a similar connection between war, now inflected with racial strife, seven years later in the second film adaptation of Matheson's novel, *The Omega Man* (dir. Boris Sagal, 1971), in which Charlton Heston plays the role of the last man. In Danny Boyle's *28 Days Later* (2002), the virus is a biological weapon that infects its victims with a concentration of human rage. And in *I Am Legend* (dir. Francis Lawrence, 2007), already the third feature adaptation of Matheson's novel, we learn in the prologue that humanity is being destroyed by a novel cancer treatment. Other examples begin in medias res, providing the exposition along the way.

Immediately after the war, there was clearly no need to remind the Polish public why the capital had been destroyed. Thus the first chapter of Miłosz's treatment begins immediately after the Warsaw Uprising, during the final evacuation. The poet had wanted to dwell immediately on the ruins, the traces of the collapsed civilization:

> An enormous column of smoke rises into the sky over the Mazovian Plain: the Polish capital is burning. Birds flying across a clear autumn sky swoop over this zone of destruction. Along main roads, among the ruins and the shattered barricades rising high above them, the crowds of the last residents, now prisoners, wander, long journeys through concentration camps before them. The air is dull, suffused with soot. This city is now a city of silence and extermination.[18]

We can see within this description how the city announces itself as the film's center, as it does in most any apocalyptic zombie film, with very few exceptions. At the core of the film's interest is the fetishization of the destruction of cities: "Emptiness, not a person. An apartment house is burning around us. A deserted courtyard filled with smoke. The gate off its hinges."[19]

In the prologue to *Warsaw Robinson Crusoe*, Piotr Rafalski, the hero in the treatment (though a minor character in Zarzycki's film), has been knocked unconscious during the evacuation by a piece of collapsing wall. His adventure begins when he wakes up to find himself an accidental "Robinson": "As Piotr Rafalski returns to consciousness, he sees the sky above him and big, fluffy clouds floating behind a wispy curtain of smoke. Complete silence all around, no sign of anyone. Not a soul."[20]

Though we in the audience might know how the protagonist has reached this point, he or she often does not. The hero awakens, bewildered, disoriented, sometimes completely unaware of how the once-familiar world has ended, or that it has ended at all. In *28 Days Later*, Jim (played by Cillian Murphy), who has been in a coma since a cycling accident, wakes up in an abandoned hospital, and it is only after he finds his way out that he learns that the entire city of London has been abandoned. Robert Kirkman's *The Walking Dead*, both the graphic novel (2003–2019) and the internationally successful television series based on it (2010–2022), introduces the exact same situation: Rick Grimes, a rural deputy shot in the line of duty, wakes up in an abandoned hospital. There are times, however, when the hero knows very well what his situation is, only it takes him a moment on waking to remember that, yes, of course, the world has ended. This is what we see in *The Last Man on Earth*: Vincent Price wakes up, then realizes that, apocalypse or no, he still needs to make breakfast. In all these instances of waking into the postapocalyptic world, the most important thing for both the hero and the audience is that fleeting moment when the hero thinks that nothing is different, that anything he might remember about the world ending was nothing more than a dream, and in a moment he'll get up, go out to see friends, go to work, and enjoy his delightfully unterrified life. But that life is over.

The treatment for *Warsaw Robinson Crusoe* underscores this fact by juxtaposing images of shocking deprivation with traces of the former life—for example, when Rafalski finds a grand piano among the ruins: "Somewhere deep in the ruins, among the demolished apartment buildings, in a landscape that suggests scenes of fantastical mountains, but at the same time also the menace of a barren, withered desert, Rafalski stumbles and falls over. As he falls, he hits his elbow against the keyboard of a piano."[21] The duality of the comforting idyll and the horrifying collapse of civilization—"a landscape that suggests scenes of fantastical mountains, but at the same time the menace of a barren, withered desert"—is essential. The danger must be ever-present, but therefore unremarkable. There must always be the risk of forgetting that the "world apart" is apart in the first place. Momentarily forgetting the danger all around him, Rafalski begins to play.

But there are dangers, and while they may not be the walking dead, their functional similarities are striking. The most basic function of a zombie is to de-individuate individuals, rendering them zombies as well. (This function distinguishes the zombies of apocalyptic narratives from the figure of the zombie in Haitian folk custom, which will not be discussed here.) In the film treatment's third chapter, entitled "Man-Eaters" (in a nod to Defoe's *Robinson Crusoe*), we encounter one of the most interesting details in the entire project: the film's main antagonist is a *Volksdeutscher*, a Polish citizen of German ethnicity, dressed in civilian clothes and speaking fluent Polish. In other words, he is presented in the film as "one of us" who has become "one of them."[22]

The zombie presents us with an inversion of ourselves; it confronts the living with the dead, the familiar with the foreign. We are not speaking here simply of monsters, for the whole notion of a zombie is predicated on the possibility that any one of us could become one. And because the allegorical repertoire of zombie apocalypse often lacks subtlety, the connection between zombies and Nazis in zombie narratives is frequently explicit: the zombies in *The Omega Man*, for example, who are conscious and call themselves "The Family," burn books and paintings at night in order to destroy the relics of a degenerated society. But it is the transformation of the individual into the zombie that remains the indispensable horror trope of these films. Virtually every zombie film features a scene in which we see a key figure *before and after* their transformation into a zombie. Those of us sitting in the audience are forced to recognize the individual absorbed into the collective, the transformation of the ally into the enemy.

Just as Robinson Crusoe must have his Friday, a consistent trope of zombie apocalypse scenarios is the junior companion, sidekick, or fellow traveler, who is sometimes another human survivor or, as often as not, a dog. It is better to be neither, since this figure is the same point of secondary focalization in these films as we find throughout camp literature, the sacrificial character whose demise offers the hero a dilemma and the audience a brief moment of tragic catharsis. This is the fate of the dog in the films *I Am Legend* (where the dog does indeed sacrifice itself to save the hero) and *The Last Man on Earth*. In Miłosz and Andrzejewski's film treatment, Rafalski encounters a dog just before the *Volksdeutscher*, called simply the "Tall One," shoots at some Poles. As we should expect, the dog sacrifices itself at the end of the film, during Rafalski's final confrontation with the Tall One.[23]

The Grotesque: On Inhuman Value

While a stock feature of the kind of apocalyptic representation we are discussing is the moment of recognizing the transformed individual, typically a loved one or ally who has been subsumed into the zombie hoard, the vast majority of the hoard is just that: an undifferentiated, dehumanized mass of dangerous matter.[24] In much the same way, literary representations of concentration camps, ghettos, and besieged cities distinguish between transformations that create "Man-Eaters," as the Miłosz/Andrzejewski film treatment terms them, and those who are all but dead, the husks of former humans shambling and moaning their way toward a seemingly inevitable inanimacy. These transformations into the inhuman, whether the kind that attacks and infects, dragging the victim with it into the abyss, or the kind that merely fades into its environment, surely reflect countless real-life personal and communal tragedies, a fact that is easy to assume when confronting their material traces in, say, the mounds of human hair displayed at Auschwitz and Majdanek, or else in the pits of once-human ashes scattered throughout Europe. Bożena Shallcross thus opens her study of the material traces of genocide in Poland by declaring, "We associate the Holocaust with human tragedy," and she goes on to argue that the material traces of this tragedy now stand among its most potent representational emblems, its "dominant metonymy."[25] Indeed, we have already seen this insistence on the *authentic* material trace—for instance, in site-specific displays like the bricks from the Warsaw Ghetto in Washington, DC. "These surviving traces attest to the fact of genocide," Shallcross continues, "*if one respects their authenticity.*"[26]

But the metonymic function of the material object—its switching on of a narrative of historical tragedy that, as Shallcross points out, *we* associate with it; its serving, in other words, a *ritual* function—has little to do with the experience of individual survival that the authors we have been discussing sought to convey. First of all, these traces are not generally of survival, and thus they represent an experiential aporia that most authors of real-life fiction are too respectful to represent. Having seen death, they can show death; not having died, they cannot play dead. Second, the tragic understanding of what happens in spaces of open confinement is always belated, when each of an individual's experiences can be generalized into a biography, various biographies into a site, and scattered sites into the narrative we already know to be tragic.

This is precisely what Gillian Rose has in mind when she refers to the "fascism of representation," the dogma that imposes a preconceived, culturally orthodox meaning both on events that, like all events in the real world, have no inherent meaning, as well as on representations of the circumstances connected with those same events. She points specifically to *Schindler's List*, declaring, "It is my own violence that I discover in this film":

> *Schindler's List* betrays the crisis of ambiguity in characterization, mythologization and identification, because of its anxiety that our sentimentality be left intact. It leaves us at *the beginning of the day*, in a Fascist security of our own unreflected predation, piously joining the survivors putting stones on Schindler's grave in Israel [at the end of the film]. It should leave us unsafe, but with *the remains of the day*. To have that experience, we would have to discover and confront our own fascism.[27]

To "confront our own fascism" would mean not only facing "the crisis of ambiguity" that Rose refers to—our own ambiguity as consumers whose "predation" of these images remains "unreflected" and unacknowledged within them—but dwelling within that ambiguity, accepting that discomfort as our own and resisting the desire, the ever-urgent need, to neutralize it with the unambiguous adjudication of victims and perpetrators. This resistance demands that we resist *sanctifying* otherwise senseless death as tragedy, where death becomes merely the symbol of tragic meaning, as it does, for example, in the film's image of "the girl in the red coat." In a film otherwise shot in black and white, according to Spielberg, to echo the visual impression of Lanzmann's *Shoah*, we see a little girl in a red-tinted coat (figure 5.1) during the liquidation of the Kraków Ghetto. Shortly thereafter, we recognize her corpse as it is being carted away (figure 5.2). The conversion of life into death, of innocence into knowledge, is clean. We know nothing of the little girl or her ordeal, because there is neither little girl nor ordeal. Serving a purely symbolic function, she has to die—*for us*. The tragic function demands it. And therein lies our fascism. We cannot discern any individual humanity in this creature, and we demand that she die in order to ratify our own sense of what is right and wrong in the world. At the same time, because she is literally no one, she could be anyone, enough so that only *after* Spielberg's film had been released to international acclaim did Roma Ligocka—Roman Polanski's cousin—publish a

Figure 5.1 In *Schindler's List*, the only figure to appear in color in the otherwise monochrome film is "the girl in the red coat," whom we first see during the liquidation of the Kraków Ghetto (01:08:50). *Source*: *Schindler's List*, dir. Steven Spielberg (Universal City, CA: Universal Pictures, 1993)

Figure 5.2 An hour after we first see her in *Schindler's List*, we catch a passing glimpse of "the girl in the red coat," now converted from symbolic life to symbolic death (02:17:18). *Source*: *Schindler's List*, dir. Steven Spielberg (Universal City, CA: Universal Pictures, 1993)

memoir in which she claims to have been "the girl in the red coat," only miraculously survived.[28]

Real-life fiction, by contrast, seeks to simulate the experience from within, so that the reader experiences the narrative in the present of its unfolding, not in an after or above that could judge its content as "tragic." When we encounter the once-human in real-life fiction, now reduced to mechanical labor or mindless brutality or human fat rendered for making soap, it is the equally horrifying and comic *absurdity* of this reality—the absurdity that such absurdity is *real*—that initially overwhelms the sense of tragedy that we have brought to the text (and not the other way around).

Primo Levi returns to this point repeatedly in *The Drowned and the Saved*, not only in his description of the "gray zone" where moral binaries break down, but in his insistence on that same experiential aporia I mentioned a moment ago, the "uncomfortable notion" that "we, the survivors, are not the true witnesses":

> We survivors are not only an exiguous but also an anomalous minority: we are those who by their prevarications or abilities or good luck did not touch bottom. Those who did so, those who saw the Gorgon, have not returned to tell about it or have returned mute, but they are the "Muslims," the submerged, the complete witnesses, the ones whose deposition would have a general significance. They are the rule, we are the exception.[29]

For Levi, the effort to represent the camp experience begins in imposture, since those who can tell cannot know, and those who know cannot tell. (Significantly, he repeatedly turns to another source, Solzhenitsyn's *The Gulag Archipelago*, for confirmation.) Only those who have completely succumbed to the conversion from human to mere flesh and labor would be able to report on what such a transmutation looks like from within.

Such people, or former people, are frequently referred to as *Muselmänner* (German, "Muslims") in literature from Nazi camps, especially Auschwitz, though the origin of the term is obscure, and others were used elsewhere in the Nazi camp system.[30] Like "Auschwitz," which has come to stand metonymically for Nazi camps in general, *Muselmann* has become its own legend, a homogenizing emblem for the many ways that malnutrition, overwork, and despair can affect the body and mind. One could return to one's humanity, as Borowski makes clear in his earliest definition of the condition, included in the glossary of camp jargon that concludes *We Were in Auschwitz*:

> MUSELMANN: a person who has been completely destroyed physically and spiritually, having neither the strength nor the will to keep fighting for life, usually with *durchfall* [severe diarrhea], phlegmons, or scabies, the ripest for the chimney. No explanations can convey

the contempt with which the *Muselmann* was regarded by his fellows. Even prisoners who relish camp autobiographies are reluctant to admit that they had been *Muselmänner* "as well."[31]

In this early description of the *Muselmann*, before the legend of the once-human husk had formed fully, the term describes a condition that one could slip into and back out of, and not the absolute relinquishment of self that Levi portrays. For Levi and others, the *Muselmann* is an absolute, a complete loss of the human. As Agamben observes, "The *Muselmann* is not only or not so much a limit between life and death; rather, he marks the threshold between the human and the inhuman."[32]

There is nothing tragic, nor is there any room for tragedy, in this image of the formerly human. This is not to say that one could not represent the physical disintegration of the human body in the camps as tragic. Of course one could, so long as the humanity remains identifiable in the body, the mortal visible within the mortification of the flesh. This is, as we have seen, how Jorge Semprún represents the death of Maurice Halbwachs, his beloved teacher, in a filthy cot in Buchenwald. The *Muselmann*, by contrast, is an object of horror, ridicule, and very often both. He is a *grotesque* body, which, in the words of Wolfgang Kayser, "depersonalizes the individual and makes him the object of something strange and inhuman, . . . its limbs not matching and each of its parts given an inhuman attribute."[33]

Isn't it precisely this *lack* of tragic framing and tone that we keep remarking when we describe these writers (and their pretenders) as "austere" or "unsettlingly raw"? Isn't our repeatedly pointing out the "brutality" and "cruelty" of writers like Borowski, Shalamov, or Kosiński a symptom of our own surprise at the incongruity of our expectation (a tragedy) and the actuality (horror, sometimes mixed with comedy)?

The stark, impersonal prose style is so typical in representing the experience of camps and besieged cities that one might be forgiven for assuming it to be the effect of trauma rather than an artistic choice on the part of the author or, for that matter, the writer's deliberate observance of a cultural script—that is, the selection of an available form appropriate to the subject matter, just as we would find in the study of an ode or an elegy. But we see this stylistic austerity clearly mandated in the so-called rubble literature (*Trümmerliteratur*) that arose in German immediately after the war and found ready analogues throughout Europe. So common does stripped-down prose become that it then assumes an air of authenticity, which authors of fraudulent texts like Wilkomirski and Defonseca would later exploit. For writers like Borowski and Shalamov, the spareness of style seems to elevate the brutality of the images and situations represented, since the narrative voice refuses to recognize the reader's horror or even to acknowledge that there is anything out of the ordinary to provoke horror in the first place. Borowski concludes "Supper" ("Kolacja"), for example, by telling us matter-of-factly that "a Muselmannified Jew from Estonia I was hauling pipes with assured me fervently all day that the human brain really is so delicate that you can eat it without cooking, completely raw."[34] "And everyone who'd managed to get hold of Solidol [American-made engine grease]," Shalamov remarks offhandedly in reference to slow starvation in Kolyma, "would lick their fingers for several hours, would swallow the minutest bits of this happiness from overseas, similar in flavor to a young stone."[35] The disjunction between the detail that provokes shock and the tone that denies it produces an effect that is not tragic, but visceral, horrifying, and at least a little bit comic. It is, in a word, *grotesque*.

The grotesque arises here as a natural symptom of the camp's ironic distance from itself, from the fact that, in the camp, one approaches the extremity of experience where horror and its metaphor, its travestying repetition, become one and the same. In all kinds of other experiential spaces—from the monotonous workplace or dreary factory to the hospital during a pandemic—one might imagine oneself living *as if* in a camp or ghetto or city under siege, one might even say so in a moment of duress, never having experienced *that* space, *that* duress, except as a metaphor. Only in the besieged city can one live not *as if*, but *within* the metaphor, "in the blockade way." Only in the camp can one inhabit what is for most of us a metaphorical image, a metonymic reference point in language, "Auschwitz," as a camp.

The Spectacle of Survival

Before the companion's demise, however, we are treated to another staple of zombie apocalypse cinema, the tour of Robinson Crusoe's quarters, a mélange of civilization and its opposite. "Just look," Rafalski says to his newfound canine friend, "how well we will live."[36] In watching a zombie film, we demand a resourcefulness from the hero that is almost superhuman. We want to see not only how she survives her solitude and deprivation, but how she triumphs over it. We require a demonstration, proof that a single human being, completely alone in the world, is capable of rebuilding an entire civilization. Sitting comfortably in a movie theater or, now more than ever, in our own homes, we enjoy watching the performance of industriousness and ingenuity, which the camera conveys to us with documentary, even fetishistic attention. What we are looking for is affirmation that a human being can survive anything.

The zombie apocalypse creates no less a spectacle of survival than we find in camp literature. More to the point, it creates the *same kind of spectacle*, observing the same conventions to tell much the same story, that of someone who survives the end of the world by recreating aspects of the old life while directly confronting the new one, all the while avoiding the "Man-Eaters," who look like us but are not us, who seek either to destroy us or to turn us into one of them.

The spectacle of survival is so powerful, in fact, that it has become a staple of global television, where one can find any number of quasi-documentaries that demonstrate lone survival strategies for all kinds of terrain and circumstances. Documentary-format shows like Canada's *Survivorman* (2005–2015) and the UK-produced *Man vs. Wild* (2006–2011) are distributed internationally and have spun off additional series. There are also gamified versions of the wilderness survival show, notably *Survivor*—which originated in Sweden in 1997 under the telling name *Expedition Robinson*, as the Polish version is also called. All of these programs serve the same purpose—namely, to reassure us through vicarious action that one can find safety and even some material comfort in the most precarious circumstances. Construed most broadly, this is one of the fundamental plotlines in Western literature, evident in the ancient epics of Greece and Iceland, and easily inclined toward satire: in the wildly popular 1960s American sitcom *Gilligan's Island*, the castaways eventually succeed in constructing a working automobile from coconuts and bamboo.[37]

We know, of course, that these narratives are not only about material survival, but moral survival as well. But as we have seen throughout this book, moral principles in a state of total isolation are barely theoretical: they are theory without the potential for actualization. In order to rebuild the moral universe, there have to be *others*. The hero of a postapocalyptic zombie film eventually meets other people, often shortly before she herself dies. She thus becomes a savior playing a role that will subsequently define her. The predictable sexual politics of this convention, with a male hero most frequently stepping in to save a younger woman or girl who then remains under his care, reflects the chauvinism of the storytellers and the audience. It has nothing to do with the demands of the genre per se.

In *Warsaw Robinson Crusoe*, Rafalski rescues a young girl, Krystyna, from a Nazi, whom he shoots on the street. From this moment on, his solitude is disrupted by Krystyna, and his goal evolves from that of personal survival to protecting the life of another. It is in this shift that we see a rebirth of an elementary sociality, the foundation for the future society. Rafalski soon meets other people who have likewise been hiding out in the ruins of Warsaw: the brothers Andrzej and Julek, the bibliophile Leon, all three having been mentioned in passing in the treatment's prologue. For his part, Rafalski is noticeably older than these newcomers—he introduces himself as "Uncle Piotr" even to "Gray," the dog, adding that this is what he had been called in the factory where he had worked before the war—and the detail is structurally significant. He naturally assumes the role of authority and paterfamilias, and he immediately realizes that, as an emissary of the past, he bears a moral obligation to protect these younger persons: "Rafalski is ever tormented by the thought that they could be discovered. Now, his resignation from life and his grudge against Andrzej for stealing Krystyna away from him are bound to a new worry. He overcomes his hurt and wants just one thing: to save the young people."[38]

From a structuralist perspective, the postapocalyptic zombie film consists of a dramatic, albeit relatively simple inversion of the hero's orientation toward the society around him. He is initially interested only in his own survival (or else in the survival of a very small group of relatives, friends, or allies). This is the part of the film that most delights in the hero's ingenuity. Later, though, after meeting the younger generation, everything changes. The hero starts to wonder whether what he had sought earlier—survival and companionship—still has the same value. He consciously determines that isolation and self-sacrifice are his destiny. This theme of Christian martyrdom can be expressed in remarkably unsubtle ways.[39]

In the hero's reorientation we can see one of the most persistent themes in Miłosz's work—that is, the difficulty of finding a clearly marked moral path. "Undoubtedly," the poet writes of Rafalski's decision, "the sacrifice here is associated with giving up. In this way we achieve a psychological framework that indicates how nobility is never as simple as it seems."[40]

The hero's isolation and sacrifice cannot be accidental. They have to have the power of resulting from a clear ethical calculation. Rafalski knows that he is facing a difficult decision. The enemies are certain to find his hideout sooner than later, and the youths will not have any chance for survival if Rafalski does not protect them. Now, just as at the beginning of the film, he is alone: "The bonds that had seemed to connect him with life again now seem to have been cut. He returns to his former level of solitude—and through this triumph he achieves peace and equilibrium."[41]

In keeping with Miłosz and Andrzejewski's long investment in questions of morality, the culmination of Rafalski's character evolution is his *triumph over himself*. The hero, who has the same right to life as anyone else, resigns from life so that others may live. This would be meaningless if Rafalski had not *wanted* to live. But he does, which is why the more he feels a desire for life and the more he enjoys the company of his new friends and the young woman, the more difficult his subsequent self-isolation and sacrifice will be. This may be why the chapter on "Rafalski's fate" is the briefest portion of Miłosz and Andrzejewski's text. After all, the most essential part of the drama, Rafalski's struggle with himself, has already been resolved. Thus the text is silent on the details of Rafalski's death. It is clear that he dies, but there is never any intention to show it in the film.

In nearly all films of this kind, the epilogue presents the young people who have been saved by the hero's sacrifice moving toward a new life of security. Safe, they leave their hideouts knowing that the worst of their ordeal has already passed; there is no longer the same menace as before, help has arrived, the antidote has been found.

Zombie apocalypse films, like the film that Miłosz wanted to make from Szpilman's account of real-life survival, are inextricably bound with the theme of war. Arguably the first appearance of the hordes of walking dead on film, in fact, is Abel Gance's 1919 film *J'accuse*, which, to underscore the senselessness of the mechanized warfare that Europe had just experienced for the first time, features a scene in which a returning soldier is chased down the road by those who have fallen on the battlefield and are now holding the living accountable for their pointless deaths.[42] Gance used real veterans to stage the scene—we can even spot Blaise Cendrars, his assistant director, who had lost an arm in the war—and montages images of the march of the dead together with documentary footage of an actual march of soldiers. In this way, Gance anticipates a stock trope of zombie apocalypse cinema, the elevation of the representation's realism through interposing footage of real-life conflict and disaster. Zarzycki does the same thing at the beginning of *The Unvanquished City*, interspersing fragments of documentary film into his otherwise staged drama.

Does this mean that we have Miłosz and Andrzejewski to thank for one of the most productive subgenres in postwar cinema? Certainly not. But we can say without question that the authors' acute sensitivity to the anxieties of postwar Europe enabled them to anticipate how those anxieties might be represented in narrative film. Their intention was never to make a drama about history. They sought instead to make a horror movie about the present.

Why Read Camp Literature?

(A Conclusion)

> On what else would our constant anguish feed if we did not all feel we had a small part in universal evil?
> —IMRE KERTÉSZ, *THE PATHSEEKER* (TRANS. TIM WILKINSON)

In 2018, while I was making a difficult journey of site visits across Poland, Germany, and France, I was talking to a bookseller at the Dachau camp museum who had stopped to ask me about my peculiar practice of entering these places and carefully photographing the selection and arrangement of the books themselves. (In fact, being preoccupied with genre, I do this quite often when I travel and enter a bookstore in a foreign city.) The bookseller was very curious about what I was doing, pointing out that of course people take lots of photographs at a place like Dachau, only they usually do so *outside* the museum store, in the site itself. We got to talking about my interest in how these sites are represented, an enthusiasm she shared, and she led me over to a table where many books were arranged (figure con.1). With a heavy sigh, she expressed her exasperation that hardly anyone ever buys *this*—and she indicated a number of books, among which I recall seeing Jan Karski's *Story of a Secret State*, one of the very first factual accounts of Nazi camps and ghettos to appear in English, as the war was still ongoing. But, she said, they sell tons of copies of *this*—and here she pointed specifically to *The Boy in the Striped Pajamas*. I was reminded of this when the Auschwitz-Birkenau State Museum issued a public statement warning the public against the very thing the bookseller lamented—namely, accepting as "true" a sentimental narrative like *The Boy in the Striped Pajamas*, an authorial invention that assumes facts about the camp experience that were not only historically inaccurate, but

Figure Con.1 The book display at Dachau includes documentary sources, fictionalized retellings, and outright inventions, offering no instruction on which is which. *Source*: photograph by the author

historically implausible and distorting. To which the novelist John Boyne, the author of *The Boy in the Striped Pajamas*, responded that fiction "cannot contain inaccuracies, only anachronisms," a self-serving defense that reveals a pathetic incomprehension of one's own activity, not to mention of genre as such.

Despite the reality of concentration camps and besieged cities as constituent institutions of life *in the present*, the concern over how to represent these spaces truthfully seems to take on more urgency as the living memory of camps in the *last century* fades. In the last decades of the twentieth century, there was already a great deal of public consternation among historians, archivists, advocates, and literary scholars that we were on the verge of losing the living memory of the spaces I discuss in this book. The death of every survivor is also the silencing of what they might have said.[1] And social research at the beginning of the twenty-first century gives us every reason to trust that these fears are well-founded. A 2021 survey of the United Kingdom found that a third of respondents "were unable to name a single one of the more than 40,000 camps or ghettos established" during the Second World War.[2] In 2018, the same organization found that close to half of the Americans surveyed were similarly ignorant.[3] A separate study from 2014 found that the "most-read book and the most-watched film about the Holocaust among students" in the United Kingdom is *The Boy in the Striped Pajamas*, John Boyne's popular and sentimental 2006 novel and its film adaptation (dir. Mark Herman, 2008), which the same study found "can reinforce an inaccurate perception of German ignorance of the Holocaust."[4] Meanwhile, in the countries of Central Europe, particularly those whose politics has been dominated in recent years by the turn toward "illiberal democracy" and neofascism, the history of camps, ghettos, and besieged cities is increasingly manipulated to serve a preconceived party narrative. In Russia, the administrative center of Memorial, the loose network of organizations and volunteers documenting the crimes of the Soviet Gulag system (and cofounded, incidentally, by Lev Razgon), was officially outlawed in April 2022, shortly after Russia invaded Ukraine and established a new system of concentration camps along its border.[5] Since the early 2010s, prisoners with a privileged position within the camp hierarchy of the Russian prison system have once again come to be called *Kapos*, just as they were in the Nazi system.

The erosion of common cultural knowledge about the history of open confinement has fueled the urgency to record as many testimonials of survival in camps, ghettos, and besieged cities as possible before time runs out. That this urgency has coincided with the rapid development of technologies for gathering, cataloguing, and archiving information has meant that we are vastly expanding our reference points to a period that is already arguably the most densely studied in the history of our species.

I am motivated here by a different urgency: my strong conviction that we have been reading these spaces incorrectly, unreflectively, and irresponsibly, especially in the anglophone literary marketplace, not recently, due to our distance from *what* these texts represent, but for more than a half-century, due to our weak understanding of *how* these texts represent. Unlike in France, Germany, or the former Soviet Bloc, where postwar political debate, collective trauma, and the task of rebuilding tended to dampen interest in written wartime accounts for a decade or more, in the United States and Britain there has been an appetite for these kinds of representations since before the Second World War ended, and since that time these texts have been divided cleanly into fiction and nonfiction, a generic boundary that is unstable, where it exists at all, in the cultures and languages from which most of these texts are generated. And because genre designations provide us with the basic instructions on how to interpret what we are reading, we often find ourselves ascribing facticity to fiction, or else assuming that what is presented as invention therefore has no value as a historical detail. This book is, then, in no small part the fruit of a certain *ressentiment* born of observing popular critics, and more than a few specialists, approve fictionalizations as fact, or outright fraud as autobiography, often with nothing more than one's own emotional attachment to the text supporting that text's claim on lived experience, as though establishing a representation's veracity could transform our feelings into truths. Woe to the author who, like James Frey, strikes that nerve and, once his narrative tricks have been exposed, forces the reader to question whether his emotional investments were also a sham.

My central argument throughout this book—an argument proffered polemically as an antidote to the irresponsible reading I have outlined—is that parallactic reading, always with an eye to comparing the present with the past and one space with another, allows us to overcome the ethical trap that sequesters this material from us, in another place, some other time, where our verdicts about good and evil and justice have already been handed down.

The Unending Urgency of Comparison

Reading the literature of concentration camps, ghettos, and besieged cities as adhering to a shared set of representational norms and, in the last chapter, suggesting that contemporary zombie horror belongs structurally to the same genre, will strike some readers as idiosyncratic, even despite the dense commonalities I have indicated throughout this study. For other readers, the very possibility of connecting the experience of survival in a Soviet labor camp and a Nazi death camp would seem to threaten the distinctiveness of one's experiences of such spaces. But the consistency in representational norms in regard to all of these spaces goes to the heart not only of how those of us who have not experienced camps firsthand come to know them through text, but also of why we should engage with these texts in the first place. Like Dante, we are guests passing through a strange universe structured concentrically, as much in its concept as in its physical layout. The question of what constitutes an appropriate use of the term "concentration camp" is naturally contained within a broader question of genres and representational norms as they pertain to these kinds of spaces, and the interrogation of these norms is contained in turn within a broader taxonomic dilemma of how to treat spaces that we interpret through more than one institution at once: the concentration camp that is also a ghetto, the ghetto that is also a besieged city, etc., and by the same token, the fiction that is also "real-life." This is a world of paradox, David Rousset's "concentration universe": "It was a world set apart, utterly segregated, a strange kingdom with its own peculiar fatality. The depths of the camps."[6]

While we must remain mindful of the historical realities that distinguish the Nazi labor and death camps from the institutions of forced "correctional" labor in the Soviet Union, as well as from the experience of survival in besieged cities or in hiding, those distinctions cannot suffice to hold separate those textual representations that are in conversation with each other and, in increasingly obvious ways, modeled on one another. The artfully awkward title of Leona Toker's excellent recent study *Gulag Literature and the Literature of Nazi Camps* reflects precisely the discomfort with the comparison between these spaces.[7] "Literature," Toker's title announces *twice*, reflecting the care she takes to emphasize that the Nazi camp *is not* the Soviet Gulag, and that what she compares in her study is the literature of the *one* with the literature of the *other*. Toker thus adopts what she calls an "intercontextual" approach—again, she is careful to maintain a historical separation between the two camp systems as institutions—and so she draws our attention to the ways in which two comparable and largely coincident phenomena generated two parallel and often self-consciously competing streams of textual production in the postwar period.

While I find Toker's work persuasive and the delineations she draws important, in my own work, which focuses on genre and the ethics of representation, the most important of those distinctions is that in the immediate postwar period most of the world did not need to be convinced that there were concentration camps and related sites of internment throughout Nazi-occupied Europe, and that these had been at the heart of a remarkably complex and effective program of forced labor and mass extermination. For a decade after the war, however, the *denial* that the Soviet Union was maintaining a vast network of forced labor camps within its own borders was the norm among intellectuals in Western Europe and especially in

France, where many writers on the left emerged from their war experiences idealizing Stalinism (or, more accurately, what they then believed Stalinism to be) as a kind of *humanizing* counterpoint to German Nazism and Italian Fascism.

In other words, while I certainly agree that it is necessary to acknowledge those differences, doing so too emphatically risks eliding the commonality of their *representational* norms. Whether we are talking about the literature that emerges from concentration camps—by which I mean forced labor, so-called correctional labor, and extermination camps, or besieged cities like Leningrad, or ghettos, the largest of which were administratively designated as *containing* concentration camps whose borders were roughly coterminous with the ghettos themselves—the representational norms are *functionally equivalent*. In each instance, the author simulates textually an experience of space, time, and agency that most people will (thankfully) find otherworldly.

Here I would note that even the historical distinctions between these spaces can themselves elide significant overlaps. For example, some major Nazi camps, including Buchenwald and Sachsenhausen, became camps of the Soviet NKVD almost immediately after the Red Amy's arrival in Germany, in a chilling demonstration of authoritarian efficiency. At the same time, the historical distinctions themselves, both between the kinds of spaces and between fact and fiction in their representation, are quickly eroding from the public consciousness.

As far as public memory is concerned, the historical distinctions between theses spaces are giving way to a single conception or, more accurately, are returning to the capacious concepts of a "concentration universe" or "world apart," a novel reality that is itself not unlike a storyworld, with permeable, fungible, or ambiguous borders, which are nevertheless defined and deadly; with enough freedom of movement and contact to foster its own peculiar social forms, which are themselves highly performative, even as it is a movement of slaves; and, but for those marked for death, with no time horizon, no foreknowledge of when this world will end. Rousset's own postwar activism against Soviet corrective labor was motivated specifically by his having become convinced that the world he had experienced in Buchenwald, a world that was supposed to have ended with the Nazi regime, lived on, hidden in plain view in the vast open spaces of the Soviet Union.

Inventing a Genre

Rousset's *L'univers concentrationnaire* lays the foundation for how this literature would be received. Its second English-language edition, appearing in 1951, is translated as *A World Apart*, establishing a less cumbersome, conceptually more expansive terminology than "the concentration universe," one that would then have renewed life in the English-language title of Herling-Grudziński's *Inny świat*. (It so happens that Herling-Grudziński's book, though written in Polish by an author then living in Naples, was first published in English in London and New York, also in 1951.) But the first English edition of Rousset's book, published in 1947 as *The Other Kingdom*, offers us an even more powerful precedent, one that is easily legible in the book's paratext. Malcolm Cowley's blurb on the front cover characterizes the book as "a brief sociological report," which would suggest that Rousset's book is a work of nonfiction. Yet the book itself is insistently novelistic and departs significantly from the author's own experience.

Since so much of my study is invested in questions of genre—and specifically in questions of the claims that highly stylized literary texts make on historical representation and collective memory, of how genre guides us in our reading of both text and experiential reality—indulge me to share just one more example of what I have sometimes called "genre dysphoria." Elie Wiesel's celebrated novel *Night*—and, though clearly autobiographical, based on the author's personal experience of survival in Auschwitz and Buchenwald, it is indeed a novel by design, self-consciously composed by a professional fiction writer according to the conventions of novelistic discourse—is about as close to "required reading" as one can find on American high school and college curricula in the decades after its publication, so chosen because it provides important insight into what it felt like to be a child in the precarious circumstance of a Nazi concentration camp. When we look to the back of the 1987 American edition, we have a very hard time determining whether this book is fiction or nonfiction. It forms the first volume of a trilogy, the second and third volumes of which—*Dawn* and *The Accident*—are designated unambiguously as "short novel" and "fiction," respectively, whereas *Night* is characterized as an "autobiographical account." Looking to the copyright page and the author's introduction—in effect, the transition from paratext to text—does little to clarify matters. We see that the text we are reading was first published in French in 1958, and that the author himself refers to all three parts of the *Night* trilogy as "narratives" and "stories." All we learn with certainty is that the author feels quite secure in the perfection of his creation, that he "would not change a single word."

Of course, he already has, and in many ways, and not only in the translation of the text from French to English (and many, many other languages besides), or in the multiple reeditions of the work, as separate volumes or as this omnibus. We also have Wiesel's earlier effort to tell the same story as *Night*, not in French or, for that matter, Romanian or German, both of which were spoken in Wiesel's home, but in Yiddish, as *And the World Kept Silent* (*Un di velt hot geshvigen*), in 1956. Needless to say, this version of what would become *Night* did not find a wide readership. It is also significantly more like a documentary text, less novelistic in its storytelling, more testamentary in its recitation of names, dates, and locations, material that was subsequently stripped away in making the version that brought Wiesel worldwide fame. The text changes over time, responding to the needs and interests of the non-Jewish audience Wiesel was intent on reaching, and in the process the line between fiction and nonfiction becomes more difficult to trace.

In the reading cultures of Central and Eastern Europe, such genre slippage would be unremarkable. First of all, mainstream journalistic practice in Europe has long made room for texts that blur the boundary between factual reporting and imaginative fancy, both in the short form ("feuilletons") and in the longer form ("reportage," which is markedly different in Russian or Polish from Anglo-American long-form journalism). When these texts enter anglophone discourse, especially as it existed in the postwar United States, they have to be subsumed into what Dwight Macdonald called "the fact-fetishism that is characteristic of the age of consumption." "Compared to the straight-forward old utilitarian attitude toward Facts," Macdonald wrote in 1957, "this new approach is decadent, even a bit perverse. Instead of being interested only in useful information, we now tend toward the opposite extreme, valuing Facts in themselves, collecting them as boys collect postage stamps, treating them, in short, as objects of consumption rather than as productive tools."[8]

As we have seen, this yields a profound potential for fraud. The very same devices used by actual survivors to make their works viscerally compelling and urgent—again, the devices of literary fiction—are also available to those who merely wish to convince readers that they have survived the same or similar circumstances. Given the difficulties posed by any effort to treat these texts as evidentiary documents memorializing actual lived experience, how can we continue to make a claim for their moral urgency?

Moral Urgency: Camps in the Present Tense

The more these texts' moral urgency is couched in instrumental terms, the more problematic it is revealed to be. At the most generic level is the argument that reading morally and aesthetically complex literature cultivates higher orders of empathy, and presumably also of moral conduct, on the part of the individual reader. Martha Nussbaum's influential reflections on this point find their counterpoint in the work of scholars like Joshua Landy, who not only questions whether there are lasting "salutary effects" of reading at all, but goes so far as to suggest that the expansion of empathic awareness that Nussbaum, Wayne Booth, and others impart to narrative could have negative consequences. After all, a sociopath who reads himself into a deeper appreciation of emotions and motivations becomes that much more dangerous as a sociopath![9]

When it comes to the literature of concentration camps, ghettos, and besieged cities, however, the notion that reading provides necessary moral instruction proves inadequate, since the state of exception that these spaces maintain, both spatially and juridically, can hardly be thought in individual terms, as the historical challenges of determining individual culpability have repeatedly demonstrated. There is no one perpetrator of the Nazi genocide of European Jewry or the Soviet offensive against ideological heterodoxy, real or imagined, just as there is no one victim or form of victimization, which is also why there can be no justice that proves satisfactory in its fairness or proportionality, no path toward retribution or restoration.

Thus we find that the instrumental morality assigned to this literature is less likely to pertain to individual ethical action and applies much more to the body politic, expressed in the notion that we (plural) must read these narratives so that the phenomena they describe never happen again. Reading collectively, so this reasoning goes, keeps the collective from becoming perpetrators of similar atrocities and may ultimately guide the same community in its efforts to prevent others from becoming perpetrators or victims themselves. But here, too, the argument collapses against a wealth of readily available data. The abundance of literary representations about the horrors of confining large civilian populations in precarity, not to mention the overwhelming accumulation of archival, journalistic, cinematic, and other sources, has not prevented these circumstances and crimes from recurring on a more or less continuing basis.

As I have been working through these sources, I have remained constantly aware of the disconnect between our near-universal condemnation of the camp as a *historical* institution and our tolerance of it in the present, whether we are talking about over a million ethnic Uighurs in reeducation camps in Xinjiang, the thirty thousand people in U.S. administrative immigration detention on any given day, or the much larger number living in detention or refugee camps throughout Europe and the Middle East. One can argue, of course, that conditions in these spaces differ greatly from those of a Nazi or Soviet camp, just as one can—and many have—that the conditions of the Gulag system differed from those of Nazi camps during the war, or that a Nazi death camp differed from a Nazi labor camp, or that a large Nazi labor camp differed from a smaller one, and so on. Again, I am not suggesting that these differences do not exist, or that they are inconsequential to a robust understanding of historical fact. Rather, I am arguing that this exceptionalist deferral of comparison—the use (or abuse) of distinctive details to forestall an active comparison of experience between past and present, there and here, them and us, he or she and I—undermines both the instrumental argument and the ethos inscribed within the literary representations.

The conventions of the genre are insistently *presentist*. Unlike an evidentiary document, these representations alternate between a clipped, "austere" approach to detail and a higher, lyrical register. They re-focalize the narrative away from the author toward third parties, who are fictional composites rather than real individuals. They are frequently composed in the present tense rather than the past. This is not simply a symptom of style, though the frequency with which these very same genre markers are held up for praise by critics suggests strongly that they are lauding not the unique power of a unique personal narrative, but rather the author's having satisfied genre expectations that we, as readers, already bring to this kind of literature. The style has been engineered for immediacy, to convey to the reader that the camp is an institution of the present. Not that this happened to me, there, and then, but that it *is* happening to someone, somewhere, right now. And it is. Focusing on the past in these texts may therefore be not only a misreading of the texts themselves, but in fact the psychological mechanism that allows these spaces to remain among modernity's constituent institutions.

In drawing this argument, I am inevitably running roughshod over several entrenched orthodoxies about the spaces I discuss and how we read them. Not least of these is that both space and representation always demand to be historicized, that a Nazi concentration camp is not the same as a Soviet forced labor camp, which is not the same as a ghetto or a besieged city, and so on. Analogously, one may continue to argue, as many have, that Nazi Germany's attempt to exterminate European Jewry was different in kind from its campaign of political repression, which was distinct in turn from the Soviet Union's. While these objections undoubtedly merit consideration in our treatment of historical data—which also includes instances of ghettos officially designated as concentration camps, as well as of Nazi camps simply being appropriated into the Gulag system after the war—the distinctions tend to dissolve in literary representation, and even in popular memory. There is an odd way in which, counter to our insistence on historical uniqueness and specificity, we are constantly folding these events into metonymy, thereby refusing to accept our own incapacity to absorb the very history we feign to protect. The Siege of Leningrad envelops the Petrograd blockade a generation earlier. Some forty thousand sites of detention and murder distributed throughout Nazi-occupied Europe assume the name "Auschwitz." The proclamation "never again" echoes worldwide, except in those sites where "again" is happening now.

Today, right now, there are millions of men, women, and children living and dying in refugee camps, concentration camps, and besieged cities. How do we understand the disconnect between the slogan "never again" and the reality? Ideology offers an easy explanation. If one maintains an ideological adherence to the notion that the Shoah was absolutely unique in human history, then it becomes impossible to recognize the Nazi genocide of European Jewry as belonging to a dense network of related or analogous phenomena, regardless of how much information and reasoned analysis we might provide to support that claim. In such a view, "never again" meets no challenge in Serbian concentration camps or the Siege of Aleppo, since the clipped slogan is shorthand for something much more narrowly defined—namely, that the Nazi regime that dominated Germany and eventually much of Europe from 1933 to 1945 will "never" commit the same atrocities against the same victims during that same period—"again." Here, the ideological excludes the paradigmatic.

Another explanation for why "never again" can remain the coeval of the very conditions it would seem to exclude, however, is that the slogan refers to events whose meaning has already been established through narrative, whereas events that are ongoing—those that, according to Mikhail Bakhtin, are the only ones to which the term "event" would apply—have no meaning. The "uncertainty principle" of the event is that it can be open and meaningless, or closed and meaningful, but one cannot know what an event means without first knowing how it ends.[10]

Required Reading

By and large, the habits of reading, or of not reading anything at all, are for the public a matter of individual tastes and preferences, simply a question of how one prefers to spend his or her time. With one exception: literature that springs from historical atrocity.

Any reader in the United States or Western Europe, or at least any *good* reader, is expected to have at least a passing familiarity with titles like *The Diary of Anne Frank* or Elie Wiesel's *Night*, which is why these texts are so frequently adopted by school curricula and local library reading groups, beyond any inclination on the reader's part to pursue Holocaust studies. As we move eastward, the moral onus shifts slightly toward Soviet oppression, to Solzhenitsyn's *One Day in the Life of Ivan Denisovich* and Shalamov's camp stories. An American reader might be surprised to learn that one of the most influential textual representations of life in Nazi concentration camps among Israeli readers in the 1960s was *House of Dolls*, a highly fictionalized text by a pseudonymous author whose depictions of sexual slavery and violence were so sensational that they helped spur an entire subgenre of "Nazisploitation" fiction and film.[11] Though the present study has been limited to how anglophone literature has received European representations of open confinement in the middle of the last century, already an expansive and internally variegated body of work, it stands to reason that other textual traditions that represent historical atrocity will be similarly interested in those events and texts most immediately pertinent to local identities and historiographic traditions, and that a small selection of canonical representations will be similarly ascribed a moral urgency not otherwise assigned to most other literature.

Even if we can identify how that moral urgency finds its home in institutions of moral instruction—the church, the university, and eventually the intellectual community—we can question what moral urgency itself means in the context of one's private reading practices. Here we cannot ignore the moral prescription to "know" history, a knowledge that, when it comes to camp existence, is always locked in brackets or scare quotes by the very paradoxes we have been touring throughout, and particularly by the fact that for the vast majority of contemporary readers the camp is both ubiquitous and nonexistent, historical and present, wholly documented and beyond one's personal experience. In the "secular age," as we have seen, the accumulation of data framed as "factual" has simply replaced the "spiritual" (which, within a spiritual cosmology, is indistinguishable from fact). Our masscult, even as a "cult of the factish gods," remains a cult nonetheless.[12] Across world religions, the community's cohesion in the present is reified by the individual's reverence for the past, demonstrated in the observance of tradition and in piety toward one's ancestors. The imperative to "know" history is no different.

Is it possible for a textual genre to accrue interpretive norms—the rules and suggestions that shape our affective posture toward the text, as well as our understanding of its relation both to the extratextual life of its readers and the intra-textual construction of its storyworld—that functionally defeat meaningful interpretation, that frustrate, mislead, or thwart? The literature of concentration camps, ghettos, and besieged cities demonstrates not only that such self-veiling is possible, but also that it can hide the mechanism of its self-distortion even from otherwise astute and inquisitive readers. It is unfortunately the case that the instrumentalist moral position has inscribed itself into the genre's interpretive norms so thoroughly that challenging it by simple reference to the world collapses all too readily into what I sometimes call "stupid discourse." We need literature about concentration camps, the moral instrumentalist says, so that "this," the necessarily amorphous, unnamable thing (or at least the unnamed, the not properly named, the never to have a satisfactorily uncontested name), this thing that has happened, the agglomeration of countless things that have happened to countless unnamed persons, these things that have coalesced into one thing for which every name proves inadequate, just as every camp has melted into the name of a place (Auschwitz) that no longer shares its name with the actual place (the Polish town of Oświęcim)—we *need* this literature so that such a place, such places, never "happen" again (and again, the place is no longer a site, but a happening). Yet these places, this place, *do* happen, they *are* now. A "stupid" discourse, not in the sense of ill-informed, small-minded, or dull-witted; even the most erudite and creative reader struggles against those biases that normalize response, that expose the ideological demons of one's interpreting consciousness. No, a "stupid" discourse because when confronted with recalcitrant data it can only ever reassert itself.

What concerns me here is the misalignment of representations we make to ourselves and the things they represent. If we say we read this in order for these phenomena not to recur, we have to confront the failure of that project or realign the project, not simply repeat the self-assurance. When the emotional temperature of reading is elevated by personal trauma or cultural postmemory, when the text resonates with the reader's preferred vision of the past or the society's designation of the "right side of history," the ideological overwhelms interpretation, it drowns out the recalcitrant data of consciousness or bends it toward itself. We read this so that what it describes will never happen again. It is happening again. But we read it so that it won't. A stupid discourse. Is there any way out of it?

There is, but it demands our attention. And I do not use the word "attention" lightly. One can read, one often does read, without paying attention, let alone "tending" to one's attention, interrogating and retuning it, performing the upkeep and adjustments necessary to continue advancing into the text. In practical terms, this would mean, among other things, asking oneself at every turn how what is read on the page relates to and, even in its inevitably belated arrival (all text being the intrusion of the author's past speech into the reader's present experience), represents the reader's actuality, the bridge between that/there/then and this/here/now. This is exhausting labor, and it is not for everyone, perhaps not for most. And that's before we have considered the ethical urgency that these connections impose on the reader, with a violence that is not entirely metaphorical. You imagined that, had you seen that/there/then with your own eyes, you would have done something, you would have saved someone, you would have sacrificed yourself, but when you are confronted with this/here/now, you do nothing, you save no one, and all thoughts of sacrifice evaporate into the entertainment of an emotional resonance. Better to keep the past in the past, even when it is present.

So, again, why read this literature at all? One response, which attempts perhaps to recover the moral instrumentalism of the "never again" argument, is that this literature constitutes a direct, concrete marshaling of speech, not only against the camp as an institution, but against the authoritarianism that underpins that institution. Blanchot remarks that a signature feature of the authoritarian is his "repetition of an imperious monologue, when he enjoys the power of being the only one to speak and, rejoicing in possession of his high solitary word, imposes it without restraint as a superior and supreme speech upon others."[13] Commenting on this same passage, Barthes remarks, not without reserved admiration, on the durability of the tyrant's monologue, the "perpetuity" of what he calls "the ideosphere"—that is, "the linguistic system of an ideology," its closed, endlessly self-referential system of meaning, to which he appends analogues: *doxosphere*, *pisteosphere* ("since it concerns discourses of faith"), and so on.[14] It is, of course, one of the truisms of humanistic research that there is no way out of ideology, that we are always speaking within, against, or toward ideology, and that this is itself ideology, of which the "truism" is an obvious marker. But since ideology is always attempting to conceal itself as such, countervailing speech serves to unveil it, allowing us to situate our subjectivity more fully within the discourses around us. In other words, the literature of concentration camps, ghettos, and besieged cities ought to be read—*ought*, since we are still in the zone of the ideological, still within its normativities—this literature ought to be read because doing so activates it over and against the autocrat's monological drone. More to the point—so goes this line of argument—this literature ought to be read in the plural: multiple tellings, multiple perspectives, a seemingly endless parade of texts providing the same basic details about the same already familiar events in the same settings as one has already encountered elsewhere—a chorus of individual voices against the one voice that seeks to convert them into a monolithic silence.

This is, for me, an attractive argument, though not one I find persuasive, since it says nothing about why I would invest what precious little time I have for new reading into texts whose features and subject matter are already familiar, and whose relationship to the very same historical events that would lend them moral urgency is troubled, to say the least. Scholarly and popular histories, survivors' diaries and testimonials, other primary source materials, documentary films, essayistic reflections from later generations—all these could serve the purpose of countering the voice of the tyrant, and they have, and they do.

Here, then, in conclusion, is a different reason to read: to train ourselves to see the spaces of open confinement now, in the present. Justice is not a matter of fact. Where, then, is it made, if anywhere? In text? In history? Only, I believe, in the embodied memory of injustice, enacted through our resistance to it in the present moment.

Why read concentration camp literature? Not to teach us about the past, but to connect us to the urgencies of the present. Not to treat today's camps the same as those of the last century. Rather, in the modest hope that we will someday treat them differently.

Notes

Have We Been Misreading the Camps?

1. A key to Winfrey's success, so exceptional that the set from her talk show now features prominently in the National Museum of African American History, is her preternatural ability to simultaneously convey and amplify the emotional response of her studio and television audiences. We trust her because she clearly feels the same way as we do, or else we find ourselves feeling what she does. The narratives that Oprah Winfrey promoted on her show were frequently about surviving extraordinarily awful circumstances. Indeed, these introductory remarks will not be Winfrey's last appearance in this book.
2. In her September 2005 announcement and the interview that followed a month later, both Frey and Winfrey remark extensively on how the book derives its power from what is "real," "raw," etc. The 2006 interview taking Frey to task for misrepresenting and exaggerating details from his life, as well as a later 2011 interview in which Winfrey publicly apologizes for her unsympathetic treatment of the author, are readily available online, but Harpo Productions, which produced *The Oprah Winfrey Show* from 1986 to 2011, has effectively removed the original interview extolling the authenticity of *A Million Little Pieces* from public access.
3. "A Million Little Lies: Exposing James Frey's Addiction Fiction," Smoking Gun, January 4, 2006, http://www.thesmokinggun.com/documents/celebrity/million-little-lies?page=0,0.

4. Motoko Rich, "James Frey and His Publisher Settle Suit Over Lies," *New York Times*, September 7, 2006, B1. *A Million Little Pieces* was subsequently reissued with a prominent disclaimer conceding that not all its details are factually accurate as reported.
5. Blakey Vermeule, *Why Do We Care About Literary Characters?* (Baltimore: Johns Hopkins University Press, 2010). Referring directly to the Frey controversy, Vermeule compares it to a recent instance of readers being so "swept away" by a novel that, despite "being told, sometimes several times, that the characters were fictional, . . . they nonetheless persisted in trying to make them real" (19–20). But while Vermeule acknowledges the strange feedback loop of readerly desire and the misattribution of reality to fictional texts—"People tend to be inspired by the stories they believe to be real. They overattribute real existence to the stories they want to believe in" (20)—she does not fully address the fundamental question of why the reader would treat a historical figure in a nonfiction book any differently from an invented one.
6. A simplistic if no less pertinent response to these questions attaches the sense of a text's authenticity to what Walter Benjamin famously described as "aura," the air of authenticity that adheres to an "original" and is diminished with each generation of a copy. See Walter Benjamin, "The Work of Art in the Age of Its Technological Reproducibility: Third Version," in *Selected Writings*, vol. 4, *1938–1940*, ed. Howard Eiland and Michael W. Jennings, trans. Harry Zohn and Edmund Jephcott (Cambridge, MA: Harvard University Press, 2003), 251–283. Such reasoning positions lived historical experience as unique to individuals or communities in a given time and place, whereas a fictional narrative can be recast and reshaped any number of times. It is easy to illustrate this framework with examples: there are any number of fictional autocrats inspired by Joseph Stalin, but there was only one Joseph Stalin.
7. Primo Levi, *The Drowned and the Saved*, trans. Raymond Rosenthal (New York: Simon and Schuster, 2017), 127.
8. Victor Shklovsky, *Theory of Prose*, trans. Benjamin Sher (Normal, IL: Dalkey Archive Press, 1990), 5.
9. Shklovsky endeavored to provide just such an "estranging" representation concurrently with his reflections on narrative technique in *Theory of Prose*. See the memoir "Petersburg During the Blockade" (1923), in his *Knight's Move*, trans. Richard Sheldon (Normal, IL: Dalkey Archive Press, 2005), 9–20, and *A Sentimental Journey: Memoirs 1917–1922*, trans. Richard Sheldon (Normal, IL: Dalkey Archive Press, 2004).
10. Phillipe Lejeune, *On Autobiography*, trans. Katherine Leary (Minneapolis: University of Minnesota Press, 1988).
11. The stages of this evolution are various, but we can trace them through the Parnassianism that opens the twentieth century with an emphasis on the

aesthetic (recovering the Romantic faith in "truth in beauty") through post-structuralism and deconstruction.
12. The Dewey decimal classification (no relation to the philosopher) does accommodate fiction, but it is common in school and municipal libraries in the United States to dispense with it altogether, using the numbered system for nonfiction books and arranging fiction alphabetically by the author's surname.
13. In borrowing the concepts of "paratext" and "peritext" as articulated by Gérard Genette, I should note Genette's own debt to Lejeune's description of the "autobiographical pact," since, as Genette indicates, "the author's name fulfills a contractual function whose importance varies greatly depending on genre: slight or nonexistent in fiction, it is much greater in all kinds of referential writing, where the credibility of the testimony, or of its transmission, rests largely on the identity of the witness of the person reporting it. . . . The maximal degree of this involvement is obviously autobiography." Gérard Genette, *Paratexts: Thresholds of Interpretation*, trans. Jane E. Lewin (Cambridge: Cambridge University Press, 1997), 41.
14. The term "fact-checking" has only recently become current in such languages as French and German, though it is still treated as an import from American media culture. To the limited extent that the term is used in the languages of Eastern and Central Europe, it usually appears either in its English form or as a direct calque from the English, and it is used narrowly in the context of political reporting. Across the region, the notion of fact-checking a poem, for example, would seem utterly absurd, though this is precisely what is done at the *New Yorker* magazine, widely regarded as embodying best practices in journalistic fact-checking. See Parker Henry and Paul Muldoon, "How Do You Fact-Check a Poem?," December 21, 2016, in *Poetry Podcast* (*New Yorker*), MP3 audio, 23:17, https://www.newyorker.com/podcast/poetry/how-do-you-fact-check-a-poem.
15. Dwight Macdonald, *Masscult and Midcult: Essays Against the American Grain*, ed. John Summers (New York: New York Review Books, 2011), 225.
16. Macdonald also suggests that American media consumers are just as unlikely to invest in a nonfiction treatment of historical realities when such a treatment demands too much interpretive effort to determine what the truth is. He illustrates this point by referring to the weak public reception of Miłosz's *The Captive Mind*. See Macdonald, *Masscult and Midcult*, 206.
17. Stephen Colbert announced the term on *The Colbert Report* on October 17, 2005. The American Dialect Society subsequently named "truthiness" their word of the year.
18. The Frey controversy occurred just as the term "truthiness" was ascendant in cultural criticism. See, for example, Julie Rak, "Memoir, Truthiness, and

the Power of Oprah," *Prose Studies: History, Theory, Criticism* 34, no. 3 (2012): 224–242, and David Carr, "How Oprahness Trumped Truthiness," *New York Times*, January 30, 2006, C1.

19. Macdonald's most colorful example is that of Senator Joseph McCarthy. But we could also point to an example from a generation earlier—namely, Orson Welles's radio play *War of the Worlds*, based on H. G. Wells's novel, which caused public panic when it was broadcast on October 30, 1938.

20. The phrase itself is interesting, since unlike "the true story of" or "a true story," which have been appended paratextually to literary texts for centuries, "based on a true story" both makes a claim on the historical record and simultaneously acknowledges that it is *not* the historical record.

21. Suetonius, *The Twelve Caesars*, trans. Robert Graves (New York: Penguin, 2003), 146.

22. Sir Thomas Browne, *Religio Medici and Urne-Buriall*, ed. Stephen Greenblatt and Ramie Targoff (New York: New York Review Books, 2012), 133.

23. Adorno's remark that "to write poetry after Auschwitz is barbaric" has become especially pernicious in our effort to understand the relationship between the reality of camp experience and its literary representations, given how frequently it is repeated by commentators who neglect any serious consideration of what it might mean, or why it is that Adorno himself tacks it onto the end of a much more general theoretical discourse. Theodore W. Adorno, *Prisms*, trans. Samuel Weber and Shierry Weber (Cambridge, MA: MIT Press, 1983), 34.

24. It is important to note that the "terminal paradoxes" that Kundera describes belong not to the literature of concentration camps, ghettos, and besieged cities, but to a broad strain of modernist literature more generally, where "all existential categories suddenly change their meaning." What I am suggesting is that the experience of survival in camps and besieged cities in the middle of the last century shifts this sudden inversion of existential categories from the real experience of individual intuition and self-concept to the collective experience of a cultural institution.

25. Imre Kertész, *The Holocaust as Culture*, trans. Thomas Cooper (London: Seagull Books, 2011), 41. The peculiarity of this detail, what he calls its "impossibility," serves as a seed for Kertész's novel *Fatelessness*. He elaborates on this shift from actual experience to fictionalization in his quasi-memoir *Dossier K.*: "I was most curious about the reality that lay behind the *Revier*, or infirmary, with the eiderdown beds; in other words, how it was possible that in the heart of Buchenwald concentration camp there could be a hospital in which patients were able to lie in separate beds with bedclothes and could receive genuine medical care." Imre Kertész, *Dossier K.*, trans. Tim Wilkinson (Brooklyn, NY: Melville House, 2006), 72.

26. Quoted in Shoshana Felman, "A Ghost in the House of Justice: Death and the Language of the Law," *Yale Journal of Law and the Humanities* 13, no. 1 (2001): 247.
27. Alexander Etkind, *Warped Mourning: Stories of the Undead in the Land of the Unburied* (Stanford, CA: Stanford University Press, 2013), 18.
28. Slavoj Žižek, *The Parallax View* (Cambridge, MA: MIT Press, 2006), 17.
29. These antecedents include, in the nineteenth century, Dostoevsky's *Notes from the House of the Dead* and Tolstoy's *War and Peace*. Earlier texts include Daniel Defoe's *Journal of the Plague Year*.

1. Fraud

1. Alicia Esteve's fraudulent tale of survival, as well as her eventual unmasking, were reported widely in the international press. For comprehensive accounts of her scheme and its aftermath, see Robin Gaby Fisher and Angelo J. Guglielmo Jr., *The Woman Who Wasn't There: The True Story of an Incredible Deception* (New York: Simon and Schuster, 2012), and the documentary film *The Woman Who Wasn't There*, dir. Angelo G. Guglielmo Jr. (New York: Meredith Viera Productions, 2012).
2. See, for example, Peter Novick, *The Holocaust in American Life* (Boston: Houghton Mifflin, 1999), 12, 207–238.
3. The sometimes surprising formal consistency of camp narratives is not evidenced only in literature and film, but is a well-attested feature of actual survivor testimony. See, for example, Brian Schiff, Heather Skillingstead, Olivia Archibald, Alex Arasim, and Jenny Peterson, "Consistency and Change in the Repeated Narratives of Holocaust Survivors," *Narrative Inquiry* 16, no. 2 (2006): 349–377.
4. Robert Pinsky, *The Inferno of Dante: A New Verse Translation* (New York: Farrar, Straus and Giroux, 1994), 19, 303.
5. Agnieszka Soltysik Monnet goes so far as to suggest that Head/Esteve's partial re-focalization of her own tale on another individual who does *not* survive elevates its cathartic potential: "The revealing thing about this hoax is that the perpetrator did not invent a story of her own miraculous escape or heroism but a story of someone else's heroic death. She intuitively sensed that self-sacrifice generates far more emotional and symbolic currency than survival, no matter how lucky." Agnieszka Soltysik Monnet, "War and National Renewal: Civil Religion and Blood Sacrifice in American Culture," *European Journal of American Studies* 7, no. 2 (2012): 6.

6. Terrence Des Pres, *The Survivor: An Anatomy of Life in the Death Camps* (Oxford: Oxford University Press, 1976), 71. The "literary" quality of life in the camp is often remarked upon by the survivors themselves, though it need not pertain to survival. "Her end was so 'literary,'" Evgeniia Ginzburg remarks of a "Comintern German" woman with whom she was interned, "that one would not have dared to invent it in a work of fiction." Eugenia Semyonovna Ginzburg (Evgeniia Ginzburg), *Journey Into the Whirlwind*, trans. Paul Stevenson and Max Hayward (San Diego, CA: Harcourt, 1995), 363.
7. The I Survived series, a popular line of children's titles authored by Lauren Tarshis for Scholastic Books, is a prime example, featuring such titles as *I Survived the Shark Attacks of 1916*, *I Survived the September 11, 2001 Attacks*, and *I Survived the Nazi Invasion*, set in the Warsaw Ghetto. The narrative arc is virtually the same in all of the titles across the series, rendering the historical contexts as functionally equivalent containers for a single story retold in different settings. We can observe much the same principle when films are remade with new contexts that are more relevant to current audiences. This is the case, for example, with the 1947 film *The Search*, about a Czech Auschwitz survivor looking for his mother in postwar Europe, and its 2014 remake, which sets the same story in Russian-occupied Chechnya. See *The Search*, dir. Fred Zinnemann (Beverly Hills, CA: Metro-Goldwyn-Mayer, 1948), and *The Search*, dir. Michel Hazanavicius (Burbank, CA: Warner Bros., 2014).
8. Des Pres, *The Survivor*, 175.
9. Unfortunately, our human frailty provides an unending stream of current examples of fraudulent attempts to seek compensation for disasters or genocide. But the frauds that are committed for no other reason than the narrative satisfaction survival narratives provide remain the most significant points of comparison here. One that especially caught my eye as I began work on this material is the case of Mamoru Samuragochi, a well-regarded composer from Hiroshima, best known for his Symphony no. 1 (*Hiroshima*), as well as for the fact that a degenerative illness left him deaf for most of his career. When his fraud was exposed, the world learned that Samuragochi's compositions had been ghostwritten by a certain Takashi Niigaki, a music school lecturer, who claims that Samuragochi is not deaf at all, and that the cane he uses in public is also merely a prop. Niigaki has described Samuragochi's deafness as "an act that he was performing for the outside world," and an editorial that ran in the *Asahi Shimbun* newspaper concludes with the following telling assessment: "The *Asahi Shimbun* has also run stories about Samuragochi and his music from time to time. He should provide a full explanation. At the same time, as a member of the media, which has a soft spot for

touching stories such as his, I think we have much to learn from this revelation. Remembering the verse 'I vow to doubt moving stories while shedding tears,' a line from a poem by Shuntaro Tanikawa, I am left with nothing but an empty feeling inside." "Vox Populi: Japan's 'Deaf Composer' May Not Be the Artist He Claims," *Asahi Shimbun*, February 6, 2014, 1.

10. See "Oprah's Questions for James," Oprah.com, accessed September 19, 2024, http://www.oprah.com/oprahshow/Oprahs-Questions-for-James/10#ixzz2saEbMKy1.

11. Laurie Friedman, *Angel Girl*, ill. Ofra Amit (Minneapolis, MN: Carolrhoda Books, 2008). Rosenblat's fraud was exposed in December 2008, three months after Friedman's children's book was released, and so the book retains the "based on a true story" boilerplate prominently on its cover. Rosenblat's complete account, *Angel at the Fence*, was never officially released.

12. The heroic narrative about Defonseca's parents has also been called into question, especially once it was revealed that her father exposed several members of the local resistance after his arrest.

13. Stefan Maechler, *The Wilkomirski Affair: A Study in Biographical Truth* (New York: Schocken, 2001).

14. "Left to ourselves, however, with benefit as our goal, we would employ harsher, less entertaining poets and story-tellers, to speak in the style of a good man and to keep their stories to the principles we originally established as lawful, when our task was the education of our militia." Plato, *Republic*, trans. Robin Waterfield (Oxford: Oxford University Press, 1993), 95.

15. This is a major theme in volume 5 of *À la recherche du temps perdu*, where Proust remarks, "Sometimes the script from which I deciphered Albertine's lies, without being ideographic, needed simply to be read backwards." Marcel Proust, *In Search of Lost Time*, vol. 5, *The Captive & The Fugitive*, trans. C. K. Scott Moncrieff and Terence Kilmartin, rev. D. J. Enright (New York: Modern Library, 1993), 112. By the same token, Marcel later remarks to Albertine, "I don't mind telling you things that would generally be regarded as false but that correspond to a truth that I'm searching for" (217).

16. Michael Riffaterre, *Fictional Truth* (Baltimore: Johns Hopkins University Press, 1990), 1.

17. Jacques Derrida, *Without Alibi*, ed. and trans. Peggy Kamuf (Stanford, CA: Stanford University Press, 2002), 34.

18. L. V. Anderson, David Haglund, Natalie Matthews-Ramo, and Jim Pagels, "Can I Make Stuff Up? A Visual Guide," *Slate*, March 21, 2012, http://www.slate.com/blogs/browbeat/2012/03/21/mike_daisey_david_sedaris_david_foster_wallace_and_other_storytellers_who_can_make_stuff_up_.html.

19. Bertold Brecht, "A Short Organum for the Theater," in *Brecht on Theater*, ed. and trans. John Willett (New York: Hill and Wang, 1992), 204.

20. Leon Trotsky, *Literature and Revolution*, ed. William Keach, trans. Rose Strumsky (Chicago: Haymarket Books, 2005), 120.
21. Józef Czapski, *Lost Time: Lectures on Proust in a Soviet Prison Camp*, trans. Eric Karpeles (New York: New York Review Books, 2018), 35.
22. Phillipe Lejeune, *On Autobiography*, trans. Katherine Leary (Minneapolis: University of Minnesota Press, 1988), 27. Lejeune's emphasis. What I have described in passing as reading fact "holographically" present within the fictional text, Lejeune presents as "stereography," referring to writers like André Gide and François Mauriac, who, "if they had not *also* written and published autobiographical texts, even 'inadequate' ones, no one would ever have seen the nature of the truth that it was necessary to look for in their novels" (27; Lejeune's emphasis).
23. The peddler of bullshit, Frankfurt argues, "is not concerned with the truth-value of what she says": "That is why she cannot be regarded as lying; for she does not presume that she knows the truth, and therefore she cannot be deliberately promulgating a proposition that she presumes to be false: Her statement is grounded neither in a belief that it is true nor, as a lie must be, in a belief that it is not true. It is just this lack of connection to a concern with truth—this indifference to how things really are—that I regard as the essence of bullshit." Harry G. Frankfurt, *On Bullshit* (Princeton, NJ: Princeton University Press, 2005), 33–34. Frankfurt's definition implies that, in its wholesale disregard for the truth-value of its own representations, bullshit functions as a genre whose only useful instruction to the audience is not to engage with it at all, since it rejects any of the consistencies that allow us to interpret it correctly. We can confirm this with our earlier example of the conventions for organizing libraries and bookstores. One can easily imagine asking a librarian or bookseller for help finding texts with mixed or troubled genres: autobiographical or historical fiction, invented histories, etc. But another query—"Where can I find the bullshit?"—even with a more delicate term substituting for Frankfurt's, is absurd on its face: there is simply no way of designating the genre of a text that is indifferent to the uses of genre.
24. Jiří Rulf uses a similar argument in his defense of Ladislav Fuks, a writer of shocking fiction about the Shoah who, as a non-Jew, never experienced it as such: "The vampiric mark that Fuks would have to bear his entire life was his homosexuality. . . . [He saw that] it was not only Jews and Roma who would vanish in the concentration camps, but homosexuals as well. People later posed the question of how it is possible for a non-Jewish writer to identify with the fates of the Jewish minority so much as to dedicate a significant portion of his work to it. The answer is precisely in the fact that Fuks, too, belonged to a threatened minority." Jiří Rulf, *Literáti: Příběhy z dvacátého století* (Prague: Paseka, 2002), 121. The essential difference between

Wilkomirski and Fuks, however, is that Fuks never presented his Holocaust-themed novels, including *Mr. Theodore Mundstock* (*Pan Teodor Mundstock* 1963) and *The Corpse-Burner* (*Spalovač mrtvol*, translated as *The Cremator*, 1969), as factual accounts of his lived experience.

25. Lionel Duroy does this to an extent in his biographical study of Monique de Wael/Misha Defonseca. Unlike Maechler, however, who is consistently interested in how Dösseker's fabrications correspond with or reflect his actual experiences, Duroy is primarily invested in reconstructing the biographical and historical facts falsified in *Surviving with Wolves*. Duroy's book is also published separately from the text it comments on. See Lionel Duroy, *Survivre avec les loups: La véritable histoire de Misha Defonseca* (Paris: XO Editions, 2011).

26. Maechler, *The Wilkomirski Affair*, 278.

27. Of course, just because Maechler provides the tools for a parallactic reading of Wilkomirski's fraud does not mean that readers will not find the effort exhausting. For a journalist's account of grappling with the layers of meaning within Wilkomirski's deception, see Blake Eskin, *A Life in Pieces: The Making and Unmaking of Binjamin Wilkomirski* (New York: Norton, 2002).

28. This recontextualization, however, cannot be attributed solely to Maechler. Other sources treat Dösseker sympathetically.

29. Roland Barthes, *Criticism and Truth*, ed. and trans. Katrine Pilcher Keuneman (London: Continuum, 2004), 37–38.

30. Barthes, *Criticism and Truth*, 38. Barthes's emphasis.

31. By much the same token, Tadeusz Borowski (in 1947) emphasizes that the work of art cannot claim a correspondence to lived experience simply by having provoked an analogous psychological response: "If the Warsaw Uprising aroused fear and terror in certain people, and a film about Frankenstein has aroused fear and terror in certain people, that is still not enough for the film to be an artistic expression of the Uprising." Orig.: "Jeżeli powstanie w Warszawie budziło w pewnych ludziach strach i grozę i film o Frankensteinie budził w pewnych ludziach strach i grozę, to to jeszcze nie wystarcza, żeby film ten był artystycznym wyrazem powstania." Tadeusz Borowski, *Pisma w czterech tomach*, vol. 4, ed. Tadeusz Drewniowski (Kraków: Wydawnictwo Literackie, 2005), 188.

32. Avishai Margalit, *The Ethics of Memory* (Cambridge, MA: Harvard University Press, 2002), 174. Margalit's emphasis.

33. Linda Hutcheon, *Irony's Edge: The Theory and Politics of Irony* (London: Routledge, 1995), 117.

34. Hans Robert Jauss, *Aesthetic Experience and Literary Hermeneutics*, trans. Michael Shaw (Minneapolis: University of Minnesota Press, 1982), 121.

35. Kevin Young, *Bunk: The Rise of Hoaxes, Humbug, Plagiarists, Phonies, Post-Facts, and Fake News* (Minneapolis, MN: Graywolf Press, 2017), 295.

36. James Frey, *A Million Little Pieces* (New York: Vintage, 2004), ii.
37. Paul Badde, "Zvi Kolitz," in Zvi Kolitz, *Yosl Rakover Talks to God*, trans. Carol Brown Janeway (New York: Vintage, 1999), 58–62.
38. Kolitz, *Yosl Rakover Talks to God*, 3.
39. For Mallow and Beeck's reestablished text of "Yosl Rakover Talks to God," which they published in an English translation, see Zvi Kolitz, "'Yossl Rakover's Appeal to God': A Story Written Especially for *Di Yiddishe* [sic] *Tsaytung*," ed. and trans. Jeffry V. Mallow and Frans Jozef van Beeck, *Crosscurrents* 44, no. 3 (Fall 1994): 362–377. Paul Badde's later edition reestablishes the text on the basis of further research.
40. The same episode had made a similarly strong impression on Oprah Winfrey, compelling her to challenge him on it specifically during Frey's second appearance on her show.
41. By "strong response," I mean one in which the visceral and emotional experiences of the text precede, or *supersede*, the intellectual engagement that would peel back the layers of that response, and that is itself motivated by the visceral and emotional—just as laughter and horror precede our awareness of *why* we are laughing or screaming.
42. K. K. Ruthven, *Faking Literature* (Cambridge: Cambridge University Press, 2001), 70.
43. Sandor Goodhart, *Möbian Nights: Reading Literature and Darkness* (New York: Bloomsbury, 2017), 119–120. Van Beeck mistakenly calls Sutzkever's reprint of "Yosl Rakover" "a pirated piece of work": "not only did the translator fail to identify himself, the story itself was presented as anonymous." Frans Jozef van Beeck, *Loving the Torah More than God? Towards a Catholic Appreciation of Judaism* (Chicago: Loyola University Press, 1989), 10. In a brief acknowledgment, van Beeck thanks Kolitz personally "for permission to reprint the first published version (1947) of his story," not realizing that the "first published version" was the Yiddish text that van Beeck took to be fraudulent. Van Beeck, ii.
44. Emmanual Levinas, "Loving the Torah More Than God," in Zvi Kolitz, *Yosl Rakover Talks to God*, trans. Carol Brown Janeway (New York: Vintage, 1999), 80.
45. Levinas, "Loving the Torah More Than God," 80.
46. Levinas's characterization of Kolitz's story as "fiction" is sufficiently ambiguous to divide commentators on his ethics. Dorota Głowacka, for example, regards Levinas's use of "fiction" as signaling that he "correctly took the story to be a work of fiction, and he recognized its merits as such." Dorota Głowacka, *Disappearing Traces: Holocaust Testimonials, Ethics, Aesthetics* (Seattle: University of Washington Press, 2012), 240n8. Miroslav Petříček, meanwhile, offers an agreeably agnostic position, pointing out that Levinas's language "testifies to his having had doubts about [the story's] authenticity as a

document, though it is apparent that the question of the author plays no fundamental role for him." Miroslav Petříček, *Filosofie en noir* (Prague: Karolinum, 2018), 156.
47. Emmanuel Levinas, *Carnets de captivité, suivi de Écrits sur la captivité et Notes philosophiques diverses*, ed. Rodolphe Calin and Catherine Chalier (Paris: Bernard Grasset/IMEC, 2009), 79.
48. Leon Wieseltier, "A Privation of Providence," in Kolitz, *Yosl Rakover Talks to God*, 89–90.
49. Alvin Rosenfeld, writing from a similar position, is quick to point out the danger that such a perspective poses to historical understanding: "Kolitz, to be sure, almost certainly did not set out to fool anyone with a dissembling text but did what writers always do—imitate reality by constructing an approximate or ideal version of it. His story is not bogus or counterfeit history, then, but no history at all. Indeed, from his standpoint, it is a realistic fiction—an imaginative projection of how such a Jew *as* his narrator *might* have comported himself in a situation *like* that of the burning ghetto. 'Like' and 'as' and 'might'—the stock-in-trade of writers—are not equivalent to 'was'—the actual or verifiable past that historians set out to reconstruct—and no one gains from a confusion of the two realms of discourse and the separate realities they represent. No one, that is, except those who are on to the current fascination with Nazism and have sought to exploit it for their own ends." Alvin H. Rosenfeld, "Holocaust Fictions and the Transformation of Historical Memory," *Holocaust and Genocide Studies* 3, no. 3 (1988) 328. Rosenfeld's emphases. The danger of willful misinformation or obfuscation, however, is clearly mitigated by the same parallactic reading that Rosenfeld performs: keeping in mind that Kolitz's story *is not* a testimony becomes the precondition for reading it productively *as if it were* testimony, as well as for understanding how that "as if" *might* be used to enrich historical understanding.
50. Levinas, "Loving the Torah More than God," 80. The question of art's status within Levinasian ethics, particularly in regard to his powerful 1948 essay "Reality and Its Shadow" ("Réalité et son ombre"), has in recent years been the subject of extensive philosophical investigation, with notable contributions by Jill Robbins and Robert Eaglestone, both of whom underscore Levinas's guarded skepticism of artistic representation, which (in a Platonic turn of which Levinas is acutely aware) threatens to supplant the real with the invented. See Jill Robbins, *Altered Reading: Levinas and Literature* (Chicago: University of Chicago Press, 1999), and Robert Eaglestone, *Ethical Criticism: Reading After Levinas* (Edinburgh: University of Edinburgh Press, 1997). My own interpretation of Levinas's approach to fictional representation aligns with that articulated by Richard Cohen, who argues that "Levinas is not

against art, he is against aestheticism," just as he also rejects positivism in science as a path toward knowing the real. Richard A. Cohen, "Levinas on Art and Aestheticism: Getting 'Reality and Its Shadow' Right," *Levinas Studies* 11 (2016): 168.

51. M. David Weiss, "How We Remember the Warsaw Ghetto," *Jewish Advocate*, April 27, 1967, A3.
52. Stephan Feuchtwang, "Loss: Transmissions, Recognitions, Authorizations," in *Regimes of Memory*, ed. Susannah Radstone and Katharine Hodgkin (London: Routledge, 2003), 89n14.
53. David Roskies, "Seeking a Spiritual Message in a Fictional Bottle: The Ghetto Fighters Become Modern Macabees," *Forward*, December 3, 1999, 11. Elsewhere, Roskies and Naomi Diamant propose a much more persuasive candidate for the reverse of the Kolitz case in Yehoshue Perle's "The Destruction of Warsaw" ("Khurbn varshe," 1943), which the poet H. Leivick publicly denounced as a fraud in 1952, though the text turned out to have been authentic. "Both in form and content," Roskies and Diamant write, "Perle's chronicle was too raw to be admissible evidence of the authentic Jewish response to catastrophe." David G. Roskies and Naomi Diamant, *Holocaust Literature: A History and Guide* (Waltham, MA: Brandeis University Press, 2012), 98.
54. Blake Eskin, "Seeking a Spiritual Message in a Fictional Bottle: Yosl Rakover's Creator Talks to a Reporter," *Forward*, December 3, 1999, 11.
55. Zvi Kolitz, quoted in Sandor Goodhart, "*Conscience*, Conscience, Consciousness: Emmanuel Levinas, the Holocaust, and the Logic of Witness," in *Remembering for the Future: The Holocaust in an Age of Genocide*, vol. 2, *Ethics and Religion*, ed. John K. Roth, Elizabeth Maxwell, Margot Levy, and Wendy Whitworth (Basingstoke, UK: Palgrave, 2001), 101.
56. Susan Stewart, *Crimes of Writing: Problems in the Containment of Representation* (Durham, NC: Duke University Press, 1994), 154.
57. Michael Rothberg, *Traumatic Realism: The Demands of Holocaust Representation* (Minneapolis: University of Minnesota Press, 2000), 101.
58. *Das Ghetto*, filmed in Warsaw in May 1942. The original film is available for online viewing at https://cdn-0.archiv-akh.de/videos_mp4/M1053_WEB.mp4 (accessed May 18, 2022).
59. Rachela Auerbach, *Pisma z getta warszawskiego*, ed. Karolina Szymaniak (Warsaw: Żydowski Instytut Historyczny, 2016), 141.
60. *Das Ghetto*, 00:49:50.
61. In what can be regarded as an effort to make the theatrical permanent, after her fraud was exposed Monique de Wael/Misha Defonseca apparently had her left arm tattooed with the number her mother received when she was deported to Ravensbrück. See Duroy, *Survivre avec les loups*, 235.
62. Lejeune, *On Autobiography*, 149.

2. Parabiography

1. Lidiia Ginzburg, *Prokhodiashchie kharaktery: Proza voennykh let, Zapiski blokadnogo cheloveka*, ed. Emily Van Buskirk and Andrei Zorin (Moscow: Novoe izdatel'stvo, 2011), 311. Hereafter cited as *PKh*. Orig.: "В годы войны люди жадно читали «Войну и мир»—чтобы проверить себя (не Толстого, в чьей адекватности жизни никто не сомневался). И читающий говорил себе: так, значит, это я чувствую правильно. Значит, оно так и есть. Кто был в силах читать, жадно читал «Войну и мир» в блокадном Ленинграде."
2. The so-called blockade diary (*blokadnyi dnevnik*) is well established as a textual subgenre in Russian, with numerous published examples and countless others in manuscript. Typically, these are impressionistic texts consisting of dated entries that are contemporaneous or nearly contemporaneous with the events and perceptions they record. That is, they are diaries in the conventional sense, most of them kept by nonprofessional writers. In her thorough study of such diaries, Alexis Peri is careful to refer to texts like *Notes of a Blockade Person* and Olga Bergholz's *Daytime Stars* (*Dnevnye zvezdy*, 1955–1959) not as "diaries" but as "diary-like accounts," recognizing that the belatedness of the texts and their play with literary form distinguishes them from the diary as a genre. Alexis Peri, *The War Within: Diaries from the Siege of Leningrad* (Cambridge, MA: Harvard University Press, 2017), 12.
3. Harrison Salsbury provides a counterexample that is worth mentioning for its peculiarity alone. He recounts how, in December 1941, Joseph Orbeli, the then director of the Hermitage Museum, had organized a scholarly meeting to mark the five hundredth anniversary of the birth of the Turkic poet Ali-Shir Nava'i (spelled "Navoi" by Salisbury, referring to his name in Russian). By this point in the blockade the Hermitage staff were subsisting on a diet of frozen potatoes fried in linseed oil and repurposed paste; several participants in the meeting were on the edge of death. In an especially dramatic moment, a young scholar named Nikolai Lebedev uses the last of his strength to recite Nava'i's poems at the gathering of scholars. He then expires. Harrison E. Salisbury, *The 900 Days: The Siege of Leningrad* (New York: Harper and Row, 1969), 430.
4. There is a long critical tradition that probes the veracity of Tolstoy's historical representations, a tradition to which Ginzburg contributed significantly, which makes her disinterest in the problem as she opens *Notes of a Blockade Person* that much more striking. For an effective digest of how Tolstoy's representations have been received, both by his contemporaries and by later critics, see especially Dan Ungurianu, "The Use of Historical Sources in *War and Peace*," in *Tolstoy on War: Narrative Art and Historical Truth in "War and*

Peace," ed. Rick McPeak and Donna Tussing Orwin (Ithaca, NY: Cornell University Press, 2012), 26–41.

5. Erich Auerbach, *Mimesis: The Representation of Reality in Western Literature*, trans. William R. Trask (Princeton, NJ: Princeton University Press, 1953), 480.
6. Hayden White, *Figural Realism: Studies in the Mimesis Effect* (Baltimore: Johns Hopkins University Press, 1999), 70. Among these "holocaustal" events, White lists "two world wars, the Great Depression, nuclear weapons and communications technology, the population explosion, the mutilation of the zoosphere, famine, genocide as a policy consciously undertaken by 'modernized' regimes, etc."
7. White, *Figural Realism*, 70.
8. Lidiia Ginzburg, *O literaturnom geroe* (Leningrad: Sovetskii pisatel', 1979), 107.
9. Ginzburg, *PKh*, 311. Orig.: "Мне нужно было показать не только общую жизнь, но и блокадное бытие одного человека. Это человек суммарный и условный (поэтому он именуется Эн), интеллигент в особых обстоятельствах."
10. Ginzburg, *O literaturnom geroe*, 107.
11. The word-level connection between literariness, the conventions of literary representation, and individual contingency are much thicker in Ginzburg's Russian than in English. In Russian, one readily hears the etymological kinship between *uslovie* (convention, contingency, etc.), *slovesnost'* (philology, literariness), and *slovo* (word).
12. Ol'ga Berggol'ts [Olga Bergholz], *Dnevnye zvezdy* (Leningrad: Sovetskii pisatel', 1960), 38.
13. Ginzburg, *PKh*, 311. Orig.: "Вернее, точка приложения обстоятельств, с которой открываются другие обстоятельства и другие люди. Этот персонаж и всё, о чём здесь рассказано, возникли из разных свидетельств, из концентрации своего и чужого опыта." Ginzburg reworked her account of the Siege of Leningrad over decades, and the several published and unpublished versions, including those in her *Literature in Search of Reality* (1987) and *The Person at the Writing Desk* (1989), feature small but significant variations, especially in statements such as this one, where the author strives to formulate the intentions of her design.
14. Emily Van Buskirk, *Lydia Ginzburg's Prose: Reality in Search of Literature* (Princeton, NJ: Princeton University Press, 2016), 68.
15. Walter Benjamin, "Experience and Poverty," in *Selected Writings*, vol. 2, pt. 2, *1931–1934*, ed. Michael W. Jennings, Howard Eiland, and Gary Smith, trans. Rodney Livingstone (Cambridge, MA: Harvard University Press, 1999), 731–735. "Erase the traces!" is Brecht's refrain in the poem that opens his *Reader for City-Dwellers* (*Lesebuch für Städtebewohner*).

16. Walter Benjamin, "The Work of Art in the Age of Its Technological Reproducibility," in *Selected Writings*, vol. 4, *1938–1940*, ed. Howard Eiland and Michael W. Jennings, trans. Harry Zohn and Edmund Jephcott (Cambridge, MA: Harvard University Press, 2003), 253.
17. Among Sandauer's chief accomplishments is his having shaped the postwar interest in the prose of Bruno Schulz and Witold Gombrowicz.
18. In translating Sandauer's title as *Notes from the City of the Dead*, I am preserving its calculated echo of Dostoevsky's *Notes from the House of the Dead*, the most common English translation of his *Zapiski iz mertvogo doma*. A more accurate translation of Dostoevsky's title would be *Notes from the Dead House*, with Sandauer's text following suit as *Notes from the Dead City*.
19. Artur Sandauer, *Proza* (Kraków: Wydawnictwo Literackie, 1972), 137–138. Orig.: "Mroziła mnie ich bezbłędna polszczyzna, ich nieskazitelne rymy i przenośnie. . . . Przez zapach rynsztoków, przez charkot handełesów, przez zawodzenie żebraków dobiegałem do schodków, na których szczycie przystawałem na chwilę, aby otrząsnąć się ze wszystkiego, co przylgnęło po drodze, usztywnić się i ucywilizować."
20. Sandauer, *Proza*, 138. Orig.: "siedlisko żydowskiej nędzy i ciemnoty—Blich; przed sobą, na wzgórzu—nasz małomiejski Rynek. Do tej dzielnicy kultury i polszczyzny musiałem—najdosłowniej—się wspinać."
21. Mandel'shtam's negative characterization of his father's language appears in *The Noise of Time* (*Shum vremeni*, 1925). Osip Mandel'shtam, *Sobranie sochinenii v chetyrekh tomakh*, vol. 2, ed. P. Nerler and A. Nikitaev (Moscow: Art-Biznes-Tsentr, 1993), 361.
22. Sandauer, *Proza*, 138–139. Orig.: "Żydzi—twierdził—przebywając wśród obcych, winni bronić się przed asymilacją, dochowując wierności sobie i swemu narodowi. Pięknie! Ale Żyd już zasymilowany i umieszczony na pograniczu dwu narodowości, którejże z nich ma być wierny? I czyż ta wierność—zwłaszcza w okresie srożącego się antysemityzmu, kiedy być dwunarodowym to jakby mieć sforę psów rozżartych w sobie—nie musi oznaczać wierności wobec własnego rozdarcia, wobec własnej— nieautentyczności? I tak—polemizując myślowo z Sartre'em—zacząłem tworzyć Mieczyława Rosenzweiga, postać—jak już z samej nazwy wynika— rozdwojoną, z jednej strony głęboko nieautentyczną, bo nienawidzącą siebie samej, z drugiej—obdarzoną jakąś autentycznością wyższego rzędu, bo wypowiadającą tę sytuację jasno i bez ogródek."
23. The same trope began appearing in Holocaust-themed films almost immediately after the war had ended, beginning with *Long Is the Road* (*Lang ist der Weg*, dir. Herbert B. Fredersdorf and Marek Goldstein, 1948), the first German-language film to address the Nazi genocide of European Jews directly. The relevant scene occurs early in the film (00:25:12).

24. Sandauer, *Proza*, 141. Orig.: "Zdaję sobie sprawę, że w tej historii, która odpowiada skądinąd wszelkim kanonom okupacyjnej poetyki (w każdej nieomal powieści z tych czasów Żydzi idąc na śmierć odmawiają *Szma Isroel*, dając tym wyraz swemu przywiązaniu do wspólnoty plemienny i optymistycznej wierze w przetrwanie narodu), że w tej historii odmowa udziału w zbiorowej modlitwie przedśmiertnej stanowi zgrzyt szczególnie rażący. A jednak mam powody, aby wierzyć, że ów gest podwójnej odmowy, z jakim ojciec mój, socjalista i niedowiarek, skłócony przez całe życie zarówno z ciemnotą Blichu, jak i ze snobizmem Rynku, odrzucił propozycję pojednania z rodzimą społecznością, że ten przekorny i samowolny uśmiech, z jakim poszedł na śmierć, nie były przywidzeniem. Również i to wspomnienie stanowi jeden z elementów 'Mieczysława Rosenzweiga.' "
25. Sandauer, 108. Orig.: "wyobrażam sobie opowieść—najchętniej autobiograficzną, w której zmiennymi byłyby nie tyle style czy fakty, co tonacje. Jedno i to samo wydarzenie z własnego życia można by podawać kolejno w przyprawie niefrasobliwej lub tragicznej, realistycznej czy groteskowej. Zakładałoby to dystans i swobodę wobec własnych przeżyć, traktowanych jedynie jako materiał, któremu można nadawać dowolne kształty, i 'parabiografia' taka zdawałaby się biec nie tyle wzdłuż, co wszerz czasu; następstwo wydarzeń ustąpiłoby w niej miejsca ich oboczności."
26. Artur Sandauer, *Pisma zebrane*, vol. 2 (Warsaw: Czytelnik, 1985), 460.
27. Artur Sandauer, *Zebrane pisma krytycyzne*, vol. 3 (Warsaw: Państwowy Instytut Wydawniczy, 1981), 671n4.
28. Sandauer, *Zebrane pisma krytycyzne*, 3:616.
29. This distinction between Sandauer and Ginzburg need not be so schematic. In particular, Ginzburg's late essay on psychological staging from stream-of-consciousness to the French *nouveau roman*, "Literature in Search of Reality" ("Literatura v poiskakh real'nosti," 1985), comports well with Sandauer's writings on autothematism in the twentieth century. See Lidiia Ginzburg, *Literatura v poiskakh real'nosti* (Leningrad: Sovetskii pisatel', 1987), 4–57.
30. Michel Foucault, *Subjectivity and Truth: Lectures at the College de France, 1980–1981*, ed. Frédéric Gros, trans. Graham Burchell (New York: Picador, 2017), 238.
31. Ginzburg, *Literatura v poiskakh real'nosti*, ii. Orig.: "В моих литературведческих книгах последнего двадцатилетия тоже порой идёт прямой разговор о проблемах жизни, о психике человека. Эссеистика иногда естественным образом переходила у меня в повествование, даже с условными вымышленными персонажами. Они нужны мне в качестве объекта анализа тех или иных фактов душевного опыта."
32. Lydia [Lidiia] Ginzburg, *On Psychological Prose*, trans. Judson Rosengrant (Princeton, NJ: Princeton University Press, 1991), 199.

33. Kertész, *Dossier K.*, 7–8.
34. In the twentieth century, Mikhail Bulgakov's *A Young Doctor's Notes* (*Zapiski iunogo vracha*, 1925–1926) and Sergei Dovlatov's *Zona: Notes of a Camp Guard* (*Zona: Zapiski nadziratel'ia*, 1965–1968) are also relevant.
35. Fedor Dostoyeffsky [F. M. Dostoevsky], *Buried Alive, or: Ten Years of Penal Servitude in Siberia*, trans. Marie von Thilo (London: Longmans, Green, and Co., 1881).
36. Ivanov grounds his "theatrical" reading of Dostoevsky's novels in their formal arrangement, whereby "all the particulars are subordinated, first of all, to the small unity of the story's separate peripeteia, and in turn these peripeteia, bundled as if into the acts of a drama, appear as iron links in the logical chain from which the basic action, the point of the whole story, hangs like some planetary body." Viacheslav Ivanov, "Dostoevskii i roman-tragediia," in *Borozdy i Mezhi: Opyty esteticheskie i kriticheskie* (Moscow: Musaget, 1916), 410. Bakhtin's study is more widely known in English under the title of its 1963 revision, *Problems of Dostoevsky's Poetics* (*Problemy poetiki Dostoevskogo*).
37. Didier Fassin, *Prison Worlds: An Ethnography of the Carceral Condition*, trans. Rachel Gomme (Cambridge: Polity, 2016), 301.
38. Fassin, *Prison Worlds*, 301. Emphasis added.
39. Dostoevsky is surely drawing on this experience when he describes the theatrical demeanor of executioners in *Notes from the House of the Dead*: "It may be that the very pomp and theatricality of the situation with which they appear before an audience on the scaffold fosters the development of a certain arrogance within them." Orig.: "Может быть, даже самая парадность и театральность той обстановки, со которою они являются перед публикой на эшафоте, способствуют развитию в них некоторого высокомерия." F. M. Dostoevskii, *Zapiski iz mertvogo doma*, in *Pol'noe sobranie sochinenii v tridtsati tomakh*, vol. 4 (Leningrad: Nauka, 1972), 156. Subsequent references to the same edition will be abbreviated as *ZiMD*, followed by the page number.
40. Orig.: "Для меня всё это было ново, и я смотрел с любопытством. Но впоследствии я узнал, что все подобные сцены были чрезвычайно невинны и разыгрывались, как в комедии, для всеобщего удовольствия; до драки же никогда почти не доходило. Всё это было довольно характерно и изображало нравы острога." *ZiMD*, 23.
41. Orig.: "Диалектик-ругатель был в уважении. Ему только не аплодировали, как актёру." *ZiMD*, 25.
42. *ZiMD*, 306.
43. Orig.: "Баклушин ещё за неделю до представления хвалился передо мной... что и в санкт-петербургском театре не видывали. Он расхаживал по казармам, хвастался немилосердно и бесстыдно, а вместе

с тем и совершенно добродушно, и иногда вдруг, бывало, отпустит что-нибудь «по-тиатральному» [sic], то есть из своей роли,—и все хохочут, смешно или несмешно то, что он отпустил." *ZiMD*, 118.

44. Orig.: "Давался целый акт, но это, видно, отрывок; начало и конец затеряны. Толку и смыслу нет ни малейшего." *ZiMD*, 125.

45. Orig.: "Наши все росходятся весёлые, довольные, хвалят актёров, благодарят унтер-офицера. Ссор не слышно. Все как-то непривычно довольны, даже как будто счастливы, и засыпают не по-всегдашнему, а почти спокойным духом,—а с чего бы, кажется? А между тем это не мечта моего воображения. Это правда, истина. Только немного позволили этим бедным людям пожить по-своему, повеселиться по-людски, прожить хоть час не по-острожному—и человек нравственно меняется, хотя быт то было на несколько только минут." *ZiMD*, 129–130.

46. An analogous term in twentieth-century Russian texts designates cultural and social formations that function "in the blockade manner" (*po-blokadnomu*).

47. Orig.: "Достоевский в «Записках из Мёртвого дома» с умилением подмечает поступки несчастных, которые ведут себя, как большие дети, увлекаются театром, по-ребячески безгневно ссорятся между собой. Достоевский не встречал и не знал людей из настоящего блатного мира." Varlam Shalamov, *Sobranie sochinenii v shesti tomakh*, vol. 1, ed. I. Sirotinskaia (Moscow: Terra, 2013), 185.

48. Orig.: "в преодолении действительности, в борьбе с мемуаром, не потерял силу мемуар." Shalamov, *Sobranie sochinenii v shesti tomakh*, 6:358. This formulation occurs in a 1963 letter from Shalamov to Boris Lesniak, in which Shalamov rejects and offers editorial advice on the latter's own narratives about survival in Kolyma.

49. Roman Gul', *Oranienburg: Chto ia videl v gitlerovskom kontsentratsionnym lagere* (Paris: Dom Knigi, 1937), 64–65.

50. Emily D. Johnson, introduction to *Gulag Letters*, by Arsenii Formakov, ed. and trans. Emily D. Johnson (New Haven, CT: Yale University Press, 2017), 12–13. Johnson goes on to note that Formakov himself attempted, and later abandoned, his own semi-fictional account of his years in the Gulag, modeling the text on Solzhenitsyn's *One Day in the Life of Ivan Denisovich*—that is, on another fiction based on personal experience.

51. Ginzburg, *PKh*, 314.

52. Ginzburg, 314.

53. Antonin Artaud, *The Theater and Its Double*, trans. Mary Caroline Richards (New York: Grove Press, 1958), 25.

54. Ginzburg, *PKh*, 325.
55. Ginzburg, 324.
56. Maurice Blanchot points to the self-annulling quality of labor in labor camps: "Work, death: equivalents. And the workplace is everywhere; worktime is all the time. When oppression is absolute, there is no more leisure, no more 'free time.' Sleep is supervised. The meaning of work is then the destruction of work in and through work. But what if, as it has happened in certain commandos, labor consists of carrying stones at top speed from one spot and piling them up in another, and then in bringing them back at the run to the starting point (Langbein at Auschwitz; the same episode in the Gulag; Solzhenitsyn)? Then, no act of sabotage can cancel work, for its annulment is work's own very purpose." Maurice Blanchot, *The Writing of the Disaster*, trans. Ann Smock (Lincoln: University of Nebraska Press, 1995), 81.
57. Yuri Dombrovsky, *The Faculty of Useless Knowledge*, trans. Alan Myers (London: Harvill Press, 1996), 470.
58. Józef Czapski, *Inhuman Land: Searching for the Truth in Soviet Russia, 1941–1942*, trans. Antonia Lloyd-Jones (New York: New York Review Books), 122–126.
59. The problem of scale offers an intriguing, if unexplored, complement to Arjun Appadurai's argument in *Fear of Small Numbers*. Appadurai describes "predatory identities" as motivated by a fear of minorities as an impurity within the body politic: "Once the project of Germanness became defined in ethno-racial terms and the logic of purity came into play, a variety of minorities became sites of rage about incomplete purity: homosexuals, the aged and infirm, Gypsies, and, above all, Jews." Arjun Appadurai, *Fear of Small Numbers: An Essay on the Geography of Anger* (Durham, NC: Duke University Press, 2006), 55. A similar logic, we should note, applies in the Soviet camp system, where political prisoners, having been accused of counterrevolutionary behavior or thought, were treated as a pollution of Soviet society, whereas those convicted of violent crime were simply serving out their sentences. When it then becomes necessary to memorialize or represent the experience of this "rage," however, it is no longer the small numbers that we resist, but the large ones. The totals of the murdered, tortured, and abused become abstractions, incapable of conveying a sense of the human experience until the scale of atrocity is reduced to clearly relatable victims.
60. Jan Błoński, Marek Edelman, Czesław Miłosz, Jerzy Turowicz, and Joanna Gromek-Illg, "Ludzkość, która zostaje: 'Campo dei Fiori' po pięćdziesięciu latach," *Tygodnik Powszechny* 18, no. 2,912 (2005): 19.
61. Whether or not Edelman knew Tajtelbaum is difficult to substantiate. Though both were active in the armed resistance within the Warsaw Ghetto, their belonging to different (and at times antagonistic) political groups—Edelman

was part of the socialist Bund, whereas Tajtelbaum belonged to the communist Gwardia Ludowa—meant that they operated in separate circles.

3. Real-Life Fiction

1. Jan Karski, *Story of a Secret State* (Boston: Houghton Mifflin, 1944), 334.
2. Among the most notorious of Kosiński's mystifications was his caginess regarding the inspiration for his novel *Being There* (1970), which was made into an acclaimed film (dir. Hal Ashby, 1979) starring Peter Sellers and Shirley MacLaine. Kosiński had based the novel on Tadeusz Dołęga-Mostowicz's *The Career of Nicodemus Dyzma* (*Kariera Nikodema Dyzmy*, 1932), which was generally unknown outside of Poland. See Benjamin Paloff, "The Career of *The Career of Nicodemus Dyzma*," in Tadeusz Dołęga-Mostowicz, *The Career of Nicodemus Dyzma*, trans. Ewa Małachowska-Pasek and Megan Thomas (Evanston, IL: Northwestern University Press, 2020), vii–xii.
3. Jerzy Kosiński, *The Painted Bird*, 2nd ed. (New York: Grove Press, 1976), xi.
4. Kosiński was sensitive to Polish accusations that the book was "slanderous," preserving in his private papers a copy of the reporting in the *New York Times* (Henry Kamm, "Poles Are Bitter About Novel Published Abroad," 12 December 1966, 2), as well as of a defensive editorial printed in the same newspaper and, in Kosiński's copy, appended with the note, "also reprinted in 27 newspapers in USA as 'From the NYT editorial page.'" Katherina von Fraunhofer-Kosiński collection of Jerzy Kosiński, Yale Beinecke Library, GEN MSS 742, Box 2, Folder "Painted Bird Correspondence."
5. Lewis Galantière, letter to Jerzy Kosiński, April 9, 1967, Katherina von Fraunhofer-Kosiński collection of Jerzy Kosiński, Yale Beinecke Library, GEN MSS 742, Box 2, Folder "Painted Bird Correspondence."
6. Roger Baldwin, letter to Jerzy Kosiński, December 2 (no year), Katherina von Fraunhofer-Kosiński collection of Jerzy Kosiński, Yale Beinecke Library, GEN MSS 742, Box 2, Folder "Painted Bird Correspondence."
7. Jerzy Kosińksi, letter to the editor, *Washington Post*, September 13, 1971, A23. Kosiński wrote the letter in reference to Henry Allen, "A Painted Bird, a Painted World: The Close Brush of Death in the Life of Jerzy Kosiński—Novelist and Cultural Hero," *Washington Post*, August 30, 1971, B1, B6.
8. Kosiński, *The Painted Bird*, 208–209.
9. For Michel Foucault, this fact of the human sciences becomes the basis by which the human being is defined, as a "living being who, from within the life to which he entirely belongs and by which he is traversed in his whole being, constitutes representations by means of which he lives, and on the basis of which he possesses that strange capacity of being able to represent to

himself precisely that life." Michel Foucault, *The Order of Things: An Archaeology of the Human Sciences* [no translator listed] (New York: Vintage, 1970), 352.
10. Kosiński, *The Painted Bird*, 125.
11. Kosiński, xxiii.
12. Alice Oswald, *Memorial: A Version of Homer's Iliad* (New York: Norton, 2011), ix.
13. Jean Améry, *At the Mind's Limits: Contemplations by a Survivor on Auschwitz and Its Realities*, trans. Sydney Rosenfeld and Stella P. Rosenfeld (Bloomington: Indiana University Press, 2009), 19.
14. Améry, *At the Mind's Limits*, 25.
15. Sima Vaisman, *A Jewish Doctor in Auschwitz: The Testimony of Sima Vaisman*, trans. Charlotte Mandell (Hoboken, NJ: Melville House, 2005), 60.
16. Elie Wiesel, *From the Kingdom of Memory: Reminiscences* (New York: Schocken, 1990), 165–166.
17. Wiesel, *From the Kingdom of Memory*, 167.
18. Wiesel, 168.
19. Pieter Geyl, *Use and Abuse of History* (New Haven, NJ: Yale University Press, 1955), 60.
20. Paul Ricoeur, *Memory, History, Forgetting*, trans. Kathleen Blamey and David Pellauer (Chicago: University of Chicago Press, 2004), 178.
21. Georges Didi-Huberman, *Images in Spite of All: Four Photographs from Auschwitz*, trans. Shane B. Lillis (Chicago: University of Chicago Press, 2008), 82. His emphasis.
22. Didi-Huberman, *Images in Spite of All*, 83. His emphasis.
23. Maurice Halbwachs, *On Collective Memory*, ed. and trans. Lewis A. Coser (Chicago: University of Chicago Press, 1992), 204.
24. The physical space of the Warsaw Ghetto, which was obliterated at the end of the 1943 Warsaw Ghetto Uprising and rebuilt in a way that largely erases its wartime infrastructure, including the movement or elimination of major traffic corridors, represents an extreme case of the non-correspondence of the physical space and the collective memory. See Benjamin Paloff, "Can You Tell Me How to Get to the Warsaw Ghetto?," *Modernism/Modernity* 24, no. 3 (September 2017): 429–460.
25. Annette Wieviorka, *The Era of the Witness*, trans. Jared Stark (Ithaca, NY: Cornell University Press, 2006), 110–111.
26. Wieviorka, *The Era of the Witness*, xii.
27. Jorge Semprún, *Literature or Life*, trans. Linda Coverdale (New York: Penguin, 1997), 199–200.
28. Semprún, *Literature or Life*, 201.
29. Jorge Semprún, *What a Beautiful Sunday!*, trans. Alan Sheridan (San Diego, CA: Harcourt Brace Jovanovich, 1982), 373.

30. Semprún, *What a Beautiful Sunday!*, 149.
31. Halbwachs, *On Collective Memory*, 40, 53.
32. Semprún, *Literature or Life*, 13.
33. Semprún, 87–88.
34. Bella Brodzki, *Can These Bones Live? Translation, Survival, and Cultural Memory* (Stanford, CA: Stanford University Press, 2007), 165–166.
35. Semprún, *Literature or Life*, 124.
36. Semprún, 165.
37. Imre Kertész, *The Holocaust as Culture*, trans. Thomas Cooper (London: Seagull Books, 2011), 51.
38. Semprún, *Literature or Life*, 216.
39. Jorge Semprún, *L'Evanouissement* (Paris: Gallimard, 1967), 7–10.
40. Clifton Fadiman, ed., *The World of the Short Story: A Twentieth Century Collection* (Boston: Houghton Mifflin, 1986), 546. I am grateful for Fadiman's note. It enticed me to read Polish fiction for the first time, in this anthology, which I later appropriated from my father's bookshelf.
41. Primo Levi, *The Drowned and the Saved*, trans. Raymond Rosenthal (New York: Simon and Schuster, 2017), 25.
42. Orig.: "в прежнюю свою душу мы и не рассчитывали вернуться. И не вернулись, конечно. Никто не вернулся." Varlam Shalamov, *Sobranie sochinenii v shesti tomakh*, vol. 1, ed. S. Sirotinskaia (Moscow: Terra, 2013), 124.
43. Semprún, *Literature or Life*, 236.
44. Orig.: "J'ai choisis cette époque parce que je la trouve . . . très représentative, et parce qu'elle prêtait d'une façon extraordinaire à mon propos. La vérité historique ou politique ne m'intéresse pas. Seule compte pour moi la vérité ontologique." Anna Langfus, "Conversation avec P. Rawicz," *L'Arche* 61 (1962): 17.
45. Orig.: "Je trouve cette époque parfaitement normale. Elle correspond à ce qu'il y a de plus profond en nous. Pour moi, cette guerre est comme la germe même de l'être, l'être à l'état pur." Langfus, "Conversation avec P. Rawicz," 17.
46. Orig.: "До него доходили уже разные слухи о мерах начальства, ещё когда он содержался под судом; он уже и тогда готовился к смерти. Но, выходив первую половину, он ободрился. Он явился в госпиталь избитый до полусмерти; я ещё никогда не видал таких язв; но он пришёл с радостью в сердце, с надеждой, что останется жив, что слухи были ложные, что его вот выпустили же теперь из-под палок, так что теперь, после долгого содержания под судом, ему уже начинали мечтаться дорога, побег, свобода, поля и леса . . . Через два дня после выпуски из госпиталя он умер в том же госпитале, на прежней же койке, не выдержав второй половины." *ZiMD*, 153.

47. Gillian Rose, *Mourning Becomes the Law: Philosophy and Representation* (Cambridge: Cambridge University Press, 1996), 49.
48. Rose, *Mourning Becomes the Law*, 50.
49. Rose, 48.
50. Michael Rothberg, *Traumatic Realism: The Demands of Holocaust Representation* (Minneapolis: University of Minnesota Press, 2000), 226.
51. Terrence Des Pres, *The Survivor: An Anatomy of Life in the Death Camps* (Oxford: Oxford University Press, 1976), 24.
52. Rose, *Mourning Becomes the Law*, 50.
53. Rose, 50.
54. Orig.: "J'ai menti, oui, mais je l'ai fait pour nous sauver. Réhabiliter mon père, donner un sens à la mort de ma mère, et me sauver, moi, en me permettant de respirer dans ce monde." Lionel Duroy, *Survivre avec les loups: La véritable histoire de Misha Defonseca* (Paris: XO Editions, 2011), 228.
55. Zofia Kossak, *Z otchłani: Wspomnienia z lagru* (Częstochowa: Wydawnictwo Księgarni Wł. Nagłowskiego, 1947), 2.
56. "Mimesis," Andrew Herscher tells us, "is another name for the process by which violence comes to represent imagined or imaginary communities, ideological positions, or political agencies." Andrew Herscher, *Violence Taking Place: The Architecture of the Kosovo Conflict* (Stanford, CA: Stanford University Press, 2010), 16.
57. Orig.: "Sądzę, że jedyną metodą jest właśnie światopogląd materialistyczny, że sens Oświęcimia w jego ramach doskonale da się rozwiązać, gdyż problem etyczny: człowiek a warunki społeczne właśnie w nim się mieści, a przecież to centralny problem Oświęcimia, stosunek więźnia do więźnia!" Tadeusz Borowski, *Pisma w czterech tomach*, vol. 4, ed. Tadeusz Drewniowski (Kraków: Wydawnictwo Literackie, 2005), 85–86.
58. In Borowski's critique of Kossak we can find a powerful analogy to later objections to the use of the term "Holocaust," which, in its reference to the "burnt sacrifice" of a religious ritual, seems to assign purpose to actions that were merely wantonly destructive. "The unfortunate term 'holocaust' (usually with a capital 'H')," Agamben writes, "arises from this unconscious demand to justify death that is *sine causa*—to give meaning back to what seemed incomprehensible." Giorgio Agamben, *Remnants of Auschwitz: The Witness and the Archive*, trans. Daniel Heller-Roazen (New York: Zone Books, 2002), 28.
59. Orig.: "Может быть, он живёт надеждами? Но ведь никаких надежд у него нет. Если он не дурак, он не может жить надеждами. Поэтому так много самоубийц." Shalamov, *Sobranie sochinenii v shesti tomakh*, 1:120.
60. Orig.: "И тут бывают дни лучше и дни хуже, дни безнадежности сменяются днями надежды. Человек живёт не потому, что он во что-то

верит, на что-то надеется. Инстинкт жизни хранит его, как он хранит любое животное." Shalamov, 153.

61. Orig.: "To właśnie nadzieja każe ludziom apatycznie iść do komory gazowej, każe nie ryzykować buntu, pogrąża w martwotę. To nadzieja rwie więzy rodzin, każe matkom wyrzekać się dzieci, żonom sprzedawać się za chleb i mężom zabijać łudzi." Tadeusz Borowski, *Pisma w czterech tomach*, vol. 2, ed. Tadeusz Drewniowski, Justyna Szczęsna, and Sławomir Buryła (Kraków: Wydawnictwo Literackie, 2004), 54.

62. Lev Razgon, *Nepridumannoe: Povest' v rasskazakh*, expanded ed. (Moscow: Ex Libris, 1991), 45.

63. Améry, *At the Mind's Limits*, 10.

64. Anatol Girs, "Od wydawcy," in *Byliśmy w Oświęcimiu* (Munich: Oficyna Warszawska na Obczyźnie, 1946), 7. Though signed by Girs, this note "from the publisher" was most likely penned by Borowski. See Borowski, *Pisma w czterech tomach*, 2:407.

65. Orig.: "Niektóre z tych krótkich opowiadań są tylko realistyczne, niektóre są błahe, inne zawierają polemikę z cudzymi postawami pisarskimi. Adresy polemiki wskazują dedykacje, ale nie wszystkie. Niektóre są tylko grzecznościowe. Nie jestem pozytywnym katastrofistą, nie znałem kapy Kwaśniaka, nie jadłem mózgów ludzkich, nie mordowałem dzieci, nie siedziałem w bunkrze, nie chadzałem z Niemcami do opery, nie piłem wina w ogrodzie, nie oddaję się infantylnym marzeniom—w ogóle byłoby mi bardzo przykro, gdyby opowiadania z *Kamiennego świata* zostały potraktowane jako kartki z intymnego pamiętnika autora tylko dlatego, że są pisane w pierwszej osobie." Borowski, *Pisma w czterech tomach*, 2:255–256.

66. While acknowledging that suicides have "quite distinct meanings, personal causes, and idiosyncratic effects," Susan Gubar, for example, tells us that "such deaths can be contextualized in terms of a Holocaust haunting that hunts down and blights survivors as well as their families," pointing to Borowski and the Polish film director Andrzej Munk as powerful examples. Susan Gubar, *Poetry After Auschwitz: Remembering What One Never Knew* (Bloomington: Indiana University Press, 2003), 41. While Gubar and I clearly agree that these authors are "haunted" by their experiences, this example nevertheless demonstrates the tendency, even among astute and dedicated readers, to impose significance on data. Strictly speaking, Borowski was not an author of the Holocaust: as a non-Jewish Pole, his camp experience differed from that of most Jewish inmates, a reality that Borowski would not elide. Munk, meanwhile, did not commit suicide at all, but rather died in a car accident while driving back from Auschwitz, where he had been shooting a film based on Zofia Posmysz's camp-themed novel *The Passenger*

(*Pasażerka*, 1962). Within Gubar's framing, the deaths of Primo Levi, Borowski, and Munk all become the same interpretable object. But the suicide of a culturally significant figure is often a cipher upon which others might project meanings of their own. This, in fact, is what Czesław Miłosz does in *The Captive Mind*, where he reads the suicide of Tadeusz Borowski (flimsily anonymized as "Beta, the Disappointed Lover") as the spiritual defeat of a Communist true believer brought down by the harsh realities of Stalinism. See Czesław Miłosz, *The Captive Mind*, trans. Jane Zielonko (New York: Vintage, 1990), 111–134.

67. Dösseker's continued commitment to his alter ego is the subject of a feature-length documentary film, *W.: What Remains of the Lie* (*W.: Was von der Lüge bleibt*, dir. Rolando Colla and Thomas Ott, 2020).
68. Quoted in Kathryn Brackney, "Remembering 'Planet Auschwitz' During the Cold War," *Representations* 144 (November 2018): 124.
69. Quoted in Brackney, "Remembering 'Planet Auschwitz' During the Cold War," 125.
70. Hannah Arendt, *Eichmann in Jerusalem: A Report on the Banality of Evil* (New York: Penguin, 1964), 223–224.
71. Arendt, *Eichmann in Jerusalem*, 224.
72. Arendt, 224.
73. Orig.: "Zey zenen bakumen fun ergets an ort, vos iz nisht bakant, khotsh men veyst, az aza ort iz faran. Vi men veyst af ayn shtern vegn di ekzistenz fun a tsveytn shtern; men veyst—ober iz dimyen ken men zikh beshum oyfn nisht farshteln vi azoy es kukt dort oys." K. Tzetnik 135633 [Yehiel Dinoor], *Dos Hoyz fun di lyalkes* (Buenos Aires: Tzentral-farband fun poylishe yidn in Argentine, 1955), 322.
74. Orig.: "Indroysn, af der menshlekher velt, iz der toyt glaykh, nor dos lebn—farsheydnartik. Dakegn, inem lager, iz dos lebn glaykh, nor der toyt—farsheydnartik. . . . Yeder lager vet do lign inem oytomobil, vi a bezundere rase; vi mustern fun farsheydene planetn. Baym lebn zenen ale geven glaykh." K. Tzetnik 135633, *Dos Hoyz fun di lyalkes*, 326.
75. Orig.: "Der zun hot gebrent hinter zayne pleytzes un es hot oysgezen vi a fayerdiker gestapo-man volt zikh aropgelozt fun a blutikn planet un shteyn-geblibn zvishn himl un erd." K. Tzetnik 135633, 195.
76. Phillipe Lejeune, *On Autobiography*, trans. Katherine Leary (Minneapolis: University of Minnesota Press, 1988), 35, 33.
77. Ginzburg, *On Psychological Prose*, 105.
78. Gustaw Herling-Grudziński, *Inny świat: Zapiskie sowietskie*, ed. Włodzimierz Bolecki (Kraków: Wydawnictwo Literackie, 2000), 69. The author specifies that, besides Dostoevsky's novel, the only texts he attempted to read were

Stalin's *Questions of Leninism* (*Voprosy leninizma*, 1926), works by the nineteenth-century stage satirist Alexander Griboyedov, and a book on folklore from the Komi Republic.
79. Herling-Grudziński, *Inny świat*, 71–75.
80. Agamben, *Remnants of Auschwitz*, 120.
81. Orig.: "Jak się później dowiedziałem, Marię, jako aryjsko-semickiego mischlinga, wywiedziono wraz z transportem żydowskim do osławionego obozu nad morzem, zagazowano w komorze krematoryjnej, a ciało jej zapewne przerobiono na mydło." Borowski, *Pisma w czterech tomach*, 2:132.
82. By the time Borowski's story appeared in 1947, the soap rumor had been sealed in legend, first in the accusation leveled against Spanner in Nuremberg, and then more forcefully in the short story "Dr. Spanner," which opens Zofia Nałkowska's 1946 collection *Medallions* (*Medaliony*).
83. Orig: "Tehdy, když dohořívaly v kamnech poslední lístky škrabanic, jimiž mělo být vymazáno jméno Josef Roubíček, jsem pochopil, že není a nebude již nikdy Josefa Roubíčka, který chtěl kličkovat, uhýbat, vykroutit se, jen aby se mohl vyhnout svobodě." Jiří Weil, *Život s hvězdou* (Prague: Nakladatelství ELK, 1949), 210.
84. Orig.: "Měl jsem zakázány určité ulice v různých dnech, do některých jsem nesměl vkročit v pátek, do jiných zase v neděli, v některých jsem musil kráčet rychle a nikde se nezastavovat, pletl jsem si názvy ulic a dny a některé ulice jsem ani neznal, představoval jsem si, že někdy vkročím náhodou do některé ulice, která se bude jmenovat Hermelínová, že odkudsi vyskočí strážník a zatkne mě, protože Hermelínová ulice je v nějakém nejnovějším seznamu zakázaných ulic, který jsem si ještě nepřečetl. Bylo mi nařízeno, že nesmím chodit do parků, ale věděl jsem, že se dobře nevyznám, co je park a co není, byly tu cesty vroubené stromy, jež mohly být považovány za sady, a také nemusily." Weil, *Život s hvězdou*, 30.
85. Orig.: "Růžena mi nemohla odpovědět, nebyla v pokoji, nebyla vůbec se mnou. Nevěděl jsem, co se s ní stalo, neviděl jsem ji již dlouho. Snad nebyla vůbec na světě, snad vůbec nikdy nežila." Weil, 5.
86. Orig.: "A také s Růženou mluvím, která je stínem, která snad nebyla nikdy na světě, patrně jsem ji stvořil v dýmu, čmoudu a zápachu, když jsem se převaloval a házel sebou celé noci ve spacím pytli, aby byla paprskem, který pronikne trhlinou zatemnění." Weil, 61.
87. Seymour Chatman, *Story and Discourse: Narrative Structure in Fiction and Film* (Ithaca, NY: Cornell University Press, 1978), 59–62.
88. In a much lesser-known diary, published as *I Looked at Their Mouths . . . : A Diary from the Warsaw Ghetto* (*Patrzyłem na usta . . . : Dziennik z warszawskiego getta*, 1943), there is more a sense of despair than dread. This may be because the author, known only by her first name, Marylia, is obscure throughout

the text, which was found after the liberation of Majdanek. The fact that only a small fragment of the larger diary survives, and that so little is known about its author, deprives the text of a story arc that could foster readerly suspense. *Patrzyłem na usta . . . : Dziennik z warszawskiego getta*, ed. Piotr Weiser (Kraków: Wydawnictwo Homini, 2008).

89. Chatman, *Story and Discourse*, 53–56.
90. Franz Stanzel, *Narrative Situations in the Novel*, trans. James P. Pusack (Bloomington: Indiana University Press, 1971), 145–157.
91. Jean-Luc Nancy, "*Eros*, Emmanuel Levinas's Novel?," in *Levinas and Literature*, ed. Michael Fagenblat and Arthur Cools (Berlin: De Gruyter, 2021), 22.
92. Orig.: "I choć wychodziliśmy poza wielką postenkettę na 'prawdziwy świat'—to jednak ciągnął się za nami nasz prawdziwy 'świat'—obóz." Borowski, *Pisma w czterech tomach*, 4:40.
93. Macdonald, *Masscult and Midcult*, 234.
94. Włodzimierz Bolecki, *Inny świat Gustawa Herlinga-Grudzińskiego* (Kraków: Universitas, 2007), 128–129. See also Bolecki's conversation with Herling-Grudziński regarding Defoe and the uses of fiction to access historical truth: Gustaw Herling-Grudziński and Włodzimierz Bolecki, *Rozmowy w Dragonei, Rozmowy w Neapolu*, in Herling-Grudziński, *Dzieła zebrane*, vol. 11, ed. Włodzimierz Bolecki, Sylwia Błażejczyk-Mucha, Zdzisław Kudelski, and Aleksandra Siwek (Kraków: Wydawnictwo Literackie, 2018), 57–65.
95. Orig: "Lekcja polegała na tym, że pewne rozdziały 'czarnej historii' ludzkości—kataklyzmy, zarazy, eksterminacje, barbarzyńskie podboje, ludobójstwa—są odtwarzalne wyłącznie piórem bezosobistego do maksimum kronikarza." Herling-Grudziński, *Dziennik pisany nocą, Vol. 1*, in *Dzieła zebrane*, 7:238.
96. Orig.: "Ale trzeba je brać niemal dosłownie: martwe światło odepchniętej świadomie gwiazdy poezji; klucz narracyjny w opisach kataklizmów i plag." Herling-Grudziński, *Dziennik pisany nocą, Vol. 1*, 420–421. Joyce offers his praise for Defoe in James Joyce, "Realism and Idealism in English Literature (Daniel Defoe—William Blake)," in *Occasional, Critical, and Political Writing*, ed. Kevin Barry (Oxford: Oxford University Press, 2000), 170.
97. Serge Klarsfeld, foreword to *David Olère 1902–1985: Un peintre au Sonderkommando à Auschwitz*, ed. Serge Klarsfeld (New York: Beate Klarsfeld Foundation, 1989), 9.
98. While survivors of the *Sonderkommando* were as rare as images and memoirs of their activities, the heightened authority of the "sole" or "only" has sometimes attached itself to Olère as well, but this is not accurate. The four photographs clandestinely made in the Auschwitz crematoria are the subject of Didi-Hubermann's *Images in Spite of All*. And a detailed firsthand account of the *Sonderkommando* can be found in Filip Müller, *Eyewitness Auschwitz: Three*

      Years in the Gas Chambers, ed. and trans. Susanne Flatauer (New York: Ivan R. Dee, 1999).
99. Améry, *At the Mind's Limits*, 36.
100. Orig.: "Tortury na śledztwie nie są stosowane jako zasada, ale jako środek pomocniczy. O co chodzi naprawdę, to nie tyle o wymuszenie na oskarżonym podpisu pod zmyślonym i fikcyjnem aktem oskarżenia, ile o kompletną dezintegrację jego osobowości. . . . Więźnia można uważać za 'spreparowanego' do ostatecznego zabiegu dopiero wtedy, gdy widać już wyraźnie, jak jego osobowość rozpada się na drobne części składowe: pomiędzy skojarzeniami powstają luki, myśli i uczucia obluzowują się w swych pierwotnych łośyskach. . . . Maszyna kręci się dalej na zwiększonych obrotach, ale nie pracuje już jak dawniej—wszystko, co wydawało się oskarżonemu przed chwilą absurdem, staje się rzeczą prawdopodobną, choć ciągle jeszcze nie prawdziwą, uczucia zmieniają barwę, napięcie woli znika." Herling-Grudziński, *Inny świat*, 118–119.
101. Orig.: "Przed nią [śmiercią] zaś, jak ostatni sakrament, chciał wziąć na siebie zbrodnię, której nie popełnił, czyn, którego nie dokonał. Przez tyle długich lat nie wiedział, za co cierpi. Dziś zapragnął się pryznać, zapragnął się zmieścić w okrutnym i niezrozumiałym wyroku losu, który mu przedłużono do podpisu siedem lat temu. Broniąc się przed nieznaną przyszłością, szamocąc się w sidłach teraźniejszości, ratyfikował nałożoną nań przeszłość. Aby choć na chwilę przed skonem uratować jeszcze poczucie realności i wartości swego gasnącego istnienia." Herling-Grudziński, 106.
102. K. K. Ruthven, *Faking Literature* (Cambridge: Cambridge University Press, 2001), 71.
103. By the same token, survivors have frequently noted how the information flowing from the "world apart" back into quotidian reality was often assumed to be fiction.
104. Approximately 4,500 children's drawings from Theresienstadt, produced under the instruction of the artist Friedl Dicker-Brandeis, are now part of the permanent collection of the Jewish Museum of Prague, which displays some of the materials locally in the Pinkas Synagogue. Over 12,000 children were interned at Theresienstadt during the war; fewer than 10 percent survived. Dicker-Brandeis, too, was deported to Auschwitz and murdered in Birkenau.
105. The major performance texts from Theresienstadt are available in English translation: Lisa Peschel, ed. and trans., *Performing Captivity, Performing Escape: Cabarets and Plays from the Terezín/Theresienstadt Ghetto* (London: Seagull Books, 2014). Many of the comedy sketches performed at Theresienstadt hinged on reenacting scenes from the absurd, ersatz versions of institutions within the camp.

106. Helga Weissová, *Draw What You See: A Child's Drawings from Theresienstadt/Terezín* (Göttingen: Wallstein Verlag, 1998), 120. Weissová survived the war and became a professional artist.
107. Jorge Semprún and Eli Wiesel, *It Is Impossible to Remain Silent: Reflections on Fate and Memory in Buchenwald*, trans. Peggy Frankston (Bloomington: Indiana University Press, 2020), 34.
108. Wieseltier, "A Privation of Providence," 91.
109. Bella Brodzki, *Can These Bones Live? Translation, Survival, and Cultural Memory* (Stanford, CA: Stanford University Press, 2007), 181.
110. Timothy Snyder, *Bloodlands: Europe Between Hitler and Stalin*, 2nd ed. (New York: Basic Books, 2022), 392–393. The afterword to the new edition of Snyder's book expands on this considerably in light of more recent developments in so-called memory policy instituted by nationalist regimes in Central Europe from the 2010s to the present.
111. Jeffrey Veidlinger, *In the Midst of Civilized Europe: The Pogroms of 1918–1921 and the Onset of the Holocaust* (New York: Henry Holt, 2021).
112. "The general opinion held that one needed to be abnormally asocial and unconcerned about general events if one was still able to interpret the whole accident as personal and individual bad luck and, accordingly, ended one's life personally and individually." Hannah Arendt, *The Jewish Writings*, ed. Jerome Kohn and Ron H. Feldman (New York: Schocken, 2007), 267–268.
113. Kosiński, *The Painted Bird*, xiv.
114. Avishai Margalit and Gabriel Motzkin outline this reasoning in their argument for the peculiarity of the Nazi genocide of European Jewry: "One unique aspect of the Holocaust is then the application of universalistic categories to the extermination of a race. One may argue that negative universalism has a parallel in the Marxist-Leninist application of universalistic categories to exclude class enemies. However, there is a crucial difference: Marxist-Leninists viewed class as an historical phenomenon that will disappear, and not as a natural kind. For them, there does exist a universal class, the proletariat, whose historical role is beneficent, and others may in principle join it. In contrast, Nazi ideology emphasized the particularity of race as well as the ubiquity of races. There are no individuals who do not belong to a race. Yet there is no universal race. Even the Germans do not constitute a universal race: each race is special. History for the Nazis is always race history; hence the Jews' role in history is antihistorical; they represent a threat to the possibility of a future race history because they advocated an illusory universal race. They corrupt the superior races by sapping their vitality with their universalistic ideological teeth." Avishai Margalit and Gabriel Motzkin, "The Uniqueness of the Holocaust," *Philosophy & Public Affairs* 25, no. 1 (Winter 1996): 72. Where this exceptionalist reading of history runs afoul of

history is in its assumption that class was *not* treated in the Soviet Union, and especially under Stalinism, as a racialized, inheritable identity marker. In practice, one's class background was, in effect, racialized: if your father was a bourgeois, you might also be considered a bourgeois, at least when it is convenient for the authorities to do so.
115. Mikhail Geller, introduction to *Kolymskie rasskazy*, by Varlam Shalamov (London: Overseas Publishing Interchange, 1978), 12.
116. Herling-Grudziński, *Dziennik pisany nocą, Vol. 1*, 494–495.

4. Comedy

1. Orig.: "И это не факт, а на самом деле." Il'ia Sel'vinskii, *Komandarm-2*, in *Sobranie sochinenii v shesti tomakh*, vol. 3 (Moscow: Khudozhestvennaia literatura, 1972), 20. Sel'vinskii deploys this memorable quote in his 1928 verse drama *Komandarm-2*, though he appears to have borrowed it from the Soviet humorist and entertainer Leonid Utesov, who is said to have repeated it often. It has since been regularly misattributed to Isaac Babel and to the Soviet playwright Konstantin Trenev. Razgon mistakenly places it in the mouth of one of Babel's characters. Razgon, *Nepridumannoe*, 114.
2. This encounter occurred on June 11, 2017. In Polish, the exchange between the boy and his father sounded like this: "Czy Hitler miał tu obóz?" "No tak." (*Pause.*) "Czy na imię miał Hitler?" "Nie, to nazwisko. Miał na imię Adolf." (*Long pause.*) "Czy miał namiot?" "NIE!!!"
3. The SS camp at Płaszów was dismantled in January 1945 as the Red Army was progressing across Poland. The foundations of camp buildings and the land depressions that once held mass graves can still be found throughout the city park that occupies the space today.
4. For a schematic summary of the taboo surrounding camp comedy, see David Slucki, Gabriel N. Finder, and Avinoam Patt, "To Tell Jokes After Auschwitz Is Barbaric, Isn't It?," in *Laughter After: Humor and the Holocaust*, ed. David Slucki, Gabriel N. Finder, and Avinoam Patt (Detroit, MI: Wayne State University Press, 2020), 1–11. See also the documentary film *The Last Laugh*, dir. Ferne Pearlstein (Los Angeles: Tangerine Entertainment, 2016).
5. See, for example, Alan Dundes and Thomas Hauschild, "Auschwitz Jokes," *Western Folklore* 42, no. 4 (October 1983): 249–260.
6. The camp could also be viewed ironically from outside, as Andrzej Bobkowski attests in a diary entry written in Paris on April 11, 1942: "I was thinking that since reserves, national parks, are created for animals, because we are concerned to prevent, if only on a limited terrain, the disappearance

of bison, bear, and reindeer, it would be high time to think about creating some reserves for people, reserves of freedom. Because the man who wants truly to be free, who truly loves the most beautiful of all creations—freedom, is now becoming as rare as the bison or reindeer. He is hunted at all seasons and with the help of ever more refined weapons, or put in the modern reserves and national parks known as concentration camps. He is being exterminated at every step of the way—*in the name of freedom*. This is perhaps the best joke of all." Andrzej Bobkowski, *Wartime Notebooks: France, 1940–1944*, trans. Grażyna Drabik and Laura Engelstein (New Haven, CT: Yale University Press, 2018), 307–308. Bobkowski's emphasis.

7. Orig.: "a bylo to jako v divadle němých, neboť všichni mluvili rukama a pusou a nebylo je slyšet." Ladislav Grosman, *Obchod na korze; Nevěsta; Z pekla štěstí*, in *Spisy*, vol. 1, ed. Marie Havránková (Prague: Acropolis, 2020), 185. Hereafter cited as *Spisy*.

8. Orig.: "Jožkovi Naščákovi jsem řekl přes okno, že kdyby byl, mohl by nyní spolu se mnou zažít veliké dobrodružství, avšak o rabínce, která mne propašuje přes hranice, jsem se nezmínil. Jožko řekl, že stejně ví všecano, i když vše tutláme, jo, vy všechno tutláte, řekl, neb jste Židi a děláte ze všeho tajnosti." Grosman, *Spisy*, 1:171.

9. Orig.: "On navíc je ještě i vegetarián, ten profesor, chci říct, stačí trochu mrkvičky a je to." Grosman, *Spisy*, 1:198.

10. Sander L. Gilman, *Jurek Becker: A Life in Five Worlds* (Chicago: University of Chicago Press, 2003), 75.

11. Pnina Rosenberg points out that Rosenthal's nod toward copyright initially strikes us as satire, yet the satire is predicated on our recognition that much more fundamental rights have been eliminated in the camp: "In circumstances where human rights have been almost entirely eliminated, he makes a point of apologizing for not having honoured the creator's rights. Beyond the obvious element of satire, this may also be seen as an attempt by Rosenthal to cling to the ethics of normal society, by admitting to a kind of copyright infringement even though it had been forced upon him. The laws of society may have been violated systematically and totally, but he refuses to be part of it." Pnina Rosenberg, "*Mickey Mouse in Gurs*—Humour, Irony and Criticism in Works of Art Produced in the Gurs Internment Camp," *Rethinking History* 6, no. 3 (2002): 287.

12. Orig.: "Mais ne croyez-pas que nous nous embêtons! Loin de là! Nous possédons même une troupe théâtrale permanente, dont le Directeur est le nommé Nathan. Depuis un an et demi, il présente toujours le même programme. Il ne change que les titres. Il fait voire aux français du camp ce que c'est le vrai esprit parisien. Non, mais . . . Comme on dit en allemand: Schall und . . . Rauch!" Joël and Didier Pasamonik, *Mickey à Gurs: Les Carnets de*

dessin de Horst Rosenthal (Paris: Calmann-Lévy/Mémorial de la Shoah, 2014), 48.

13. "Nathan" is likely Alfred Nathan (1909–1976), a Jewish cabaret performer from Berlin who gained fame under the stage name "Peter Pan." "Rauch" has an additional significance, referring to Ruth Rauch (1922–1942), a Jewish dancer from Berlin who was subsequently deported from Gurs to Auschwitz. See Rosenberg, "*Mickey Mouse in Gurs*," 282–283.

14. Edmond-François Calvo, *La bête est morte!: La guerre mondiale chez les animaux* (Paris: Gallimard, 1995).

15. Orig.: "Když je lešená, řekl pan Kurt Brisch, tam nemá nikdo zemžít. Zemžít má člověk mezi deset a dvanáct hodin dopoledne. To je pšijímací hodin. // Řekl to sice ironicky, ale pánům to nepřipadalo zas tak divné. V ghettu bylo vydáno tolik nelogických nařízení. Nedávno, jak tvrdil pan Löwy, vydala například komandantura příkaz, že žádný neárijec se nesmí procházet v ghettě se psem po nábřeží. A přitom za prvé žádný žid nesměl přece mít psa, za druhé žádný žid se přece nesměl procházet po nábřeží, za třetí každý žid podléhal pracovní povinnosti, takže i kdyby se směl procházet po nábřeží a měl psa, neměl by na to čas, za čtvrté každý žid, i kdyby měl na to čas, nemohl by tam chodit se psem, poněvadž měl dost starostí s tím, aby se na židovské příděly uživil sám, natož živit ještě psa, a za páté v ghettě žádné nábřeží nebylo. (Netekla tam žádná řeka.) Proč by se tedy páni měli divit tomu, kdyby bylo vydáno nařízení, že se v ghettě musí umírat mezi desátou a dvanáctou hodinou dopolední." J. R. [Jiří Robert] Pick, *Spolek pro ochranu zvířat: Humoristická—pokud je to možné—novela z ghetta* (Prague: Československý spisovatel, 1969), 76–77.

16. Orig.: "V tom je zas ta jejich pitomá německá logika. Když umřeš v klidu a pokoji, tak tě spálí v krematoriu. Ale když něco provedeš, pohřbí tě důstojně na hřbitově." Pick, *Spolek pro ochranu zvířat*, 91.

17. Aristotle writes, "As for Comedy, it is (as has been observed) an imitation of men worse than the average; worse, however, not as regards any and every sort of fault, but only as regards one particular kind, the Ridiculous, which is a species of the Ugly." Aristotle, *The Basic Works of Aristotle*, ed. Richard McKeon (New York: Modern Library, 2001), 1459.

18. Orig.: "'Vayl s'iz nisht geven azoy.' 'Avade nisht.' 'Oreme layt in geto hot azoy nisht oysgezen. Oreme layt in geto hot man nisht bashonken zayn khales." *Undzere kinder*, dir. Natan Gross (Warsaw: Kinor, 1946), 00:14:10.

19. Orig.: "Oy, di bone, / Kh'vel gibn nisht avek di bone, / Kh'vil a bisile lebn, / Di bone nisht opgebn." *Undzere kinder*, 00:15:30.

20. Orig.: "Mamish a khval . . . Keyn shoyshpiler vet finden in dosiker shtof nisht aroys bekivn dos vos di dosike kinder. Ikh zog dir, mir darfn bai di kinder lernen, der azoy tsu shpiln in geto." *Undzere kinder*, 00:16:38.

21. Orig.: "Mir hobn bashlosn avektsuforn in a hinter-shtotisher kinder-kolonie, in Helenuvek, k'dey tsu kumen a bisl tsu zikh. In der kolonie hot men eyngezamelt di geratevete yidishe yesoymim. Zey zenen geven tseshpreyt bay guthartsike kristn, in kloysters, oder stam farvorfn in shtaln un shayern beys der daytsher okupatsie. Ot zenen zey umgeloft iber dem grozikn shetekh, zikh geshpilt in baheltenish—vi kinder. Azoy vi zey voltn nokh nisht genug geven bahaltn. Kh'bin geshtanen in a vinkl, nokhgekukt undzere moyshelekh, shayndelekh, un der troyer hot gegrizshet mayn gemit. Eyntslne zenen zey geblibn fun mishpokhes. . . . Ot di kinder, hob ikh getrakht, zenen undzer hemshekh—af tsu lekhakes di soynim un fartiliker. Far zey, di kinder, iz keday vayter mamshikh tsu zayn un boyen dos lebn fundosnay. Dos kleynvarg hot undz gegebn koyekh opshokeln fun zikh di eygene groyln, af vifl dos hot zikh gelozt." Shimon Dzigan, *Der koyekh fun yidishn humor* (Tel Aviv: Gezelshaftlekher komitet tsu fayern 40 yor tetikeyt fun Shimon Dzshigan af der Yidishe bine, 1974), 270–271.
22. Maurice Blanchot, *The Writing of the Disaster*, new ed., trans. Ann Smock (Lincoln: University of Nebraska Press, 1995), 82.
23. Natan Gross, *Film żydowski w Polsce* (Kraków: Rabid, 2002), 129.
24. Diane Ackerman, *The Zookeeper's Wife* (New York: Norton, 2007), 189; *The Zookeeper's Wife*, dir. Niki Caro (Universal City, CA: Universal Pictures, 2017).
25. Lawrence Langer, *Preempting the Holocaust* (New Haven, NJ: Yale University Press, 1998), 158.
26. See Shalamov's letter outlining his initial reaction to the novel in Aleksander Solzhenitsyn, *Sobranie sochinenii v tridtsati tomakh*, vol. 1, ed. Nataliia Solzhenitsyna (Moscow: Vremia, 2007), 580.
27. Tzvetan Todorov, *Voices from the Gulag: Life and Death in Communist Bulgaria*, trans. Robert Zaretsky (University Park: Pennsylvania State University Press, 1999), 13.
28. Orig.: "humor un satire in dem nayem rezshim vet nisht zayn keyn gangbare skhoyre." Dzigan, *Der koyekh fun yidishn humor*, 272.

5. Horror

1. Orig.: "Potem wywózki. Pawiaki. Nie tak od pierwszego tygodnia obozy. To narastało. Potem zaczęło się getto. I ta ściana na placu Krasińskich, w Wielki Wtorek—20 kwietnia—drugiego dnia powstania w getcie. Niemiec strzelał chyba spod Garnizonowego, przy Miodowej, z armaty, w getto, w Bonifraterską. Tam spadali ludzie. . . . To zaczęło działać. Ale na placu

Krasińskich był taki lunapark. Karuzele. Huśtawki. No i trochę naszej publiczki kręciło się i na tych huśtawkach i młynkach. W tym dymie gęstym. Bo szedł. I szedł. Z Bonifraterskiej. I Nowolipek. Z Dzielnej. Świętojerskiej. Przejazdu. Powstanie w getcie przecież trwało i trwało. Pierwsze jaskółki. W maju ujrzałem wtedy w tych dymach i usłyszałem, jak piszczały. Gdzieś 10-go, pamiętam. To już dwa dni po zbiorowym samobójstwie żydowskiego dowództwa. W bunkrze na Miłej. Niemcy ich wykryli." Miron Białoszewski, *Pamiętnik z powstania warszawskiego*, in *Utwory zebrane*, vol. 3 (Warsaw: Państwowy Instytut Wydawniczy, 1988), 80–81.

2. Terrence Des Pres, *The Survivor: An Anatomy of Life in the Death Camps* (Oxford: Oxford University Press, 1976), 7.

3. Krzysztof Ziarek, *The Historicity of Experience: Modernity, the Avant-Garde, and the Event* (Evanston, IL: Northwestern University Press, 2001), 245.

4. See Benjamin Paloff, "Can You Tell Me How to Get to the Warsaw Ghetto?," *Modernism/Modernity* 24, no. 3 (September 2017): 452–453.

5. Czesław Miłosz, *New and Collected Poems (1931–2001)* (New York: Ecco, 2001), 33–34.

6. Orig.: "Pszczoły obudowują czerwoną wątrobę, / Mrówki obudowują czarną kość, / Rozpoczyna się rozdzieranie, deptanie jedwabi, / Rozpoczyna się tłuczenie szkła, drzewa, miedzi, niklu, srebra, pian / Gipsowych, blach, strun, trąbek, liści, kul, kryształów— / Pyk! Fosforyczny ogień z żółtych ścian / Pochłania ludzkie i zwierzęce włosie. // Pszczoły obudowują plaster płuc, / Mrówki obudowują białą kość, / Rozdzierany jest papier, kauczuk, płótno, skóra, len, / Włókna, materie, celuloza, włos, wężowa łuska, druty, / Wali się w ogniu dach, ściana i żar ogarnia fundament. / Jest już tylko piaszczysta, zdeptana, z jednym drzewem bez liści / Ziemia." Czesław Miłosz, *Wiersze, tom 1* (Kraków: Znak, 2001), 213. Translation by Czesław Miłosz, from Miłosz, *New and Collected Poems*, 63.

7. Kazimierz Wyka, "Ogrody lunatyczne i ogrody pasterskie," in *Wśród poetów*, ed. Marta Wyka (Kraków: Wydawnictwo Literackie, 2000), 33.

8. Helen Vendler, "A Lament in Three Voices," *New York Review of Books*, May 31, 2001, http://www.nybooks.com/articles/archives/2001/may/31/a-lament-in-three-voices/. It is doubtful that Vendler had been aware of Wyka's remark. She notes a similar principle of montage among a diverse selection of contemporary American poets as well, including Rita Dove and Frank Bidart. See Helen Vendler, *The Music of What Happens: Poems, Poets, Critics* (Cambridge, MA: Harvard University Press, 1988), 430, 452.

9. Czesław Miłosz, *Visions from San Francisco Bay* (New York: Farrar, Straus and Giroux, 1982), 58. Miłosz's understanding of Manicheanism in film Westerns seems to have been quite limited. One can easily find the non-Manichean vision of humanity that Miłosz desires in many Westerns, including the

so-called spaghetti Westerns of Sergio Leone, in the films of Clint Eastwood, and in the work of James Cruze, who directed the 1936 screen adaptation of Cendrars's novel.

10. Marian Marek Drozdowski, "Przedmowa," in *Exodus Warszawy: Ludzie i miasto po Powstaniu 1944*, vol. 1, ed. Emilia Borecka et al. (Warsaw: Państwowy Instytut Wydawniczy, 1992), 16.
11. Orig.: "Wycofałem moje nazwisko dowiedziawszy się o cudownym rozmnożeniu się postaci. . . . ." Czesław Miłosz, "Wyjaśnienia po latach," *Dialog* 29, no. 9 (1984): 117.
12. Czesław Miłosz, *Kontynenty* (Kraków: Znak, 1999), 365.
13. Miłosz, *Kontynenty*, 366.
14. Orig.: "Oryginalny pomysł nie miał prawie nic z tego, co rozumie się potocznie przez 'akcję.' Chodziło o postawienie znaku równania pomiędzy przyrodą, w której znalazł się Robinson Crusoe i której musiał stawić czoło—i ruinami cywilizacji sprowadzonej do stanu pierwotnej dzikości. Tak więc *przetrwanie* i potrzebny do tego dar improwizacji, nacisk na *szczegóły* bytowania (woda, żywność, legowisko), tudzież unikanie ciągłych niebezpieczeństw." Miłosz, "Wyjaśnienia po latach," 116–117.
15. Czesław Miłosz, *Prywatne obowiązki* (Kraków: Wydawnicto Literackie, 2001), 317–318.
16. Władysław Szpilman, *Śmierć miasta*, ed. Jerzy Waldorff (Warsaw: Spółdzielnia Wydawnicza "Wiedza," 1946), 8.
17. Szpilman, *Śmierć miasta*, 8.
18. Orig.: "Na równinie mazowieckiej wznosi się ku niebu olbrzymi słup dymów—to płonie stolica Polski. Ptaki lecące niebem pogodnej jesieni omijają tę sferę zniszczenia. Wylotowymi ulicami wśród ruin i strzaskanych wysoko piętrzących się barykad idą tłumy ostatnich mieszkańców, obecnie już więźniów, mających przed sobą długą wędrówkę po obozach. Powietrze jest przyćmione, nasycone sadzą. To miasto już teraz jest miastem milczenia i zagłady." Jerzy Andrzejewski and Czesław Miłosz, "Robinson warszawski: Nowela filmowa," *Dialog* 29, no. 9 (September 1984): 6.
19. Orig.: "Pustka, nie ma nikogo. Dom płonie dokoła. Podwórze wymarłe, całe w dymu. Zawalona brama." Andrzejewski and Miłosz, "Robinson warszawski," 7.
20. Orig.: "Kiedy Piotr Rafalski budzi się z omdlenia, widzi nad sobą wysokie niebo i wielkie pierzaste obłoki, płynące za zasłoną przerzedzonych dymów. Dokoła zupełna cisza, żadnego śladu. Pustka bezludzia." Andrzejewski and Miłosz, 7.
21. Orig.: "Oto gdzieś w głębi ruin, wśród zburzonych domów, w pejzażu, który ma w sobie coś z dekoracji fantastycznych gór, a jednocześnie i coś z grozy jałowej, wyschniętej pustyni, Rafalski potyka się i przewraca. Upadając uderza łokciem w klawiaturę fortepiana." Andrzejewski and Miłosz, 8.

22. Andrzejewski and Miłosz, 15.
23. Andrzejewski and Miłosz, 16.
24. Recent zombie apocalypse narratives take the non-differentiation of the zombie masses literally, such that the zombies not only act as a single force, but literally merge together into increasingly menacing monstrosities. See, for example, Junot Diaz, "Monstro," *New Yorker*, June 4–11, 2012, 106–118. See also the zombie character designs in popular video game franchises like *The Last of Us* (2013).
25. Bożena Shallcross, *The Holocaust Object in Polish and Polish-Jewish Culture* (Bloomington: Indiana University Press, 2011), 1.
26. Shallcross, *The Holocaust Object*, 1. My emphasis.
27. Gillian Rose, *Mourning Becomes the Law: Philosophy and Representation* (Cambridge: Cambridge University Press, 1996), 48.
28. Roma Ligocka and Iris von Finckenstein, *Das Mädchen im roten Mantel* (Munich: Droemer, 2000).
29. Primo Levi, *The Drowned and the Saved*, trans. Raymond Rosenthal (New York: Simon and Schuster, 2017), 70.
30. See Giorgio Agamben, *Remnants of Auschwitz: The Witness and the Archive*, trans. Daniel Heller-Roazen (New York: Zone Books, 2002), 44–45.
31. Orig.: "MUZUŁMAN: człowiek całkowicie zniszczony fizycznie i duchowo, nie mający ani sil, ani woli do dalszej walki o życie, zazwyczaj z durchfallem, flegmonami lub krecą, najzupełniej dojrzały do komina. Żadne objaśnienia nie mogą oddać pogardy, z jaką muzułman był traktowany w obozie przez towarzyszy. Nawet więźniowie, lubujący się w autobiografiach obozowych, niechętnie przyznają się do tego, że byli kiedyś 'także' muzułmanami." Tadeusz Borowski, *Pisma w czterech tomach*, vol. 2, ed. Tadeusz Drewniowski, Justyna Szczęsna, and Sławomir Buryła (Kraków: Wydawnictwo Literackie, 2004), 399.
32. Agamben, *Remnants of Auschwitz*, 55.
33. Wolfgang Kayser, *The Grotesque in Art and Literature*, trans. Ulrich Weisstein (Bloomington: Indiana University Press, 1963), 197n12.
34. Orig.: "Zmuzułmaniały Żyd z Estonii, który nosił wraz ze mną rury, przez cały dzień zapewniał mnie żarliwie, jakoby mózg ludzki naprawdę był tak delikatny, że można go jeść bez gotowania, zupełnie na surowo." Borowski, *Pisma w czterech tomach*, 2:278.
35. Orig.: "И все, кому удалось коснуться солидола, несколько часов облизывали пальцы, глотали мельчайшие кусочки этого заморского счастья, по вкусу похожего на молодой камень." Varlam Shalamov, *Sobranie sochinenii v shesti tomakh*, vol. 1, ed. I. Sirotinskaia (Moscow: Terra, 2013), 395.

36. Orig.: "Zobaczysz, jak będziemy mieszkać." Andrzejewski and Miłosz, "Robinson warszawski," 10. The description appears as follows: "Mieszkanie Rafalskiego. Rzeczywiście wygląda teraz całkiem inaczej, niż z początku. Jest to chyba najdziwniejsze mieszkanie na świecie. Luksus łączy się tu z przypadkowością i z nieporządkiem. Rzeczy mają charakter tylko użytkowy. Podłogę zaścielają grube puszyste dywany, na ścianach wiszą makaty. Klubowy fotel. W kącie posłanie z miękkich materaców. Ale jednocześnie pośrodku pokoju walają się unurzane w ziemi kartofle wysypane z kosza. Dalej puste puszki po konserwach, skorupki od jajek." [NB: We do not know where he has obtained eggs.]
37. In this regard, it is worth noting that Danny Boyle, the director of *28 Days Later*, is especially interested in telling stories about individual survival in extreme conditions, as we also see in his films *Sunshine* (2007; the Irish actor Cillian Murphy plays the lead role both here and in *28 Days Later*) and *127 Hours* (2010).
38. Orig. "Rafalskiego ciągle dręczy myśl, iż mogą zostać odkryci. Teraz jego rezygnacja z życia i pewien żal do Andrzeja za zabranie Krystyny łączą się z nową troską. Przezwycięża swój uraz i chce jednego: uratować młodych." Andrzejewski and Miłosz, "Robinson warszawski," 16.
39. See, for example, the conclusion of *The Omega Man*, where a dead Charlton Heston is shown lying in the pose of Christ crucified.
40. Orig.: "Niewątpliwie poświęcenie skojarzone jest tu z załamaniem się. W ten sposób uzyskuje się podbudowę psychologiczną, wskazującą, że szlachetność nie bywa nigdy taka prosta jak się zdaje." Andrzejewski and Miłosz, "Robinson warszawski," 16.
41. Orig.: "Więzy, które zdawały się na nowo łączyć go z życiem, teraz zostały jakby przecięte. Wraca na swój poprzedni etap samotności—i przez to przezwyciężenie odzyskuje spokój i równowagę." Andrzejewski and Miłosz, 16.
42. See also Walter Benjamin, "The Work of Art in the Age of Its Technological Reproducibility," in *Selected Writings*, vol. 4, *1938–1940*, ed. Howard Eiland and Michael W. Jennings, trans. Harry Zohn and Edmund Jephcott (Cambridge, MA: Harvard University Press, 2003), 221.

Why Read Camp Literature?

1. Kertész, by contrast, takes a more sanguine view of this reality. See Imre Kertész, "Who Owns Auschwitz?," trans. John MacKay, *Yale Journal of Criticism* 14, no. 1 (2001): 267–272.

2. "New Study Reveals U.K. Respondents Believe Two Million or Fewer Jews Were Killed in the Holocaust," Conference on Jewish Material Claims Against Germany, November 10, 2021, https://www.claimscon.org/uk-study/.
3. "Claims Conference Survey Finds a Significant Lack of Holocaust Knowledge in the United States," Conference on Jewish Material Claims Against Germany, accessed October 9, 2024, https://www.claimscon.org/our-work/allocations/red/holocaust-study/.
4. Stuart Foster et al., *What Do Students Know and Understand About the Holocaust: Evidence from English Secondary Schools* (London: Centre for Holocaust Education, University College London, 2014), 71.
5. In Russian, these camps are designated as *fil'tratsionnye lageria*, or "filtration camps," similar to those used by the Russian Federation during its wars in Chechnya. The term and model for the "filtration camp" were first used by the Soviet Union in 1941, with hundreds of thousands of inmates being transferred directly into the Gulag system.
6. David Rousset, *A World Apart*, trans. Yvonne Moyse and Roger Senhouse (London: Secker and Warburg, 1951), 12.
7. See Leona Toker, *Gulag Literature and the Literature of Nazi Camps: An Intercontextual Reading* (Bloomington: Indiana University Press, 2019).
8. Dwight Macdonald, *Masscult and Midcult: Essays Against the American Grain*, ed. John Summers (New York: New York Review Books, 2011), 206.
9. Martha Nussbaum, *Poetic Justice: The Literary Imagination and Public Life* (Boston: Beacon Press, 1995); Joshua Landy, *How to Do Things with Fictions* (Oxford: Oxford University Press, 2012); Wayne C. Booth, *The Company We Keep: An Ethics of Fiction* (Berkeley: University of California Press, 1988).
10. For an elaboration on this principle in the philosophy of narrative, see Benjamin Paloff, *Bakhtin's Adventure: An Essay on Life Without Meaning* (Evanston, IL: Northwestern University Press, 2025).
11. The pulp novels in this genre, called *Stalags*, were written by Israeli authors as pseudo-translations of purportedly American texts.
12. Bruno Latour, *On the Modern Cult of the Factish Gods* (Durham, NC: Duke University Press, 2010).
13. Maurice Blanchot, *The Infinite Conversation*, trans. Susan Hanson (Minneapolis: University of Minnesota Press, 1993), 75.
14. Roland Barthes, *The Neutral*, trans. Rosalind E. Krauss and Dennis Hollier (New York: Columbia University Press, 2005), 92, 86.

Bibliography

Ackerman, Diane. *The Zookeeper's Wife*. New York: Norton, 2007.
Adorno, Theodore W. *Prisms*. Translated by Samuel Weber and Shierry Weber. Cambridge, MA: MIT Press, 1983.
Agamben, Giorgio. *Remnants of Auschwitz: The Witness and the Archive*. Translated by Daniel Heller-Roazen. New York: Zone Books, 2002.
Allen, Henry. "A Painted Bird, a Painted World: The Close Brush of Death in the Life of Jerzy Kosiński—Novelist and Cultural Hero." *Washington Post*, August 30, 1971, B1, B6.
Améry, Jean. *At the Mind's Limits: Contemplations by a Survivor on Auschwitz and Its Realities*. Translated by Sydney Rosenfeld and Stella P. Rosenfeld. Bloomington: Indiana University Press, 2009.
Anderson, L. V., David Haglund, Natalie Matthews-Ramo, and Jim Pagels. "Can I Make Stuff Up? A Visual Guide." *Slate*, March 21, 2012. http://www.slate.com/blogs/browbeat/2012/03/21/mike_daisey_david_sedaris_david_foster_wallace_and_other_storytellers_who_can_make_stuff_up_.html.
Andrzejewski, Jerzy, and Czesław Miłosz. "Robinson warszawski: Nowela filmowa." *Dialog* 29, no. 9 (September 1984): 5–17.
Appadurai, Arjun. *Fear of Small Numbers: An Essay on the Geography of Anger*. Durham, NC: Duke University Press, 2006.
Arendt, Hannah. *Eichmann in Jerusalem: A Report on the Banality of Evil*. New York: Penguin, 1964.
———. *The Jewish Writings*. Edited by Jerome Kohn and Ron H. Feldman. New York: Schocken, 2007.

Aristotle. *The Basic Works of Aristotle*. Edited by Richard McKeon. New York: Modern Library, 2001.

Artaud, Antonin. *The Theater and Its Double*. Translated by Mary Caroline Richards. New York: Grove Press, 1958.

Auerbach, Erich. *Mimesis: The Representation of Reality in Western Literature*. Translated by William R. Trask. Princeton, NJ: Princeton University Press, 1953.

Auerbach, Rachela. *Pisma z getta warszawskiego*. Edited by Karolina Szymaniak. Warsaw: Żydowski Instytut Historyczny, 2016.

Badde, Paul. "Zvi Kolitz." In *Yosl Rakover Talks to God*, by Zvi Kolitz, translated by Carol Brown Janeway, 58–62. New York: Vintage, 1999.

Barthes, Roland. *Criticism and Truth*. Edited and translated by Katrine Pilcher Keuneman. London: Continuum, 2004.

———. *The Neutral*. Translated by Rosalind E. Krauss and Dennis Hollier. New York: Columbia University Press, 2005.

Benjamin, Walter. "Experience and Poverty." In *Selected Writings*. Vol. 2, pt. 2, *1931–1934*, edited by Michael W. Jennings, Howard Eiland, and Gary Smith, translated by Rodney Livingstone, 731–735. Cambridge, MA: Harvard University Press, 1999.

———. "The Work of Art in the Age of Its Technological Reproducibility: Third Version." In *Selected Writings*. Vol. 4, *1938–1940*, edited by Howard Eiland and Michael W. Jennings, translated by Harry Zohn and Edmund Jephcott, 251–283. Cambridge, MA: Harvard University Press, 2003.

Berggol'ts, Ol'ga [Olga Bergholz]. *Dnevnye zvezdy*. Leningrad: Sovetskii pisatel', 1960.

Białoszewski, Miron. *Pamiętnik z powstania warszawskiego*. Utwory zebrane, vol. 3. Warsaw: Państwowy Instytut Wydawniczy, 1988.

Blanchot, Maurice. *The Infinite Conversation*. Translated by Susan Hanson. Minneapolis: University of Minnesota Press, 1993.

———. *The Writing of the Disaster*. New ed. Translated by Ann Smock. Lincoln: University of Nebraska Press, 1995.

Błoński, Jan, Marek Edelman, Czesław Miłosz, Jerzy Turowicz, and Joanna Gromek-Illg. "Ludzkoś ć, która zostaje: 'Campo dei Fiori' po pię ćdziesięciu latach." *Tygodnik Powszechny* 18, no. 2912 (2005): 19.

Bobkowski, Andrzej. *Wartime Notebooks: France, 1940–1944*. Translated by Grażyna Drabik and Laura Engelstein. New Haven, CT: Yale University Press, 2018.

Bolecki, Włodzimierz. *Inny świat Gustawa Herlinga-Grudzińskiego*. Kraków: Universitas, 2007.

Bonito Oliva, Achille. *The Ideology of the Traitor: Art, Manner and Mannerism*. Translated by Mark Eaton and Paul Metcalfe. Milan: Electa, 1998.

Booth, Wayne C. *The Company We Keep: An Ethics of Fiction*. Berkeley: University of California Press, 1988.

Borowski, Tadeusz. *Pisma w czterech tomach*, vol. 2. Edited by Tadeusz Drewniowski, Justyna Szczęsna, and Sławomir Buryła. Kraków: Wydawnictwo Literackie, 2004.

———. *Pisma w czterech tomach*, vol. 4. Edited by Tadeusz Drewniowski. Kraków: Wydawnictwo Literackie, 2005.

Boyle, Danny, dir. *28 Days Later*. Los Angeles: Fox Searchlight, 2002.

Boyne, John. *The Boy in the Striped Pajamas*. New York: Random House, 2006.

Brackney, Kathryn. "Remembering 'Planet Auschwitz' During the Cold War." *Representations*, no. 144 (November 2018): 124–153.

Brecht, Bertold. "A Short Organum for the Theater." In *Brecht on Theater: The Development of an Aesthetic*, edited and translated by John Willett, 179–205. New York: Hill and Wang, 1992.

Brodzki, Bella. *Can These Bones Live? Translation, Survival, and Cultural Memory*. Stanford, CA: Stanford University Press, 2007.

Browne, Sir Thomas. *Religio Medici and Urne-Buriall*. Edited by Stephen Greenblatt and Ramie Targoff. New York: New York Review Books, 2012.

Calvo, Edmond-François. *La bête est morte!: La guerre mondiale chez les animaux*. Paris: Gallimard, 1995.

Caro, Nick, dir. *The Zookeeper's Wife*. Universal City, CA: Universal Pictures, 2017.

Carr, David. "How Oprahness Trumped Truthiness." *New York Times*, January 30, 2006, C1.

Chatman, Seymour. *Story and Discourse: Narrative Structure in Fiction and Film*. Ithaca, NY: Cornell University Press, 1978.

"Claims Conference Survey Finds a Significant Lack of Holocaust Knowledge in the United States." Conference on Jewish Material Claims Against Germany. Accessed October 9, 2024. https://www.claimscon.org/our-work/allocations/red/holocaust-study/.

Cohen, Richard A. "Levinas on Art and Aestheticism: Getting 'Reality and Its Shadow' Right." *Levinas Studies* 11 (2016): 149–194.

Colla, Rolando, and Thomas Ott, dirs. *W.: Was von der Lüge bleibt*. Zurich: Peacock Film A. G., 2020.

Czapski, Józef. *Inhuman Land: Searching for the Truth in Soviet Russia, 1941–1942*. Translated by Antonia Lloyd-Jones. New York: New York Review Books, 2018.

———. *Lost Time: Lectures on Proust in a Soviet Prison Camp*. Translated by Eric Karpeles. New York: New York Review Books, 2018.

Das Ghetto. Warsaw, May 1942. Accessed May 18, 2022. https://cdn-0.archiv-akh.de/videos_mp4/M1053_WEB.mp4.

Derrida, Jacques. *Without Alibi*. Edited and translated by Peggy Kamuf. Stanford, CA: Stanford University Press, 2002.

Des Pres, Terrence. *The Survivor: An Anatomy of Life in the Death Camps*. Oxford: Oxford University Press, 1976.

Diaz, Junot. "Monstro." *New Yorker*, June 4–11, 2012, 106–118.

Didi-Huberman, Georges. *Images in Spite of All: Four Photographs from Auschwitz*. Translated by Shane B. Lillis. Chicago: University of Chicago Press, 2008.

Dombrovsky, Yuri. *The Faculty of Useless Knowledge*. Translated by Alan Myers. London: The Harvill Press, 1996.

Dostoyeffsky, Fedor [F. M. Dostoevskii]. *Buried Alive, or: Ten Years of Penal Servitude in Siberia*. Translated by Marie von Thilo. London: Longmans, Green, and Co., 1881.

Dostoevskii, F. M. *Zapiski iz mertvogo doma*. In *Pol'noe sobranie sochinenii v tridtsati tomakh*, vol. 4, 5–232. Leningrad: Nauka, 1972.

Duroy, Lionel. *Survivre avec les loups: La véritable histoire de Misha Defonseca*. Paris: XO Editions, 2011.

Dzigan, Shimon. *Der koyekh fun yidishn humor*. Tel Aviv: Gezelshaftlekher komitet tsu fayern 40 yor tetikeyt fun Shimon Dzshigan af der Yidisher bine, 1974.

Eaglestone, Robert. *Ethical Criticism: Reading After Levinas*. Edinburgh: University of Edinburgh Press, 1997.

Eskin, Blake. *A Life in Pieces: The Making and Unmaking of Binjamin Wilkomirski*. New York: Norton, 2002.

———. "Seeking a Spiritual Message in a Fictional Bottle: Yosl Rakover's Creator Talks to a Reporter." *Forward*, December 3, 1999, 11.

Etkind, Alexander. *Warped Mourning: Stories of the Undead in the Land of the Unburied*. Stanford, CA: Stanford University Press, 2013.

Fadiman, Clifton, ed. *The World of the Short Story: A Twentieth Century Collection*. Boston: Houghton Mifflin, 1986.

Fassin, Didier. *Prison Worlds: An Ethnography of the Carceral Condition*. Translated by Rachel Gomme. Cambridge: Polity, 2017.

Felman, Shoshana. "A Ghost in the House of Justice: Death and the Language of the Law." *Yale Journal of Law and the Humanities* 13, no. 1 (2001): 241–282.

Feuchtwang, Stephan. "Loss: Transmissions, Recognitions, Authorizations." In *Regimes of Memory*, edited by Susannah Radstone and Katharine Hodgkin, 76–89. London: Routledge, 2003.

Fisher, Robin Gaby, and Angelo J. Guglielmo Jr. *The Woman Who Wasn't There: The True Story of an Incredible Deception*. New York: Simon and Schuster, 2012.

Friedman, Laurie. *Angel Girl*. Illustrated by Ofra Amit. Minneapolis, MN: Carolrhoda Books, 2008.

Foster, Stuart, Alice Pettigrew, Andy Pearce, Rebecca Hale, Adrian Burgess, Paul Salmons, and Ruth-Anne Lenga. *What Do Students Know and Understand About the Holocaust: Evidence from English Secondary Schools*. London: Centre for

Holocaust Education, University College London, 2014. https://holocausteducation.org.uk/wp-content/uploads/What-do-students-know-and-understand-about-the-Holocaust-2nd-Ed.pdf.

Foucault, Michel. *The Order of Things: An Archaeology of the Human Sciences.* New York: Vintage, 1970.

———. *Subjectivity and Truth: Lectures at the College de France, 1980–1981.* Edited by Frédéric Gros. Translated by Graham Burchell. New York: Picador, 2017.

Frankfurt, Harry G. *On Bullshit.* Princeton, NJ: Princeton University Press, 2005.

Fredersdorf, Herbert B., and Marek Goldstein, dirs. *Lang ist der Weg.* Berlin: U.S. Army Information Control Division, 1948.

Frey, James. *A Million Little Pieces.* New York: Vintage, 2004.

Gance, Abel, dir. *J'accuse.* Los Angeles: United Artists, 1919.

Geller, Mikhail. Introduction to *Kolymskie rasskazy*, by Varlam Shalamov, 5–16. London: Overseas Publishing Interchange, 1978.

Genette, Gérard. *Paratexts: Thresholds of Interpretation.* Translated by Jane E. Lewin Cambridge: Cambridge University Press, 1997.

Geyl, Pieter. *Use and Abuse of History.* New Haven, CT: Yale University Press, 1955.

Gilman, Sander L. *Jurek Becker: A Life in Five Worlds.* Chicago: University of Chicago Press, 2003.

Ginzburg, Lidiia. *Literatura v poiskakh real'nosti.* Leningrad: Sovetskii pisatel', 1987.

———. *O literaturnom geroe.* Leningrad: Sovetskii pisatel,' 1979.

——— [as Lydia Ginzburg]. *On Psychological Prose.* Translated by Judson Rosengrant. Princeton, NJ: Princeton University Press, 1991.

———. *Prokhodiashchie kharaktery: Proza voennykh let, Zapiski blokadnogo cheloveka.* Edited by Emily Van Buskirk and Andrei Zorin. Moscow: Novoe Izdatel'stvo, 2011.

Girs, Anatol. "Od wydawcy." In *Byliśmy w Oświęcimiu*, 7–9. Munich: Oficyna Warszawska na Obczyźnie, 1946.

Głowacka, Dorota. *Disappearing Traces: Holocaust Testimonials, Ethics, Aesthetics.* Seattle: University of Washington Press, 2012.

Goodhart, Sandor. "*Conscience*, Conscience, Consciousness: Emmanuel Levinas, the Holocaust, and the Logic of Witness." In *Remembering for the Future: The Holocaust in an Age of Genocide.* Vol. 2, *Ethics and Religion*, edited by John K. Roth, Elizabeth Maxwell, Margot Levy, and Wendy Whitworth, 1024–1039. Basingstoke, UK: Palgrave, 2001.

———. *Möbian Nights: Reading Literature and Darkness.* New York: Bloomsbury, 2017.

Grosman, Ladislav. *Obchod na korze; Nevěsta; Z pekla štěstí.* In *Spisy*, vol. 1. Edited by Marie Havránková. Prague: Acropolis, 2020.

Gross, Natan. *Film żydowski w Polsce.* Kraków: Rabid, 2002.

———, dir. *Undzere kinder*. Warsaw: Kinor, 1946.
Gubar, Susan. *Poetry After Auschwitz: Remembering What One Never Knew*. Bloomington: Indiana University Press, 2003.
Guglielmo, Angelo G., Jr., dir. *The Woman Who Wasn't There*. New York: Meredith Viera Productions, 2012.
Gul', Roman. *Oranienburg: Chto ia videl v gitlerovskom kontsentratsionnym lagere*. Paris: Dom Knigi, 1937.
Halbwachs, Maurice. *On Collective Memory*. Edited and translated by Lewis A. Coser. Chicago: University of Chicago Press, 1992.
Hazanavicius, Michel, dir. *The Search*. Burbank, CA: Warner Bros., 2014.
Henry, Parker, and Paul Muldoon. "How Do You Fact-Check a Poem?" *Poetry Podcast (New Yorker)*. MP3 audio, 23:17, December 21, 2016. https://www.newyorker.com/podcast/poetry/how-do-you-fact-check-a-poem.
Herling-Grudziński, Gustaw. *Dziennik pisany nocą*, vol. 1. In *Dzieła zebrane*, vol. 7. Edited by Włodzimierz Bolecki, Sylwia Błażejczyk-Mucha, Zdzisław Kudelski, and Aleksandra Siwek. Kraków: Wydawnictwo Literackie, 2017.
———. *Inny świat: Zapiskie sowietskie*. Edited by Włodziemierz Bolecki. Kraków: Wydawnictwo Literackie, 2000.
Herling-Grudziński, Gustaw, and Włodzimierz Bolecki. *Rozmowy w Dragonei, Rozmowy w Neapolu*. In *Dzieła zebrane*, vol. 11. Edited by Włodzimierz Bolecki, Sylwia Błażejczyk-Mucha, Zdzisław Kudelski, and Aleksandra Siwek. Kraków: Wydawnictwo Literackie, 2018.
Herscher, Andrew. *Violence Taking Place: The Architecture of the Kosovo Conflict*. Stanford, CA: Stanford University Press, 2010.
Hersonski, Yael, dir. *A Film Unfinished*. New York: Oscilloscope Laboratories, 2011.
Hutcheon, Linda. *Irony's Edge: The Theory and Politics of Irony*. London: Routledge, 1995.
Ivanov, Viacheslav. *Borozdy i Mezhi: Opyty esteticheskie i kriticheskie*. Moscow: Musaget, 1916.
Jauss, Hans Robert. *Aesthetic Experience and Literary Hermeneutics*. Translated by Michael Shaw. Minneapolis: University of Minnesota Press, 1982.
Johnson, Emily D. Introduction to *Gulag Letters*, by Arsenii Formakov, edited and translated by Emily D. Johnson, 1–48. New Haven, CT: Yale University Press, 2017.
Joyce, James. "Realism and Idealism in English Literature (Daniel Defoe—William Blake)." In *Occasional, Critical, and Political Writing*, edited by Kevin Barry, 163–182. Oxford: Oxford University Press, 2000.
Kamm, Henry. "Poles Are Bitter About Novel Published Abroad." *New York Times*, December 12, 1966, 2.
Karski, Jan. *Story of a Secret State*. Boston: Houghton Mifflin, 1944.

Kayser, Wolfgang. *The Grotesque in Art and Literature*. Translated by Ulrich Weisstein. Bloomington: Indiana University Press, 1963.
Kertész, Imre. *Dossier K*. Translated by Tim Wilkinson. Brooklyn, NY: Melville House, 2006.
———. *The Holocaust as Culture*. Translated by Thomas Cooper. London: Seagull Books, 2011.
———. *The Pathseeker*. Translated by Tim Wilkinson. Brooklyn, NY: Melville House, 2008.
———. "Who Owns Auschwitz?" Translated by John MacKay. *Yale Journal of Criticism* 14, no. 1 (2001): 267–272.
Klarsfeld, Serge. Foreword to *David Olère 1902–1985: Un peintre au Sonderkommando à Auschwitz*, edited by Serge Klarsfeld, 8–10. New York: Beate Klarsfeld Foundation, 1989.
Kolitz, Zvi. "'Yossl Rakover's Appeal to God': A Story Written Especially for *Di Yiddishe* [sic] *Tsaytung*." Edited and translated by Jeffry V. Mallow and Frans Jozef van Beeck. *Crosscurrents* 44, no. 3 (Fall 1994): 362–377.
———. *Yosl Rakover Talks to God*. Translated by Carol Brown Janeway. New York: Vintage, 1999.
Kosiński, Jerzy. Letter to the editor. *Washington Post*, September 13, 1971, A23.
———. *The Painted Bird*. 2nd ed. New York: Grove Press, 1976.
Kossak, Zofia. *Z otchłani: Wspomnienia z lagru*. Częstochowa: Wydawnictwo Księgarni Wł. Nagłowskiego, 1947.
Kotek, Joël, and Didier Pasamonik, eds. *Mickey à Gurs: Les Carnets de dessin de Horst Rosenthal*. Paris: Calmann-Lévy/Mémorial de la Shoah, 2014.
K. Tzetnik 135633 [Yehiel Dinoor]. *Dos Hoyz fun di lyalkes*. Buenos Aires: Tzentralfarband fun poylishe yidn in Argentine, 1955.
Landy, Joshua. *How to Do Things with Fictions*. Oxford: Oxford University Press, 2012.
Langer, Lawrence. *Preempting the Holocaust*. New Haven, CT: Yale University Press, 1998.
Langfus, Anna. "Conversation avec P. Rawicz." *L'Arche*, no. 61 (1962): 16–17.
Latour, Bruno. *On the Modern Cult of the Factish Gods*. Durham, NC: Duke University Press, 2010.
Lawrence, Francis, dir. *I Am Legend*. Burbank, CA: Warner Bros, 2007.
Lejeune, Phillipe. *On Autobiography*. Translated by Katherine Leary. Minneapolis: University of Minnesota Press, 1988.
Levi, Primo. *The Drowned and the Saved*. Translated by Raymond Rosenthal. New York: Simon and Schuster, 2017.
Levinas, Emmanuel. *Carnets de captivité, suivi de Écrits sur la captivité et Notes philosophiques diverses*. Edited by Rodolphe Calin and Catherine Chalier. Paris: Bernard Grasset/IMEC, 2009.

———. "Loving the Torah More Than God." In *Yosl Rakover Talks to God*, by Zvi Kolitz, translated by Carol Brown Janeway, 79–87. New York: Vintage, 1999.

Ligocka, Roma, and Iris von Finckenstein. *Das Mädchen im roten Mantel*. Munich: Droemer, 2000.

Macdonald, Dwight. *Masscult and Midcult: Essays Against the American Grain*. Edited by John Summers. New York: New York Review Books, 2011.

Maechler, Stefan. *The Wilkomirski Affair: A Study in Biographical Truth*. New York: Schocken, 2001.

Mandel'shtam, Osip. *Sobranie sochinenii v chetyrekh tomakh*, vol. 2. Edited by P. Nerler and A. Nikitaev. Moscow: Art-Biznes-Tsentr, 1993.

Margalit, Avishai. *The Ethics of Memory*. Cambridge, MA: Harvard University Press, 2002.

Margalit, Avishai, and Gabriel Motzkin. "The Uniqueness of the Holocaust." *Philosophy & Public Affairs* 25, no. 1 (Winter 1996): 65–83.

"A Million Little Lies: Exposing James Frey's Addiction Fiction." *Smoking Gun*, January 4, 2006. http://www.thesmokinggun.com/documents/celebrity/million-little-lies?page=0,0.

Miłosz, Czesław. *The Captive Mind*. Translated by Jane Zielonko. New York: Vintage, 1990.

———. *Kontynenty*. Kraków: Znak, 1999.

———. *New and Collected Poems (1931–2001)*. New York: Ecco, 2001.

———. *Prywatne obowiązki*. Kraków: Wydawnicto Literackie, 2001.

———. *Visions from San Francisco Bay*. New York: Farrar, Straus and Giroux, 1982.

———. *Wiersze, tom 1*. Kraków: Znak, 2001.

———. "Wyjaśnienia po latach." *Dialog* 29, no. 9 (1984): 116–117.

Müller, Filip. *Eyewitness Auschwitz: Three Years in the Gas Chambers*. Edited and translated by Susanne Flatauer. New York: Ivan R. Dee, 1999.

Nancy, Jean-Luc. "*Eros*, Emmanuel Levinas's Novel?" In *Levinas and Literature*, edited by Michael Fagenblat and Arthur Cools, 21–35. Berlin: De Gruyter, 2021.

"New Study Reveals U.K. Respondents Believe Two Million or Fewer Jews Were Killed in the Holocaust." Conference on Jewish Material Claims Against Germany, November 10, 2021. https://www.claimscon.org/uk-study/.

Novick, Peter. *The Holocaust in American Life*. Boston: Houghton Mifflin, 1999.

Nussbaum, Martha. *Poetic Justice: The Literary Imagination and Public Life*. Boston: Beacon Press, 1995.

"Oprah's Questions for James." Oprah.com. Accessed September 19, 2024. http://www.oprah.com/oprahshow/Oprahs-Questions-for-James/10#ixzz2saEbMKy1.

Oswald, Alice. *Memorial: A Version of Homer's Iliad*. New York: Norton, 2011.

Paloff, Benjamin. *Bakhtin's Adventure: An Essay on Life Without Meaning*. Evanston, IL: Northwestern University Press, 2025.

———. "Can You Tell Me How to Get to the Warsaw Ghetto?" *Modernism/Modernity* 24, no. 3 (September 2017): 429–460.

———. "The Career of *The Career of Nicodemus Dyzma*." In *The Career of Nicodemus Dyzma*, by Tadeusz Dołęga-Mostowicz, translated by Ewa Małachowska-Pasek and Megan Thomas, vii–xii. Evanston, IL: Northwestern University Press, 2020.

Pearlstein, Ferne, dir. *The Last Laugh*. Los Angeles: Tangerine Entertainment, 2016.

Peri, Alexis. *The War Within: Diaries from the Siege of Leningrad*. Cambridge, MA: Harvard University Press, 2017.

Peschel, Lisa, ed. and trans. *Performing Captivity, Performing Escape: Cabarets and Plays from the Terezín/Theresienstadt Ghetto*. London: Seagull Books, 2014.

Petříček, Miroslav. *Filosofie en noir*. Prague: Karolinum, 2018.

Pick, J. R. [Jiří Robert]. *Spolek pro ochranu zvířat: Humoristická—pokud je to možné—novela z ghetta*. Prague: Československý spisovatel, 1969.

Pinsky, Robert. *The Inferno of Dante: A New Verse Translation*. New York: Farrar, Straus and Giroux, 1994.

Plato. *Republic*. Translated by Robin Waterfield. Oxford: Oxford University Press, 1993.

Proust, Marcel. *In Search of Lost Time*. Vol. 5, *The Captive & The Fugitive*. Translated by C. K. Scott Moncrieff and Terence Kilmartin, revised by D. J. Enright. New York: Modern Library, 1993.

Ragona, Ubaldo B., and Sidney Salkow, dirs. *The Last Man on Earth*. Beverly Hills, CA: American International Pictures, 1964.

Rak, Julie. "Memoir, Truthiness, and the Power of Oprah." *Prose Studies: History, Theory, Criticism* 34, no. 3 (2012): 224–242.

Razgon, Lev. *Nepridumannoe: Povest' v rasskazakh*. Expanded ed. Moscow: Ex Libris, 1991.

Rich, Motoko. "James Frey and His Publisher Settle Suit Over Lies." *New York Times*, September 7, 2006, B1.

Ricoeur, Paul. *Memory, History, Forgetting*. Translated by Kathleen Blamey and David Pellauer. Chicago: University of Chicago Press, 2004.

Riffaterre, Michael. *Fictional Truth*. Baltimore: Johns Hopkins University Press, 1990.

Robbins, Jill. *Altered Reading: Levinas and Literature*. Chicago: University of Chicago Press, 1999.

Rose, Gillian. *Mourning Becomes the Law: Philosophy and Representation*. Cambridge: Cambridge University Press, 1996.

Rosenberg, Pnina. "*Mickey Mouse in Gurs*—Humour, Irony and Criticism in Works of Art Produced in the Gurs Internment Camp." *Rethinking History* 6, no. 3 (2002): 273–292.

Rosenfeld, Alvin H. "Holocaust Fictions and the Transformation of Historical Memory." *Holocaust and Genocide Studies* 3, no. 3 (1988): 323–336.

Roskies, David. "Seeking a Spiritual Message in a Fictional Bottle: The Ghetto Fighters Become Modern Macabees." *Forward*, December 3, 1999, 11.

Roskies, David G., and Naomi Diamant. *Holocaust Literature: A History and Guide*. Waltham, MA: Brandeis University Press, 2012.

Rothberg, Michael. *Traumatic Realism: The Demands of Holocaust Representation*. Minneapolis: University of Minnesota Press, 2000.

Rousset, David. *A World Apart*. Translated by Yvonne Moyse and Roger Senhouse. London: Secker and Warburg, 1951.

Rulf, Jiří. *Literáti: Příběhy z dvacátého století*. Prague: Paseka, 2002.

Ruthven, K. K. *Faking Literature*. Cambridge: Cambridge University Press, 2001.

Sagal, Boris, dir. *The Omega Man*. Burbank, CA: Warner Bros, 1971.

Salisbury, Harrison E. *The 900 Days: The Siege of Leningrad*. New York: Harper and Row, 1969.

Sandauer, Artur. *Pisma zebrane*, vol. 2. Warsaw: Czytelnik, 1985.

———. *Proza*. Kraków: Wydawnictwo Literackie, 1972.

———. *Zebrane pisma krytycyzne*, vol. 3. Warsaw: Państwowy Instytut Wydawniczy, 1981.

Schiff, Brian, Heather Skillingstead, Olivia Archibald, Alex Arasim, and Jenny Peterson. "Consistency and Change in the Repeated Narratives of Holocaust Survivors." *Narrative Inquiry* 16, no. 2 (2006): 349–377.

Sel'vinskii, Il'ia. *Sobranie sochinenii v shesti tomakh*, vol. 3. Moscow: Khudozhestvennaia literatura, 1972.

Semprún, Jorge. *L'Evanouissement*. Paris: Gallimard, 1967.

———. *Literature or Life*. Translated by Linda Coverdale. New York: Penguin, 1997.

———. *What a Beautiful Sunday!* Translated by Alan Sheridan. San Diego, CA: Harcourt Brace Jovanovich, 1982.

Semprún, Jorge, and Eli Wiesel. *It Is Impossible to Remain Silent: Reflections on Fate and Memory in Buchenwald*. Translated by Peggy Frankston. Bloomington: Indiana University Press, 2020.

Shalamov, Varlam. *Sobranie sochinenii v shesti tomakh*, vol. 1. Edited by I. Sirotinskaia. Moscow: Terra, 2013.

———. *Sobranie sochinenii v shesti tomakh*, vol. 6. Edited by I. Sirotinskaia. Moscow: Terra, 2013.

Shallcross, Bożena. *The Holocaust Object in Polish and Polish-Jewish Culture*. Bloomington: Indiana University Press, 2011.

Shklovsky, Viktor. "Petersburg During the Blockade" [1923]. In *Knight's Move*, translated by Richard Sheldon, 9–20. Normal, IL: Dalkey Archive Press, 2005.

———. *A Sentimental Journey: Memoirs 1917–1922*. Translated by Richard Sheldon. Normal, IL: Dalkey Archive Press, 2004.

———. *Theory of Prose.* Translated by Benjamin Sher. Normal, IL: Dalkey Archive Press, 1990.

Slucki, David, Gabriel N. Finder, and Avinoam Patt. "To Tell Jokes After Auschwitz Is Barbaric, Isn't It?" In *Laughter After: Humor and the Holocaust,* edited by David Slucki, Gabriel N. Finder, and Avinoam Patt, 1–11. Detroit: Wayne State University Press, 2020.

Snyder, Timothy. *Bloodlands: Europe Between Hitler and Stalin.* 2nd ed. New York: Basic Books, 2022.

Soltysik Monnet, Agnieszka. "War and National Renewal: Civil Religion and Blood Sacrifice in American Culture." *European Journal of American Studies* 7, no. 2 (2012): 1–17.

Solzhenitsyn, Aleksander. *Sobranie sochinenii v tridtsati tomakh,* vol. 1. Edited by Nataliia Solzhenitsyna. Moscow: Vremia, 2007.

Spiegelman, Art. *Maus: A Survivor's Tale.* Vol. 2, *And Here My Troubles Began.* New York: Pantheon, 1991.

Spielberg, Steven, dir. *Schindler's List.* Universal City, CA: Universal Pictures, 1993.

Stanzel, Franz. *Narrative Situations in the Novel.* Translated by James P. Pusack. Bloomington: Indiana University Press, 1971.

Stewart, Susan. *Crimes of Writing: Problems in the Containment of Representation.* Durham, NC: Duke University Press, 1994.

Suetonius. *The Twelve Caesars.* Translated by Robert Graves. New York: Penguin, 2003.

Szpilman, Władysław. *Śmierć miasta.* Edited by Jerzy Waldorff. Warsaw: Spółdzielnia Wydawnicza "Wiedza," 1946.

Todorov, Tzvetan. *Voices from the Gulag: Life and Death in Communist Bulgaria.* Translated by Robert Zaretsky. University Park: Pennsylvania State University Press, 1999.

Toker, Leona. *Gulag Literature and the Literature of Nazi Camps: An Intercontextual Reading.* Bloomington: Indiana University Press, 2019.

Trotsky, Leon. *Literature and Revolution.* Edited by William Keach. Translated by Rose Strumsky. Chicago: Haymarket Books, 2005.

Ugrešić, Dubravka. *The Culture of Lies: Antipolitical Essays.* University Park: Pennsylvania State University Press, 1998.

Ungurianu, Dan. "The Use of Historical Sources in *War and Peace.*" In *Tolstoy on War: Narrative Art and Historical Truth in "War and Peace,"* edited by Rick McPeak and Donna Tussing Orwin, 26–41. Ithaca, NY: Cornell University Press, 2012.

Vaisman, Sima. *A Jewish Doctor in Auschwitz: The Testimony of Sima Vaisman.* Translated by Charlotte Mandell. Hoboken, NJ: Melville House, 2005.

van Beeck, Frans Jozef, S. J. *Loving the Torah More Than God? Towards a Catholic Appreciation of Judaism.* Chicago: Loyola University Press, 1989.

Van Buskirk, Emily. *Lydia Ginzburg's Prose: Reality in Search of Literature*. Princeton, NJ: Princeton University Press, 2016.

Veidlinger, Jeffrey. *In the Midst of Civilized Europe: The Pogroms of 1918–1921 and the Onset of the Holocaust*. New York: Henry Holt, 2021.

Vendler, Helen. "A Lament in Three Voices." *New York Review of Books*, May 31, 2001. http://www.nybooks.com/articles/archives/2001/may/31/a-lament-in-three-voices/.

———. *The Music of What Happens: Poems, Poets, Critics*. Cambridge, MA: Harvard University Press, 1988.

Vermeule, Blakey. *Why Do We Care About Literary Characters?* Baltimore: Johns Hopkins University Press, 2010.

"Vox Populi: Japan's 'Deaf Composer' May Not Be the Artist He Claims." *Asahi Shimbun*, February 6, 2014, 1.

Weiser, Piotr, ed. *Patrzyłem na usta . . . : Dziennik z warszawskiego getta*. Kraków: Wydawnictwo Homini, 2008.

Weiss, M. David. "How We Remember the Warsaw Ghetto." *Jewish Advocate*, April 27, 1967, A3.

Weissová, Helga. *Draw What You See: A Child's Drawings from Theresienstadt/Terezín*. Göttingen: Wallstein Verlag, 1998.

White, Hayden. *Figural Realism: Studies in the Mimesis Effect*. Baltimore: Johns Hopkins University Press, 1999.

Wiesel, Elie. *From the Kingdom of Memory: Reminiscences*. New York: Schocken, 1990.

———. *The Night Trilogy: Night, Dawn, The Accident*. Translated by Stella Rodway, Frances Frenaye, and Anna Borchardt. New York: Hill and Wang, 1987.

Wieseltier, Leon. "A Privation of Providence." In *Yosl Rakover Talks to God*, by Zvi Kolitz, translated by Carol Brown Janeway, 89–99. New York: Vintage, 1999.

Wieviorka, Annette. *The Era of the Witness*. Translated by Jared Stark. Ithaca, NY: Cornell University Press, 2006.

Wyka, Kazimierz. *Wśród poetów*. Edited by Marta Wyka. Kraków: Wydawnictwo Literackie, 2000.

Young, Kevin. *Bunk: The Rise of Hoaxes, Humbug, Plagiarists, Phonies, Post-facts, and Fake News*. Minneapolis, MN: Graywolf Press, 2017.

Zbigniew Libera: Work from 1984–2004. Ann Arbor: University of Michigan School of Art and Design and Center for Russian and East European Studies, 2005.

Ziarek, Krzysztof. *The Historicity of Experience: Modernity, the Avant-Garde, and the Event*. Evanston, IL: Northwestern University Press, 2001.

Zinnemann, Fred, dir. *The Search*. Beverly Hills, CA: Metro-Goldwyn-Mayer, 1948.

Žižek, Slavoj. *The Parallax View*. Cambridge, MA: MIT Press, 2006.

Index

28 Days Later (film), 166–167, 231n37
Ackerman, Diane, 150
Adorno, Theodore, 10, 198n23
Agamben, Giorgio, 48, 108, 145, 173, 217n58
Aleichem, Sholem, 150–152
allegorical parallelism, 24, 29, 41, 165, 168
Alter, Wiktor, 74
Améry, Jean, 80, 90, 99, 118
Anders, Władysław, 116
Andrzejewski, Jerzy, 159, 161–165, 168–169, 177–178. See also *Warsaw Robinson Crusoe*
Angel at the Fence (Rosenblat), 22, 46, 81, 201n11
Angel Girl (Friedman), 23, 43, 201n11
Appadurai, Arjun, 213n59
Arendt, Hannah, 12, 103–105, 129, 223n112
Artaud, Antonin, 72
"At Our Place, Auschwitz" ("U nas, w Auschwitzu...," Borowski), 98, 100
Auerbach, Erich, 50–51

Auerbach, Rachela, 43, 150
aura (Benjamin), 43, 70, 196n6
Auschwitz, 13, 16, 80–83, 92–93, 97–100, 102–103, 117, 121–123, 125–126, 129, 131, 135, 138, 142–143, 146, 149 169, 172, 174, 179, 185, 189, 191, 198n23, 200n7, 213n56, 218n66, 221n98, 222n104, 226n13
authenticity, 8, 19, 27–40, 43, 53–54, 56–57, 61, 69–70, 77, 117, 124, 137, 164, 169, 173, 195n2, 196n6, 204n46, 206n53
authorial discourse, 114
autobiographical pact (Lejeune), 5, 26, 71, 100, 197n13
automatization (Shklovsky), 4
autothematism, 58–61, 210n29

Babel, Isaac, 224n1
Badde, Paul, 34–35, 204n39
Bakhtin, Mikhail, 66, 145, 190, 211n36
banality of evil (Arendt), 12, 103
bare life, 13, 142

[245]

Barthes, Roland, 30, 41, 193
The Beast Is Dead! (La béte est morte!, Calvo), 143
Becker, Jurek, 135–136, 139, 141, 146, 153
Being There (Kosiński), 214n2
Bełżec, 57
Benigni, Roberto, 135–136, 140
Benjamin, Walter, 54, 82, 196n6
Benny, Jack, 136
Bergen-Belsen, 87
Bergholz, Olga, 52, 207n2
Białoszewski, Miron, 157–159
Birkenau, 117, 122, 179, 222
Blanchot, Maurice, 1, 149, 193, 213n56
Bloomberg, Michael, 18
Bobkowski, Andrzej, 224n6
Booth, Wayne C., 187
Borowski, Tadeusz, 13, 92, 97–101, 109–110, 112–114, 116–117, 129, 148, 172–174, 203n31, 217n58, 218n64, 218n66, 220n82
Borowski, Tadeusz, works of: "At Our Place, Auschwitz" ("U nas, w Auschwitzu…"), 98, 100; "A Day in Harmenz" ("Dzień na Harmenzach"), 114–115; *Farewell to Maria (Pożegnania z Marią)*, 100, 109–110; "The People Who Went" ("Ludzie, którzy szli"), 100; *The Stone World (Kamienny świat)*, 100–101, 109–110; "Supper" ("Kolacja"), 174; "A Tale from Real Life" ("Opowiadanie z prawdziwego życia"), 101; "This Way to the Gas, Ladies and Gentlemen" ("Proszę państwa do gazu"), 116
The Boy in the Striped Pajamas (Boyne), 81, 179–181
Boyle, Danny, 166, 231n37
Boyne, John, 81, 180–181
Brecht, Bertold, 26–27, 54, 208n15
Brickhill, Paul, 122

Brodzki, Bela, 91, 127
Brooks, Mel, 155
Browne, Thomas, 10–11
Buchenwald, 12, 22, 81, 87–88, 90, 93, 117, 125, 129, 131–132, 173, 184–185, 198n25
Bulgakov, Mikhail, 211n34
bullshit (Frankfurt), 27, 31, 33, 202n23

Calvo, Edmond-François, 143
"Campo dei Fiori" (Miłosz), 159–160
Camus, Albert, 158
Captive Mind, The (Zniewolony umysł, Miłosz), 6, 197n16, 218n66
carousel outside the Warsaw Ghetto, 157, 159–160
Cendrars, Blaise, 162–163, 177, 228n9
Chatman, Seymour, 113–114
Chernyshevsky, Nikolai, 63
Colbert, Stephen, 7, 197n17
collective memory, 28, 83, 89–90, 101, 125, 185, 215n24
character, composite, 15, 42, 50–54, 72, 115, 188
Chomsky, Marvin J., 86
correspondence theory of truth. *See* truth-in-correspondence
Cowley, Malcolm, 185
Crowther, Welles, 18
Cruze, James, 228n9
Czapski, Józef, 26, 73–74, 88

Dachau, 83, 85, 87, 92, 100, 132, 179–180
Danzig Anatomical Institute, 110
Das Ghetto (film), 43, 121
"Day in Harmenz, A" ("Dzień na Harmenzach," Borowski), 114–115
Day the Clown Cried, The (film), 136
de Wael, Monique. *See* Defonseca, Misha
Defoe, Daniel, 115–116, 166, 168, 199n29, 221n94, 221n96

Defoe, Daniel, works of: *Journal of the Plague Year,* 115–116, 199n29; *Robinson Crusoe,* 115, 166, 168
Defonseca, Misha (Monique de Wael), 22–23, 27–30, 40–41, 43–44, 46, 53, 97, 174, 201n12, 203n25, 206n61
Derrida, Jacques, 25
Des Pres, Terrence, 10, 21, 96, 158
Dewey decimal classification, 197n12
Dewey, John, 5
Diaz, Juno, 230n24
Dicker-Brandeis, Friedl, 222n104
Didi-Huberman, Georges, 82, 86, 88, 90, 106, 119, 221n98
Dinoor, Yehiel. *See* Ka-Tzetnik 135663
Dołęga-Mostowicz, Tadeusz, 214n2
Dombrovsky, Yuri, 73
Dösseker, Bruno. *See* Wilkomirski, Binjamin
Dossier K. (*K. dosszié,* Kertész), 62, 198n25
Dostoevsky, Fyodor, 63–72, 94, 99, 108, 146, 199n29, 209n18, 211n36, 211n39, 219n78
Dostoevsky, Fyodor, works of: *Notes from the House of the Dead* (*Zapiski iz mertvogo doma*), 63–72; 94, 99, 108, 146, 199n29, 209n18, 211n39, 219n78; *Notes from Underground* (*Zapiski iz podpol'ia*), 64
Dostoevsky, Mikhail, 64
double focus (Halbwachs), 83, 106
Dovlatov, Sergei, 211n34
dramatic reenactment, 43–44, 51, 55, 66, 74, 95, 98, 114, 150–153, 222n105
dual action (Didi-Huberman), 82–83, 88, 106, 119
Duroy, Lionel, 203n25
Dzigan, Shimon, 147–155

Eastwood, Clint, 228n9
Edelman, Marek, 74–76, 213n61
Ehrlich, Henryk, 73–74

Eichmann, Adolf, 13, 86, 102–105
Eichmann in Jerusalem (Arendt), 103–105
enargeia, 79–80, 90, 92
epitext, 32
Esteve, Alicia. *See* Head, Tania
Etkind, Alexander, 13
Expedition Robinson (television series), 175

fact-checking, 7, 23, 197n14
facticity, 3–8, 62, 67, 78, 182
Fainting (*L'Évanouissement,* Semprún), 92
Farewell to Maria (*Pożegnania z Marią,* Borowski), 100, 109–110
Fassin, Didier, 66–67
Fatelessness (*Sorstalanság,* Kertész), 91, 198n25
Feuchtwang, Stephan, 38
fiction and nonfiction, separation of, 5–6, 24, 70, 181, 185–186, 196n5, 197n12
figural discourse, 114
Film Unfinished, A (film), 43–45
Formakov, Arsenii, 212n50
Fortunoff Video Archive of Holocaust Testimony, 86
Foucault, Michel, 61, 66, 145, 214n9
Fragments (*Bruchstücke,* Wilkomirski), 22–24, 27–31, 33–35, 38–40, 42–44, 53, 79, 102
Frank, Anne, 113, 190
Frankfurt, Harry, 27, 31, 33–34, 202n23
Freud, Sigmund, 13
Frey, James, 1–3, 7, 22, 25, 32, 35, 71, 117, 182, 195n2, 196n4, 196n5, 197n18, 204n40
Friedman, Laurie, 43, 201n11
Fuks, Ladislav, 202n24
The Führer Gives the Jews a City (*Der Führer schenkt den Juden eine Stadt,* film). *See Theresienstadt: A Documentary Film from the Jewish Settlement*

Gance, Abel, 177
Geller, Mikhail, 129
Genette, Gérard, 197n13
Geyl, Pieter, 81–82
Gide, André, 202n22
Gilligan's Island (television series), 175
Gilman, Sander, 141
Ginzburg, Evgeniia, 71, 200n6
Ginzburg, Lidiia, 48–55, 59, 61–64, 66, 71–73, 79, 106–107, 148, 207n4, 208n11, 208n13, 210n29
Ginzburg, Lidiia, works of: *Notes of a Blockade Person* (*Zapiski blokadnogo cheloveka*), 48–54, 59, 62, 66, 72, 79, 207n2, 207n4; *Literature in Search of Reality* (*Literatura v poiskakh real'nosti*), 61–62, 208n13, 210n29; *The Person at the Writing Desk* (*Chelovek za pis'mennym stolom*), 208n13
girl in the red coat, 170–171
Girs, Anatol, 100, 218n64
Giuliani, Rudy, 18
Goffman, Erwin, 66
Gogol, Nikolai, 64
Gombrowicz, Witold, 60, 209n17
Goodhart, Sandor, 36
Goskind, Saul, 149–150
gray zone (Levi), 92–99, 108, 172
Great Escape, The (film), 122, 131, 132
Great Plague of 1665, 115–116
Griazovets, 26
Griboyedov, Alexander, 219n78
"Grishka Logun's Thermometer" ("Termometr Grishki Loguna," Shalamov), 93
Grosjean, Bruno. *See* Wilkomirski, Binjamin
Grosman, Ladislav, 128, 139–141, 145–146, 153
Grosman, Ladislav, works of: *Lucky as Hell* (*Z pekla štěstí*), 139–140, 145–146, 153–154; *The Shop on Main Street* (*Obchod na korze*), 128; 140
Gross, Natan, 149–150, 153
Gubar, Susan, 218n66
Gul, Roman, 70
Gulag Archipelago, The (*Arkhipelag GULAG*, Solzhenitsyn), 98, 172
Gurs, 123, 129, 141–143, 226n13

Halbwachs, Maurice, 83, 89–90, 93, 106, 173
Head, Tania, 18–21, 199n5
Herling-Grudziński, Gustaw, 13, 70–71, 88–89, 99–100, 108, 113–116, 118–120, 129, 148, 185, 219n78
Herling-Grudziński, Gustaw, works of: *A World Apart* (*Inny świat*), 70–71, 88–89, 99–100, 108, 118–120, 185, 219n78
Herman, Mark, 181
Hero of Our Time, A (Lermontov), 101
Herscher, Andrew, 217n56
Hersonski, Yael, 43, 45
Herzen, Alexander, 62
heteronymic depersonalization, 108–110
hiding, 16, 41, 77, 111, 113, 128, 136, 138–140, 146, 148, 150, 153, 155, 176, 183
historicity, 8–9, 11, 91
Hitler, Adolf, 133–134
Hogan's Heroes (television series), 137
Holocaust (television miniseries), 86
Holy Week (Andrzejewski), 159
House of Dolls (*Dos hoyz fun di lyalkes*, Ka-Tzetnik 135663), 102, 104, 117, 190
Hutcheon, Linda, 31

ideosphere, 193
I Am Legend (Matheson), 166
I Am Legend (film), 166, 168

illeism, 107
irony, 30–31, 42, 47, 60, 69, 95, 101, 131, 138
Ivanov, Viacheslav, 66, 211n36

J'accuse (film), 177
Jakob the Liar (Becker), 135–136, 139, 141, 146–147, 153
Jacobson, Leon, 130–131
James, William, 5
Jauss, Hans Robert, 31
Johnson, Alan, 155
Johnson, Emily, 70, 212n50
Jojo Rabbit (film), 154
Journal of the Plague Year (Defoe), 115, 199n29

Kadár, Ján, 128
Kamińska, Ida, 128
Karski, Jan, 76, 179
"Kasrilevke Is Burning" (Kasrilekve brent," Aleichem), 150–152
Ka-Tzetnik 135663, 13, 86, 101–105
Keneally, Thomas 96
Kertész, Imre, 11–12, 62–63, 90–91, 158, 179, 198n25, 231n1
Kertész, Imre, works of: Dossier K. (K. dosszié), 62, 198n25; Fatelessness (Sorstalanság), 91, 198n25; The Pathseeker (A nyomkereső), 179
Kirkman, Robert, 167
kitsch, 81, 86, 96, 99
Klos, Elmar, 128
Koch, Ilse, 117–118
Kochina, Elena, 113
Koestler, Arthur, 76
Kolitz, Zvi, 34–41, 204n43, 204n46, 205n49, 206n53
Kolyma, 16, 98, 129, 174, 212n48
Kolyma Tales (Kolymskie rasskazy, Shalamov), 98, 129

Kosiński, Jerzy, 76–79, 102, 116–117, 129, 173, 214n2, 214n4
Kosiński, Jerzy, works of: Being There, 214n2; The Painted Bird, 76–79, 117, 129
Kosovo, 127
Kossak, Zofia, 97–98, 217n58
Kraków Ghetto, 150, 170–171
Kundera, Milan, 11, 198n24

Landy, Joshua, 187
Langer, Lawrence, 152
Langfus, Anna, 93–94
Last Laugh, The (film), 155
Last Man on Earth, The (film), 165–168
Last of Us, The (video game), 230n24
Lanzmann, Claude, 96, 170
Lawrence, Francis, 166
Lebedev, Nikolai, 207n3
"Legend of the Monster-City, The" ("Legenda miasta-potwora," Miłosz), 164
Lejeune, Philip, 5, 26, 47, 100, 107, 113, 197n13, 202n22
Leone, Sergio, 228n9
Lermontov, Mikhail, 101
Levi, Primo, 4, 92–95, 101, 109, 172–173, 218n66
Levinas, Emmanuel, 35–38, 114, 204n46, 205n50
Lewinkopf, Józef. See Kosiński, Jerzy
Lewis, Jerry, 136
Libera, Zbigniew, 130–131
Life Is Beautiful (La vita è bella, film), 135, 139, 154
Life or Theater (Leben oder Theater, Salomon), 123–126
Life with a Star (Život s hvězdou, Weil), 79, 110–114
Ligocka, Roma, 170–171

INDEX [249]

Literature in Search of Reality (*Literatura v poiskakh real'nosti,* Ginzburg), 61–62, 208n13, 210n29
Literature or Life (*L'Écriture ou la vie,* Semprún), 76, 87–92
Łódź Ghetto, 130–131, 136, 147–148
Lombard, Carol, 136
London, Artur, 73
Long Is the Road (*Lang ist der Weg,* film), 209n23
Lucky as Hell (*Z pekla štěstí,* Grosman), 139–140, 145–146, 153–154

Macdonald, Dwight, 7, 115, 186, 197n16, 198n19
Maechler, Stefan, 23–24, 27–30, 33, 35, 44, 203n25, 203n27, 203n28
Mallow, Jeffry V., 34
Man vs. Wild (television series), 175
Mandel'shtam, Osip, 56
Margalit, Avishai, 30, 32, 223n114
Matheson, Richard, 166
Mauriac, François, 202n22
Maus (Spiegelman), 83, 142–143
Mauthausen, 87
McCarthy, Joseph, 198n19
McQueen, Steve, 122, 132
Memoir of the Warsaw Uprising, A (*Pamiętnik z powstania warszawskiego,* Białoszewski), 157–159
Memorial (human rights organization), 101
Million Little Pieces, A (Frey), 2, 22, 32, 35, 195n2, 196n4
Miłosz, Czesław, 6, 157, 159–169, 176–178, 197n16, 218n66, 228n9
Miłosz, Czesław, works of: "Campo dei Fiori," 159–160; *The Captive Mind* (*Zniewolony umysł*), 6, 197n16, 218n66; "The Legend of the Monster-City" ("Legenda miasta-potwora"), 164; "A Poor Christian Looks at the Ghetto" ("Biedny chrześcijanin patrzy na getto") 160–161; "A Song on the End of the World"("Piosenka o końcu świata"), 157; *Warsaw Robinson Crusoe* (*Warszawski Robinson Crusoe*), 162–168, 175–178
mimesis, 42, 97, 152, 217n56
model, 47, 51, 70–71, 99, 115, 121–124, 127, 129–132, 137–138, 159, 183, 212n50, 232n5
Monument to the Heroes of the Warsaw Ghetto, 147
Motzkin, Gabriel, 223n114
Müller, Filip, 221n98
Munk, Andrzej, 218n66
Murphy, Cillian, 167, 231n37
Muselmann, 172–174
"My Ration Card" ("Di bone," song), 147

Nałkowska, Zofia, 220n82
Nathan, Alfred, 226n13
notes (genre). See *zapiski*
Notes from the House of the Dead (*Zapiski iz mertvogo doma,* Dostoevsky), 63–72; 94, 99, 108, 115, 146, 199n29, 209n18, 211n39, 219n78
Notes from the City of the Dead (*Zapiski z martwego miasta,* Sandauer), 55–59, 79, 209n18
Notes from Underground (*Zapiski iz podpol'ia,* Dostoevsky), 64
Notes of a Blockade Person (*Zapiski blokadnogo cheloveka,* Ginzburg), 48–54, 59, 62, 66, 72, 79, 207n2, 207n4
Nussbaum, Martha, 187

Oflag II-D, 82
Olère, David, 117–118, 221n98

Omega Man, The (film), 166, 168, 231n39
One Day in the Life of Ivan Denisovich (*Odin den' Ivana Denisovicha*, Solzhenitsyn), 70, 89, 155, 190, 212n50
Oprah's Book Club, 2. *See also* Winfrey, Oprah
Oprah Winfrey Show, The (television series). *See* Winfrey, Oprah
Oranienburg, 70
ostranenie (Shklovsky), 14
Oswald, Alice, 79
Our Children (*Undzere kinder*, film), 16, 147–155
Oyneg Shabes, 150

Painted Bird, The (Kosiński), 76–79, 117, 129
parallactic reading, 14–16, 25–28, 30–31, 33, 38, 42, 44, 46, 52, 60, 82–83, 95, 100, 119, 182, 203n27, 205n49
parajournalism, 115
paratext, 6, 32, 43, 65–66, 79, 92, 100–101, 106–107, 185, 197n13, 198n20
The Passenger (*Pasażerka*, Posmysz), 218n66
Pathseeker, The (*A nyomkereső*, Kertész), 179
Pataki, George, 18
Pearlstein, Ferne, 155
"People Who Went, The" ("Ludzie, którzy szli," Borowski), 100
peritext, 4, 6, 34–35, 79, 197n13
Person at the Writing Desk, The (*Chelovek za pis'mennym stolom*, Ginzburg), 208n13
Petrashevsky Circle, 63, 67
Pianist, The (film), 158–159, 162
Pick, Jiří Robert, 143–146, 148, 153, 155
phantasmatic pact, 26, 100

Płaszów, 133–134, 224n3
Plato, 8–9, 24, 32, 80, 93, 205n50
Polanski, Roman, 158, 162, 170
"Poor Christian Looks at the Ghetto, A" ("Biedny chrześcijanin patrzy na getto," Miłosz), 160–161
Posmysz, Zofia, 218n66
possible worlds (subgenre), 158–159
postapocalyptic fiction, 16, 159, 165, 167, 175–176
postmemory, 192
post-truth, 33
pragmatism, 5
Price, Vincent, 165–167
Proust, Marcel, 24, 26, 80, 201n15

Rapoport, Natan, 147
Rauch, Ruth, 226n13
Rawicz, Piotr, 93–94
Razgon, Lev, 98, 101, 181, 224n1
reality effect, 41
refocalization, 106–110, 116
responsible reading, 10, 14–17, 21, 23, 27, 34, 42–44, 46, 62, 182
Ricoeur, Paul, 82
Riffaterre, Michael, 24–25, 32, 42
Ringelblum, Emanuel, 150
Robinson Crusoe (literary character), 163, 168, 174
Robinson Crusoe (Defoe), 115, 166, 168
Robinsonade, 41, 145. *See also* "Robinson Crusoe" (literary character)
Rose, Gillian, 95–97, 170
Rosenblat, Herman, 22–23, 27–29, 40–41, 43–44, 46–47, 81, 97, 201n11
Rothberg, Michael, 41, 96
Rousset, David, 13, 183–185
rubble literature, 173
Rulf, Jiří, 202n24
Rundo, Maria, 110

Russian invasion of Ukraine, 2022, 101
Ruthven, K. K., 35, 120
Ružomberok, 146

Sachsenhausen, 16, 123, 132, 136, 184
Salmonì, Rubino Romeo, 139
Salomon, Charlotte, 123–126, 129
Salsbury, Harrison, 207n3
Sambor (Sambir), 55, 57
Samuragochi, Mamoru, 200n9
Sandauer, Artur, 55–61, 79, 106, 209n17, 209n18, 210n29
Sartre, Jean-Paul, 56
Schindler's Ark (Keneally), 96
Schindler's List (film), 86, 96, 133, 170–171
Schlieben, 22–23
Schulz, Bruno, 60, 209n17
science fiction, 16, 25, 69, 158–159
Sel'vinski, Il'ia, 133, 224n1
Semprún, Jorge, 13, 76, 87–93, 95, 105, 124–127, 129, 131, 173
Semprún, Jorge, works of: *Fainting* (*L'Évanouissement*), 92; *Literature or Life* (*L'Écriture ou la vie*), 76, 87–92; *What a Beautiful Sunday!* (*Quel beau dimanche!*), 88–89
September 11, 2001 (terrorist attacks), 18, 21, 200n7
"Seraphim" ("Serafim," Shalamov), 98
Shalamov, Varlam, 70–71, 93, 98–99, 113, 117, 129, 148, 155, 173–174, 190, 212n48, 227n26
Shalamov, Varlam, works of: "Grishka Logun's Thermometer" ("Termometr Grishki Loguna"), 93; *Kolyma Tales* (*Kolymskie rasskazy*), 98, 129; "Seraphim" ("Serafim"), 98
Shallcross, Bożena, 169
Shema (prayer), 57
Shklovsky, Viktor, 4, 13–14, 26, 80, 196n9

Shoah (film), 96, 170
Shop on Main Street, The (*Obchod na korze,* film and novel), 128; 140
Shumacher, Israel, 147–152
Siege of Leningrad, 48, 54, 82, 113, 189, 207n3, 208n13. See also Ginzburg, Lidiia
Siege of Petrograd, 4, 189
simulation, 39, 41, 59, 68, 73, 89, 118, 120–123, 138, 145–146, 153, 158, 171, 184
situational comedy, 135–137, 175
Slovak National Uprising, 146
Smoking Gun, The (website), 2
Snyder, Timothy, 127, 223n110
soap made from human fat, 109–110, 171–172, 220n82
Society for the Protection of Animals: A Humorous Novella from the Ghetto, Insofar as That Is Possible, The (*Spolek pro ochranu zvířat: Humoristická— pokud je to možné—novela z ghetta,* Pick), 143–146, 148, 153, 155
Solzhenitsyn, Alexander, 13, 70–71, 89, 98, 129, 155, 172, 190, 212n50, 213n56
Sonderkommando, 117, 221n98
"Song on the End of the World, A" ("Piosenka o końcu świata," Miłosz), 157
Soviet NKVD Special Camp Number 7, 132
Spanner, Rudolf, 110, 220n82
Spiegelman, Art, 83, 142–143
Spielberg, Steven, 86, 96, 170–171
Stalag Luft III, 122, 131–132
Stalag novels, 102, 232n11
Stalag XI-B, 114
Stalin, Joseph, 70, 74, 119–120, 196n6
Stanzel, Franz, 114
Stone World, The (*Kamienny świat,* Borowski), 100–101, 109–110

stupid discourse (Paloff), 191–192
Stutthof, 109
supplement (Ruthven), 35–36, 120
Suetonius, 9–10
"Supper" ("Kolacja," Borowski), 174
Survivor (television series), 175
Survivorman (television series), 175
Szpilman, Władysław, 162–164, 177

Tajtelbaum, Niuta, 75, 213n61
Talese, Nan, 1–2
"Tale from Real Life, A" ("Opowiadanie z prawdziwego życia," Borowski), 101
Tarshis, Lauren, 200n7
terminal paradox (Kundera), 11, 114, 198n24
theatricality, 12, 66–71, 73–74, 102–103, 105, 120–121, 123–124, 131, 135, 142, 146, 149, 151, 153, 206n61, 211n36, 211n39
Theresienstadt, 16, 111, 120–122, 143, 222n104, 222n105
Theresienstadt: A Documentary Film from the Jewish Settlement (Theresienstadt: Ein Dokumentarfilm aus dem jüdischen Siedlungsgebiet, film), 121–122
"This Way to the Gas, Ladies and Gentlemen" ("Proszę państwa do gazu," Borowski), 116
Time (journal), 64
To Be or Not to Be (1942 film), 111, 135–136, 139
To Be or Not to Be (1983 remake), 155
Todorov, Tzvetan, 10, 155
Toker, Leona, 183
Tolstoy, Lev, 48–49, 63, 199n29, 207n4
Trenev, Konstantin, 224n1
truth-in-correspondence, 24–30, 40–41, 49, 79; Borowski's critique of, 203n31

truthiness, 7, 197n17, 197n18
Turgenev, Ivan, 64

Ugrešić, Dubravka, 18
Uighurs in detention, 188
Unvanquished City, The (Miasto nieujarzmione, film), 161–165, 178
USC Shoah Foundation Archive, 44–47, 86
Utesov, Leonid, 224n1

Vaisman, Sima, 80
van Beeck, Frans Jozef, 34, 36, 204n39, 204n43
Van Buskirk, Emily, 53
Veidlinger, Jeffrey, 127
Vendler, Helen, 161, 228n8
veridiction (Foucault), 61

W.: What Remains of the Lie (film), 219n67
Waititi, Taika, 154
Wajda, Andrzej, 159
Waldorff, Jerzy, 164
Walking Dead, The (graphic novel and television series), 167
War and Peace (Tolstoy), 48–50, 69, 199n29, 207n4
Warsaw Ghetto, 16, 30, 34, 36–40, 43, 74–75, 83–84, 132, 135, 147, 150–152, 169, 200n7, 213n61, 215n24, 220n88
Warsaw Ghetto Uprising, 16, 21, 38, 157–158
Warsaw Robinson Crusoe (type), 162
Warsaw Robinson Crusoe (Warszawski Robinson Crusoe, Andrzejewski and Miłosz), 162–168, 175–178
Warsaw Uprising, 16, 157–158, 166, 203n31
We Were in Auschwitz (Byliśmy w Auschwitzu, anthology), 100, 172

Weil, Jiří, 79, 110–114
Weissová, Helga, 121, 223n106
Welles, Orson, 198n19
Wells, H. G., 76, 198n19
What a Beautiful Sunday! (Quel beau dimanche!, Semprún), 88–89
Wiesel, Elie, 80–81, 90, 124–127, 129, 185–186, 190
Wiesel, Elie, works by: *And the World Kept Silent (Un di velt hot hot geshvigen)*, 186; *Night (La Nuit)*, 185–186, 190
Wieseltier, Leon, 35, 38, 127
Wieviorka, Annette, 83–86, 89
Wilkomirski, Binjamin, 22–24, 27–35, 39, 41, 43–46, 53, 79, 102, 174, 202n24, 203n27
Winfrey, Oprah, 1–2, 22, 32, 195n1, 195n2, 204n40
World Apart, A (Inny świat, Herling-Grudziński), 70–71, 88–89, 99–100, 108, 118–120, 129, 185, 219n78

World Apart, A (L'Univers concentrationnaire, Rousset), 183, 185
World Trade Center, 18
World Trade Center Survivors' Network, 18
Wyka, Kazimierz, 161, 228n8

Young, Kevin, 32
"Yosl Rakover Talks to God" ("Yosl Rakover redt tsu got," Kolitz), 34–41, 204n39, 204n43

zapiski (genre), 62–66, 70, 209n18, 211n34
Zarzycki, Jerzy, 162, 164, 166, 177–178
Ziarek, Krzysztof, 158
zombie, 159, 165, 168–169
zombie apocalypse, 161, 165–166, 168, 174–177, 182, 230n24
Zookeeper's Wife, The (Ackerman), 150

GPSR Authorized Representative: Easy Access System Europe, Mustamäe tee
50, 10621 Tallinn, Estonia, gpsr.requests@easproject.com

www.ingramcontent.com/pod-product-compliance
Lightning Source LLC
Chambersburg PA
CBHW022045290426
44109CB00014B/986